Zoro's book activates the dreamer in all of u ... *have a corresponding plan of action that bri...* ... *felt book informs, educates, directs, and cha...* ... *be all we were created to be. Filled with dee[...* ...ne *of the most thorough, absorbing and insightful texts written on the art of being an artist that I have ever read. If you want a blueprint for a successful and purposeful life and want to truly understand what it takes to live the dream, I highly recommend you read this book. You will be inspired beyond your imagination, in a profoundly deep and meaningful way.*

> —QUINCY JONES, Grammy Award-Winning Producer for such
> legends as Michael Jackson, Frank Sinatra, and Ray Charles

Regardless of your chosen profession, the business principles revealed in The Big Gig *will empower you with the necessary vision to begin the journey and equip you with the tools needed to complete the task of climbing to the top. A masterpiece of motivation for everyone!*

> —PHILIPPE SCHAEFFER, President, Rolex (France)

Although Zoro has played around the world as a premier drummer, his greater purpose is one of a motivator. ... His music and life lessons are about using your God-given talents to the maximum. ... [This book] was created as an act of love from a humble servant who would love to see you follow your vision and turn your dreams into reality.

> —LENNY KRAVITZ, Grammy Award-Winning Recording Artist

From my first encounter with Zoro, his zeal has been motivating, powerful and infectious. I hope Zoro's unique experiences and the wisdom he has acquired through the years will be a blessing to you, as I believe Zoro to be one of the true gifts to pure artistry.

> —STEPHEN BALDWIN, Actor, Film Maker, Author

The Big Gig *is a story of persistence, diligence, and faith, as well as a wealth of information. It's an inspirational book packed full of tools for anyone wanting to do great things in life.*

> —JOYCE MEYER, Best-Selling Author and Bible Teacher

Zoro and I grew up on different ends of the country and in different time periods, but we share one huge trait in common—we are both dreamers. Another amazing parallel is that just like me Zoro was inspired as a kid by Frank Sinatra. Like the Chairman of the Board, both Zoro and I were blessed to live our dreams. And now Zoro's book, The Big Gig, *can be a terrific guide for the road to YOUR dreams.*

> —FRANKIE VALLI, Lead Singer of Frankie Valli and the Four Seasons;
> Co-Creator of *Jersey Boys* Broadway Musical

One of the keys to succeeding in life is to serve others wholeheartedly with the gift you have been given. However, there is an art to excelling at that which few understand. In The Big Gig, Zoro reveals that there is an art to every aspect of the creative and purposeful life. Throughout the book, he serves readers well by equipping them with motivating principles that will help them understand the many stages of development and giving them keys to unlocking their hidden potential. This book is a must-read for anyone who is chasing a dream and longs to strike that quintessential balance between life and art.

—STEVE GADD, Drummer for such artists as Eric Clapton, Paul Simon, and Paul McCartney

Zoro is one of the best drummers with whom I've ever worked and one of the nicest people I have ever met. And the fact that he would take his years of expertise about the music business and write them down solely for the benefit of others is a little mind bending, because it's no easy task. Encouragement, putting people in the right direction, and giving nods and pats on the back are easy. But to really share your life with people is another story. That's what a person does when he really cares. Success happens when preparation and opportunity meet. In this book, Zoro shows you how to be more prepared and how to look for better opportunities.

—PAUL JACKSON JR., Guitarist for American Idol, The Tonight Show with Jay Leno, America's Got Talent, and such artists as Michael Jackson, Elton John, and Aretha Franklin

The Big Gig, the really Big Gig, is our life and how we choose to live it. This book has many practical and powerful tips for learning and growing as a musician, but it also helps you connect your music to who you are as a person and challenges you to learn and grow as a fully rounded human being.

—ROGER BROWN, President, Berklee College of Music

Inspiring, sincere and honest. Zoro's The Big Gig goes right to the heart of the matter—you. Much more than a "how to get a gig" guide, this book addresses the core issues critical for success in any creative field.

—MICHAEL KENYON, Executive Director, Percussive Arts Society

You don't meet guys like Zoro often. He's an extremely talented artist with a heart for helping people reach their potential. The Big Gig is a must read.

—JASON KENNEDY, Weekend Anchor, E! Entertainment Television

As a young man, Zoro captivated me with his drumming and natural ability to communicate verbally. Now, he captivates us all with the powerful thoughts and masterful instruction contained in this book. I believe The Big Gig is the most comprehensive and inspiring book in print on the art, business, and soul of being a musician.

—AL McKAY, Grammy Award-Winning Guitarist for Earth, Wind & Fire; Songwriter

The Big Gig *is a philosophy of accomplishment. In it, Zoro opens his head and his heart to life in the music lane.*

　　　　—VIC FIRTH, President, Vic Firth Company

Because of his success and longevity as a player, author, educator, clinician, and motivational speaker, Zoro is the only one I can think of who is legitimately qualified to cover the broad scope of this book with total authority. Zoro does an extraordinary job of merging the art of performing with the art of commerce and gives a blueprint for connecting heart, soul, mind, and body to your craft and life's purpose.

　　　　—DAVEY JOHNSTONE, Musical Director and Guitarist for Elton John

Incredibly inspirational. True American success story. Strong family values with a wonderful mother who truly inspired her children!

　　　　—GEORGE WEISS, Founder, Say Yes to Education

The Big Gig *could easily be considered a manual—a must-read for ALL musicians who desire to get a further glimpse into the music business as well as specific tools for developing the skills to get to the next level or levels you hope and pray to achieve.*

　　　　—RON TUTT, Drummer for Elvis Presley

In His infinite grace, God has granted His children specific gifts to be used for His pleasure and to His Glory! Zoro does just that as a highly skilled musician who not only exhibits what he obviously was created to do but also inspires young adults to realize and fulfill their God-given dreams and potential. In The Big Gig, *Zoro passionately shares his love for music as well as life-earned lessons about the path to meaningful relationships and true success. This book will touch your heart, and I highly recommend it.*

　　　　—DR. WESS STAFFORD, President and CEO,
　　　　Compassion International

The Big Gig—*a totally inspiring read—sums up the drive of someone following his dream. The book explains how everyone—whether a musician like Zoro or any other professional following what the Good Lord has gifted him with—can deal with the ups and downs, good and bad, bumps and bruises, and the rewards. It is about time a book like this is written. Gracias, Zoro. Keep up the love.*

　　　　—LUIS CONTE, Percussionist for *Dancing with the Stars* and such
　　　　artists as Madonna, Celine Dion, and James Taylor

Zoro has a way—from his personal journey—of conveying all the inner truths of inspiration, mechanics, pitfalls, and secrets of the world of music making. A must-read. Take the journey!

　　　　—WILL LEE, Grammy Award-Winning Bassist on *The Late Show*
　　　　With David Letterman and for such artists as James Brown, Mick Jagger,
　　　　and Aretha Franklin

If anyone could write a book on this topic with the wisdom of having lived it, Zoro would be my choice. The book is a Godsend to anyone looking for a lasting career in the music business.

—MARK NELSON, Vice President, Drums and Percussion Division, Guitar Center, Inc.

This book is written in an unusual fashion by an unusual man, who loves the Lord and his family in an unusually wonderful way. He has written a textbook for life that everyone should read. My prayer for Zoro and this book is that everyone who sees it or hears about it will not miss the chance to read it.

—KEN BARUN, Senior Vice President, Billy Graham Evangelistic Association

The inner workings of the music industry can be hard to understand. In this book, Zoro tackles many of the pitfalls and issues a young artist might face. It's always good to have a roadmap or a GPS. The Big Gig can serve as a guide to those looking to navigate an ever-changing road.

—MICHAEL W. SMITH, Grammy Award-Winning Recording Artist and Songwriter

Zoro is an extraordinary performer and teacher. Under his guidance, our students have flourished not only as musicians but as human beings of vision and faith. The Big Gig offers the same inspiring message of personal achievement to countless others.

—DR. CYNTHIA CURTIS, Dean, College of Visual and Performing Arts, Belmont University

I cannot imagine what my life in this business would have been like if I'd had THIS book when I was starting out. But like all things God-given, it comes at the perfect time ... right now.

—TOMMY SIMS, Bassist, Producer, and Songwriter for such artists as Eric Clapton, Garth Brooks, Bruce Springsteen, and Bonnie Raitt

Zoro has put together a very fascinating read which, for the first time, thoroughly explains the details inside the music industry from a sideman's (hired musician) perspective. The Big Gig will educate, motivate, inspire, and enlighten anyone with the dream of becoming a successful musician. This is a must read!

—KEITH CARLOCK, Drummer for such artists as John Mayer, Sting, Steely Dan and James Taylor

In his book, Zoro gives thanks to "Big Brothers Big Sisters of America for allowing me the privilege of partnering with them in the great work they do around the world to change the lives of children." The thanks go both ways, and we appreciate Zoro's work with children facing adversity in the Big Brothers Big Sisters program. As an educator, inspiration, and mentor, Zoro adds to his life's work as a musician. With the publication of The Big Gig, writer is one more title he now acquires!

—KAREN MATHIS, President and CEO, Big Brothers Big Sisters of America

Of the thousands of musicians I've contracted [to play with famous recording artists], one rose to the top and that is Zoro. As a friend, Zoro is in my heart. As a businessman, Zoro is in my mind. And as a drummer, Zoro is in my soul

—**STEVE TRUDELL,** Trudell Orchestras' National Contractor for such artists as Josh Groban, Barry Manilow, and Michael Bublé

I believe there is a universal human desire to make music. And yet, so many give up on their dream or worse—they never even try. Zoro's life story and his sources of inspiration shared in The Big Gig *can be a key to unlock your musical dreams. Whether you aspire to tour and play on the world's great stages, have a recording career or express your musical dreams as a music educator or member of your local church band, Zoro's message is clear: Believe in yourself and believe in music!*

—**JOE LAMOND,** President and CEO, National Association of Music Merchants

The Big Gig *is a wonderful message of triumph wrought by the perennial insistence that goodness and a genuinely joyful spirit can and will conquer life's challenges. This book is easy to read because it is written with the language of simple truth and the intimacy of a real and friendly voice.*

—**ABRAHAM LABORIEL,** Bassist for such artists as Stevie Wonder, Barbra Streisand, and Ray Charles

I have known Zoro for a very long time. Every time we're together, I happily discover new things about drumming and, more importantly, about life. This is not a drumming book, but rather a life book. He provides a blueprint for "making it" in this very difficult business of music. The core principles Z lays out—dedication, passion, discipline, service, selflessness—are sound life principles which also will make you a heck of a musician. As a teacher, I was particularly taken by the Art of Practicing chapter, which provides wonderful observations and sound strategies for improvement. Get this book! It may change your drumming, your life, and make you smile.

—**STEVE HOUGHTON,** Professor of Jazz and Percussion, Indiana University; Percussive Arts Society Past President

Zoro is a master. He has walked boldly, faithfully, and with the confidence of victory being his reward. Lock into Zoro's insight and wisdom, which only the God of heaven could impart.

—**PETER FURLER,** Songwriter, Artist, Producer, and Former Lead Singer of Newsboys

The Big Gig *ignites, delights, and will help you soar to the highest of heights. An essential and exciting read for everyone. Let Zoro funkify your life in a way that only the Minister of Groove could do!*

—**SINBAD,** Comedian, Actor, Television Producer

Zoro's genius extends far beyond the throne behind the drum kit. He knows that creating great music is only one piece of creating a great life. This book is not only for musicians eager to perfect their craft, it's for anyone who wants to know how the soul, body, heart, and mind are meant to work in harmony to form a life rich with meaning and purpose.

> —IAN MORGAN CRON, Author of *Chasing Francis: A Pilgrim's Tale* and *Jesus, My Father, the CIA and Me: A Memoir...Of Sorts*

Some of us share all the wisdom we have acquired in our journey to inspire the next generation. This book is a "one stop" for all. I will be using this for my educational programs.

> —EDDIE BAYERS, Drummer for such artists as Kenny Chesney, Alan Jackson, Trisha Yearwood, and Vince Gill

The Big Gig *is written from the heart. It encourages, inspires and educates.*

> —ED SOPH, Professor in Jazz Studies and Performance Divisions, University of North Texas

Zoro's vast experience provides a rare insider's look at the highs and lows of a musician's journey. This book is a real inspiration for anyone who wants to know what it takes to survive in the jungle that is the music business.

> —SHAWN PELTON, Drummer for the *Saturday Night Live Band* and such artists as Shawn Colvin, Kelly Clarkson, and Brecker Brothers

The Big Gig *is a roadmap to your destination in the music industry. Wherever you choose to go, there are words of wisdom that will help get you there. Zoro reminds us that while the music industry is in a state of change the fundamental principles of success are not. Zoro takes a complex subject and breaks it down into simple, easy-to-understand truths.*

> —CLIFF CASTLE, Co-Founder, Audix Microphones

Anyone reading The Big Gig *and taking seriously Zoro's ideas and recommendations can undoubtedly improve their lives, professions, and relationships. It also gives those who already have successful lives an opportunity to reflect and better understand how they achieved their own goals.* The Big Gig *is a classic read for everyone.*

> —DON M. ESSIG, PH.D., Author and Motivational Speaker

To live the dream while maintaining a servant's heart describes Zoro and his book, The Big Gig. *If you want to find success in all aspects of life and have a life that is purpose driven, read this book.*

> —DR. JEFF KIRK, Associate Dean, Performance Studies, Belmont University

In today's culture, one rarely looks to celebrities as role models or for inspiration. I truly appreciate Zoro's book, which works to inspire a generation of young people and musicians with reliable standards of right and wrong based on faith and with good advice on how to turn dreams into reality. Musicians and non-musicians alike will appreciate his book, replete with the hope that a talent from God can become a career with meaning and purpose.

> —GARY BAUER, President, American Values

The Big Gig will connect to the heart of every reader because it's real and genuinely relatable. If you want to be a winner in the game of life, you need to read this book.

> —T.G. SHEPPARD, Country Music Recording Artist

Zoro may seem like another rock star drummer. But once you talk with him, it becomes quickly apparent that Zoro is an anointed man of God. Zoro is a phenomenal husband, father, musician, speaker, and author, with wisdom about how to do all these things with excellence. His words and thoughts hold great value.

> —ED CASH, Producer and Songwriter for auch artists as Amy Grant, Chris Tomlin, and Steven Curtis Chapman

Zoro is one of the most unique people I have ever met, and I mean that in the most positive sense possible. He is an amazing combination of artist, educator, devoted family man, friend, and encourager. His book, The Big Gig, *is sure to challenge and inspire you in life-changing ways. I encourage anyone looking to live his or her life with a greater sense of purpose to read it. I am grateful to call Zoro a friend. He is truly one of a kind.*

> —LINCOLN BREWSTER, Recording Artist and Songwriter

From the very first time I met Z, it was apparent we both share a passion for Christ and a mission to empower kids. His testimony as a former little brother in the Big Brothers Big Sisters program is both powerful and entertaining. This book displays the depth of the man and his dedication to taking his own unique gifting to the maximum and inspiring others to their own level of greatness.

> —LOWELL PERRY JR., CEO Big Brothers Big Sisters of Middle Tennessee

Zoro is one spectacular individual. His principles revealed in The Big Gig *are solid, his thinking is clear and his passion for life, music and others is obvious. How can you not like a book from a guy who is rooting so much for you to win in life?*

> —BRUCE ADOLPH, Publisher, *Christian Musician* Magazine

THE
BIG GIG

Big-Picture Thinking
for Success

By

With Amy Hammond Hagberg

Alfred Music Publishing
LEARN · TEACH · PLAY

LOS ANGELES

For my beautiful and amazing wife, Renee,
our precious children, Jarod and Jordan, and the
wonderful memory of my loving mother, Maria.
You are all proof of God's undeniable love and
His unmerited favor on my life.

CONTENTS

....

FOREWORD

I met Zoro one hot and sunny Los Angeles day after school on the lawn of my high school. I walked out of class and headed across the grass as usual to find myself staring at a character dressed in designer clothes, shades, a gold chain, and a mother-of-pearl watch on an alligator strap. He was playing rhythms on a drum practice pad to Earth, Wind & Fire on a boom box. He had an attitude to match the look.

Z looked like a professional studio musician, and I knew he didn't go to my school. I had to find out who this cat was and why he was there. Well, without going into the whole thing—and to make a long story short—the answer is vision.

Whether Zoro fully comprehended it at the time, he was following The Voice that spoke to him. He was told to sit on the lawn of that school because he had an appointment that would change his life forever. We both did.

After getting to know Z and hearing him play an actual set of drums, I realized he had an exceptional gift. He had a funky pocket and a repertoire of grooves that were superior to any of the drummers I had played with. I quickly showed him off to all the best musicians at my school, and I talked my music teacher into letting Zoro play with us in class. I was his agent. Z's look may have gotten him the initial attention on the lawn of my school that day, but Zoro's heart, discipline, and passion are what propelled him to greatness.

Within weeks, I even arranged for Zoro to go to (Motown Records founder) Berry Gordy Jr.'s house to display his skills. After a short time, we formed a strong musical and personal relationship. We played in bands together and started a mobile disco business, deejaying parties on the weekends.

When I moved out of my house at age 15 (over a rift with my father because he wouldn't let me go to a Buddy Rich concert), Zoro picked me up and helped me move. We were together all of the time after that, driving aimlessly around L.A. listening to funk music.

http://4wrd.it/A.BGForeword

He would make me drive so he could use the dashboard of his Oldsmobile Omega as a drum pad, which he completely destroyed.

A couple of years after high school when I was recording demos around L.A., I was asked by Jheryl Busby of MCA Records if I knew a drummer who could go on tour with The New Edition. I sent Z, and the rest is history. The legend of Zoro the Drummer was born. He created a persona for himself that made him more than just a "drummer."

Zoro became an integral part of their show. And before you knew it, he was gracing the pages of teen magazines. When Bobby Brown left the group, he took Zoro along—featuring Z on the road and in videos.

Soon thereafter, I recorded my first album, *Let Love Rule*, and asked Zoro to go on tour with me. It was full circle from high school to playing together professionally. It was a dream come true.

Now, with all of this history to give you some background, Zoro's backstory is not what this is about. It is about Zoro's character and the vision I spoke of earlier. Although he has played around the world as a premier drummer, Z's greater purpose is one of a motivator. This desire was always in his spirit.

I remember walking the streets of New York with Z late one night for hours, when he told me about the details of this very book. That was 20-some years ago. In recent years, Zoro has spent much of his time as a mentor to young people. His music and life lessons are about using your God-given talents to the maximum. Z wants to see people follow their vision, turn their dreams into reality, and follow that Voice.

With all of this said, I can tell you that I have the utmost respect for Zoro as a friend, musician, family man, and educator. He is an inspiration to so many people around the world. I hope you find this book helpful. It was created as an act of love from a humble servant who would love to see you follow your vision and turn your dreams into reality.

—**LENNY KRAVITZ**
Grammy Award-Winning Recording Artist

Acknowledgements

THANKS TO GOD, THE SOURCE OF ALL THINGS

First and foremost, I humbly give thanks to God the Father for the gifts of life, music, and all creative abilities He has bestowed upon mankind. To the Holy Spirit for teaching me how to fulfill the dreams the Father has placed in my heart, and for giving me the strength and courage necessary to pursue those visions to completion. To my Lord and Savior Jesus Christ, I thank you for enduring the cross so I could have eternal life and experience abundance and victory in this one.

MY WIFE, CHILDREN, AND MOTHER

I thank my incredible wife, Renee, for her love, support, and faithfulness, and all she does to bless my life and the lives of our children. Thank you Jarod and Jordan for filling my life with unspeakable joy and inspiration; it is a privilege to be your father. I thank God for allowing me to be a steward over your lives each and every day. I would like to thank my dearly departed mother, Maria, for being the absolute light of my life and the greatest mother a boy could have. She was a tremendous source of encouragement, inspiration, and love. It is an honor to be her son. None of my success would have been possible without her! Thank you my dear, sweet mother for filling my heart with big dreams and high hopes, for believing in me the way you did, and for being the wind beneath my wings.

FAMILY

I also extend my deepest gratitude to all my brothers and sisters. The six of you have played an integral role in what I have been able to achieve, and you have enriched my life through the vast experiences and incredible adventures we have shared together. Thank you to Armando for being my protector; Maria for teaching me how to stand up and fight; Ricardo for the greatest of adventures; Patricia for investing in me like no other, believing in me, and showing me the world; Bobby for being my absolute best friend; and Lisa for being my pal and always laughing at my jokes. I would also like to say thanks to my niece Lydia Bravo for all her love, support, and advice, and thanks to all the rest of my nieces and nephews, Anna, Corina, Linda, Armando Jr., Anthony, Travis, Gina, Jordyn, Calvyn, Stephanie, André, and Angelina for being who you are. Thanks to my in-laws Wil and Sandy Strong for their unbelievable faith, and for being such a tremendous blessing through the years in every way. A special thanks to my brother-in-law, George Weiss, for his generosity and kindness.

EDITORIAL AND PUBLISHER

I express my deepest gratitude to my coauthor, Amy Hagberg, for her dedication to excellence on this book and all her editorial input. I genuinely appreciate everything you have done, Amy, to make *The Big Gig* what it is, for being so patient, and also for being a great teacher. You're the best! Heartfelt thanks goes to all my friends at Alfred Music Publishing for their faith in this book: Ron Manus, Lindsey Harnsberger, Antonio Ferranti, Holly Anzalone-McGinnis, Gwen Bailey-Harbour, Rich Lackowski, Ted Engelbart, Holly Sieu Fraser, Kate Westin, Mark Burgess, Robert Hirsh, Donnie Trieu, Greg Dills, Gilbert Paez, Renee Cunning, Marina Terteryan, Dave Black, Michael Finkelstein, Jordan Bell, Jonni Murphy, Karissa Read, Ann Miranda, Samantha Ordonez, Mark Malone, and the entire Alfred staff for their hard work and support of all I aspire to do.

FOREWORD

I wish to thank my dear brother and life-long friend Lenny Kravitz for honoring me with his heartfelt words of love in the foreword that he wrote for this book. You believed in me more than anyone else, Lenny, and helped to usher in God's destiny for my life. Thanks for blessing me in the countless ways that you have throughout the years and for the genuine friendship that you have displayed. Truly my life would not be the same without you, and I love you like a brother!

PARTNERS

I sincerely thank other partners I am privileged to have worked with throughout the years, in order of their appearance in my life: Robert Donnelly, Lenny Kravitz, Jerry Hammack, Brian Mason, Russ Miller, Amy Hagberg, Daniel Glass, Greg Johnson, Ken Gire, and Lisa Cieslewicz. Your friendship, inspiration, wisdom, and generosity have enriched my life so very much. You have made the fruit that I endeavor to bear much sweeter, and each of you has played a pivotal role in the success I have been fortunate enough to experience. THANK YOU!

MENTORS

Much love, honor, and respect go out to my early mentors who played key roles in shaping my formative years and helped me become the person I am today: Pearl Jones; Reverend Williamson from Faith Baptist Church in Grants Pass, Oregon; James Worthington; Joe Kantola; Eric Christianson; Bill and Beverly Large; the Big Brothers Big Sisters of America program; Kent Clinkingbeard; Donn Essig; Ralph Johnson and Al McKay of Earth, Wind & Fire; Jack Smith and the staff at Wilderness Trails Camp in Oregon. I would also like to thank the following churches for helping my family and me in every way: Our Lady of Victory, St. Anne's, Christian Assembly, and Overcomers Faith Church. Extra thanks to my spiritual mother, Beverly Afifi, for her impact on my life and the lives of my family. Each of you has greatly blessed me, and I thank you from the bottom of my heart for the love you so faithfully demonstrated to me. I also extend my deepest gratitude to my friend, Frank DaMatto, a man who picked me up when I was down, a man who taught me the meaning of the word faith and how to believe and trust God, a man who made my life better because of his. I'll see you in heaven, Frank!

BIG GIG TESTIMONIALS

I thank legendary music producer Quincy Jones for his loving support and personal endorsement of *The Big Gig*, in addition to his heartfelt testimonial featured on the first page of this book. Thank you from the bottom of my heart, Q, for being the person you are and for the important work you are doing with the Quincy Jones Musiq Consortium. Also, thanks to everyone who provided a testimonial, quote, or endorsement, or who otherwise helped publicize this book. My utmost gratitude belongs to all of you for giving me your valuable time in such a selfless manner. Lending your highly respected and revered names to my work has truly been one of the greatest honors I have ever been given and a gift I will cherish for the rest of my life!

FAITHFUL FRIENDS & SUPPORTERS

In appreciation for blessing me with their friendship and support, my sincere thanks goes to all of the following individuals, in order of their appearance in my life: David Watts; Clayton Sasser; Paul Baker; Bill Newman; Cory Graper; Dave Day; Cindy Johnson; Lynda J. Person Kauffman; Kathy Cunningham Cappelli; Barry Anderson; Ken Burns; Pat, Gordon and Kevin Robell; Sandra Frederiksen; Alphonse Mouzon; Lenny Kravitz; Kennedy Gordy; Osama, Lolita and Mustoffa Afifi; Vadim Zilberstein; Richard Allen; Dan Donifrio; Bruce, Artie and John Soto; Jeanette Jurado; Lynn Espinosa; Alex Cabrera; George Segerman; Mark and Denice Guzman; Bob Wilson; Ray Brych; Glenn Noyes; Dave Whiterman; Mark Nelson; Kenric Knecht; Robby and Rex Robinson; Frankie Valli; Dennis and Anita Tinerino; Keith and Heidi Hershey; Cheryl Benedick; Angus and Catherine Keith; Russ and Christine Miller; Allen Rhodes; Jusden Aumand; Carlo Krouzian; Tim Fogerty; Eric and Shannon Rhodes; Victoria Kemper; Robert Jolly; Jerry and Barb Andreas; Steve and Sally Petree; George and Jenny Parks; Steve Trudell; Bruce Adolph; Matt Kees; Gary and Fay Asher; Anthony and Rosanne Albanese; Bill and Linda Johnson; Bob Cashier; Rebekah Hubbell; Jackie Monaghan; Kyle Prins; Dustin Ransom; Eric Anthony; Lisa and Bill Cieslewicz; Jules Follet; Marty and Tracy Layton; Ken and Sethea Barun; Larry and Debbie Miller; Kim Clement; Bob and Joyce Robertson; Doug Coe; Bill and Robin Siren; Mark and Tricia Arnold; Michael and Kristi Hamrick; Leslie Scruggs; Dr. Burton Elrod; Dave, Joyce and Danny Meyer; Lisa Unge; Kraig and LaSandra Wall; Roger and Bobbi Hodges; Luke McKee; Steve Weiss; Janet White; and Lu Hanessian.

ORGANIZATIONS

Thanks to Compassion International and Big Brothers Big Sisters of America for allowing me the privilege of partnering with them in the great work they do around the world to change the lives of children. My gratitude to Dr. Chris Norton, Dr. Jeff Kirk, Dr. Cynthia Curtis, Chester Thompson, Lisa Davis, April Simpkins, Joan Eakin, and all staff at Belmont University in Nashville, Tennessee, where I have the honor of teaching. A heartfelt thanks to Berklee College of Music in Boston, Massachusetts, for the great training they provided, and to the American Federation of Musicians and the American Federation of Television Radio Artists for the work they do on behalf of musicians and vocalists. I also would like to say thanks to everyone at the Percussive Arts Society and National Association of Music Merchants for the great work they do and their support throughout my career.

RECORDING ARTISTS AND MUSICIANS

My deepest thanks to all the recording artists and countless musicians I have had the privilege of playing with over the years. Each of you inspired me so much personally, and I am grateful for your contribution to my life experiences in addition to the honor of being able to make music with you.

MUSIC PUBLICATIONS

I also extend my appreciation to the following magazines for their support and friendship throughout my career: *Modern Drummer*; *Drum!*; *Rhythm*; *Drum Head*; *Classic Drummer*; *Drummer*; *Todo Percussion*; *Bateria*; *Batera & Percussao*; *Slagwerkkrant*; *Sticks*; *Drums & Percussion*; *Rhythm & Drums*; *Drum Club*; *Drums etc.*; *Batteur*; *Drum Scene*; *Percussiioni*; Bernhard Castiglioni at drummerworld.com; and all other drum publications throughout the world.

MUSICAL EQUIPMENT MANUFACTURERS

My sincere thanks to the following companies and their staffs for their friendship, incredible and innovative equipment, and amazing clinic support throughout the years: Drum Workshop, Sabian, Evans Drumheads, Vic Firth, Latin Percussion, Audix Microphones, SKB Cases, and Danmar Percussion. It's an honor to be associated with you and represent you around the world. You guys rock!

CLINIC SUPPORT

Thanks to all drum shops, music stores, music chains (Guitar Center, Sam Ash), drum schools, professors, educators, music colleges, and music festivals throughout the world for inviting me to share my passion at clinics and educational events around the globe. It has been a privilege to spread the gospel of groove and joy of drumming with those entrusted to you. I thank you sincerely for allowing me the opportunity to share my passion and heart.

QUOTE SOURCES

I extend my deepest love and appreciation to all the significant individuals, past and present, quoted throughout this book for their words of wisdom, inspiration, and amazing contributions to our world. Special thanks goes out to *Modern Drummer* magazine for the use of the Steve Gadd and Bernard Purdie quotes. (Steve Gadd quote © April 1996, Modern Drummer Publications, Inc. Used by permission, all rights reserved. Bernard Purdie quote © May/June 1979, Modern Drummer Publications, Inc. Used by permission, all rights reserved.)

PHOTO CREDITS

Cover photo by David Hindley. "About the Author" photo by Peter Muller. All other photos used in the QR code video segments throughout the book are from Zoro's personal collection.

QR CODE DRUMMING FOOTAGE

A special thanks goes to my friends Rob Wallis and Paul Siegel of Hudson Music and Modern Drummer Publications for the use of the drumming footage featured throughout the QR code segments of this book. The majority of the footage featured throughout was excerpted from the DVD *The Modern Drummer Festival 2005,* by Hudson Music (© 2005, Hudson Music LLC/ Modern Drummer Publications, Inc. Used by permission, all rights reserved.) Thank you guys for all your support and friendship throughout the years!

QR Codes

HOW TO EXPERIENCE THE WHOLE BIG GIG

Throughout this book, you will find small codes, called QR codes, that look like this:

http://4wrd.it/A.BGQR

QR stands for "Quick Response." These codes allow you to view additional content from *The Big Gig*, such as videos and photos, using your smartphone.

Each chapter has a unique QR code that unlocks exclusive video in which Zoro discusses the concepts presented in the book. The QR code at the end of the Big Gig Picture Book (p. 397) links to a selection of additional photos from Zoro's collection. On the back cover, the QR code accesses The Big Gig Quiz.

Search for a QR code scanner app in your app store. There are several to choose from, and many are free.

If you don't have a smartphone, the website printed below each QR code allows you to access all the additional features using a standard Internet browser.

Preface: The Gift of Music

*The aim and final end of all music should be none other
than the glory of God and the refreshment of the soul.*
—Johann Sebastian Bach

Since the dawn of mankind, the expression of music has been with us in one form or another. Music is synonymous with humans; our ability to make it separates us from the animal kingdom. On its most basic level, music is of a spiritual nature because it satisfies our innate desire to connect with God. We somehow know intuitively that music connects our spirits, minds, and bodies in some magical way to the divine life force from which it miraculously originates.

Unlike any other force on the planet, music beckons us down its endless path of creative expression. We use it to express emotion, whether a call to love or a call to war. We use it to express adoration or disdain toward things about which we feel strongly. Sometimes only the lyric of a song can best describe how we feel deep inside about a particular thing. Like poetry, lyrics speak of our joy and laughter, pain and suffering, hopes and dreams.

Music can spark the soul and drive away depression and sadness by the mere striking of a celestial chord. Conversely, a chord on the darker side of the spectrum can stop the laughter and evoke powerful feelings of fear or sadness, bringing about tears for no apparent reason. No one can fully explain the miracle of music—and we cannot take credit for inventing it—we are simply vessels of its limitless and divine expression.

Musicians are inseparable from the music because it is pre-wired into our DNA. We were created with an incredible desire to express the creative flow of music in one way or another. How, where, and why we do it is not as important as that we do it.

In the garden of music, things work much like they do in a vegetable garden. At the beginning of the season, farmers plow the earth and then carefully plant the seeds

http://4wrd.it/A.BGPreface

into the life-giving soil. To ensure that they grow healthy and strong, the plants are consistently watered and fertilized. Gardeners go to great lengths to protect their crops from harmful elements that might prevent the reaping of a harvest. If they do what's required to sustain it, their fields will produce an abundant crop. It is a laborious process.

In the end, the bounty of the harvest is determined by the farmers' faithfulness and diligence to do their part. They understand, however, that they neither created the seed, nor produced the miracle of that tiny seed growing into a mature, edible plant. They are merely the stewards of the seed. The farmer's role is to abide by the governing principles that bring forth life.

So it is with all types of creative people, particularly musicians. We have to take the seed of the talent that God gave us and develop it by studying, practicing, and performing. That laborious process causes our seed to grow.

The person who renders loyal service in a humble
capacity will be chosen for higher responsibilities, just as
the biblical servant who multiplied the one pound given
by his master was made ruler over ten cities.
—B.C. Forbes

Just like a farmer fights off the birds of the air that come to devour the seed, or covers the plants with plastic to protect them from freezing, we, too, have to combat the negative elements that threaten the productivity of our talent. Whether it's doubt, laziness, or discouraging messages delivered by those who try to talk us out of our dreams, our job is to persevere in order that our gifts glorify God, multiply, and produce something of beauty for others to enjoy.

Although most people enjoy music in some fashion, whether it is singing, clapping, or dancing to its rhythms, far fewer have the genetic gifting in their DNA to express themselves through its magical and mystical stream. Those who are endowed with that gift are not spiritually satisfied unless the divine flow is being channeled through them and out to others where its joy is manifest and its purpose fulfilled. When we abandon this call on our lives, we cease to be fulfilled because music is what God created us to do.

Each musician is given a particular song to sing. Your job is to sing your song, not anyone else's. A thousand drummers can play the same exact drum beat notated on manuscript paper, but each will play it in his or her own unique way. Likewise, one hundred of the greatest actors of all time can play the role of Elvis Presley, but they will all present the character with their own special type of authenticity.

You have the privilege of putting your own signature on whatever music you play. You don't have to try and be unique or original because you already are! Just be yourself. Like a potter takes a lump of clay and fashions it into a beautiful vase or bowl, through time you will be shaped into an even better version of who you were originally—but only if you are willing to undergo the process.

I believe that dreams are divinely placed in the hearts of all human beings. They are not really even our dreams, but the dreams that God placed within us in order that we might bless others with our talents and experience the fulfillment that comes from doing so. The problem is that very few people ever take hold of their dreams. Most miss out because they fail to rise up and walk into their destinies, and because of that, those who would have benefited from that creative expression miss out. The reason so few live out their dreams is that it takes deliberate steps to bring them into a state of reality.

Although an initial gifting has already been deposited in everyone, only the courageous will bring it to life. Only those who understand what it takes to succeed, and are willing to fight for it, stand the chance of seeing the dream come to pass.

Just as a farmer encounters countless obstacles to produce a great harvest, each creative person also faces tremendous challenges to bring forth a musical harvest. None of this is easy, but it is definitely possible.

Death isn't the greatest loss in life. The greatest loss is
what dies inside of us while we live.
—Norman Cousins

Although there are no guarantees with any endeavor, certain strategies can increase your chances of being successful. True, lasting achievement requires vision, perseverance, patience, and above all—faith.

My goal in writing *The Big Gig* is to share what the process of success looks like and demonstrate how a strategic effort can make all the difference in the outcome. So join me on this adventure toward living out the musician's dream. It is an honor and privilege to share with you what I have learned on the fantastic journey I have been fortunate enough to travel.

INTRODUCTION

*A man is a success if he gets up in the morning
and gets to bed at night, and in between he does
what he wants to do.*

—Bob Dylan

Music is therapy for the soul. Without it, the world would be an empty and lifeless place; in a spiritual sense it would be dead. Music, the rhythmic force of the universe, touches upon every human emotion and plays an important role in nearly every culture that shares this planet.

When Albert Einstein was asked about the inspiration for his theory of relativity, he replied, "It occurred to me by intuition, and music was the driving force behind that intuition. My discovery was the result of musical perception." In other words, music is crucial to our progress as human beings.

Musicians are a special breed, indeed, and I absolutely love being a part of that culture. I like to think of us as the chosen ones; chosen to make the world a more vibrant place through the wondrous sounds of melody, harmony, and rhythm. In doing so, we bring forth the only truly universal language…music.

But where does this talent come from? I believe our talents are given to us by God. If talent were something we could obtain through our own methods and by acts of will, we would all choose the type of talent we wanted and that would be the end of the story. We don't have a choice what our gifts are…they just are.

Talent does not come from us; its power freely flows through us like an electrical current. We are merely the wire and conduits through which talent is displayed. While your talent is certainly a free gift, developing it to its full potential does have a cost. The decision to pay that price lies entirely with you. Developing your gift is not a burden; it is a divine privilege.

Let me give you an illustration that might help shed some light on this. Imagine a set of human lungs. One

http://4wrd.it/A.BGIntro

of them is completely full, representing your talent or gifting. The other lung is totally empty. That is your potential. You were born with one lung bursting with talent, but reaching your potential and filling up the other lung is left completely up to you. Whether you do so or not is your choice—reaching your potential is an act of free will and requires desire, faith, and action. True fulfillment in life only comes when you are utilizing the gifts you have been given, in the manner in which they were intended to be used.

The tragedy of life doesn't lie in not reaching your goals.
The tragedy lies in having no goal to reach.
—Benjamin Mays

Throughout my travels around the world, I have met countless musicians, aspiring and professionals alike. The question I have been asked most frequently is: "How did you make it?" Ultimately, they wanted to know how they could break into the music business and score the big gig. The answer is multifaceted and one I intend to divulge in great detail throughout this book.

The Big Gig is for musicians at all stages of their careers; from beginners just learning to play, to advanced players trying to break into the business, to professionals who have never gotten their big breaks and are reaching for higher ground and looking for inspiration.

The book offers a full and frank discussion of the music industry from the perspective of a freelance musician. It's not about how to get a record deal with a band; it's about how to become a successful player and make a living as an independent musician. I felt a personal calling to write this book in hopes that other musicians could live out their dreams as I have. My goal is to teach you how to develop a vision, design a master plan for success, and see it through to the end.

While the book is more specific in terms of becoming a successful player, the principles are the same for achieving anything significant; the only difference is the specific skill sets needed to succeed. Even though the music industry is in a constant state of change, and from time to time undergoes rigorous periods of reinvention, the principles revealed in this book are timeless. If applied properly, they will yield positive results year after year, because the basic strategies for making a name as an independent musician will always remain the same.

For years, the process of successfully breaking into the business as a player has been insider's knowledge only. What all aspiring players need is a successful musician to show them the industry ropes. Consider The Big Gig to be your own personal mentor that will teach you how to become a Jedi master. My aim with this book is to demystify what has largely remained unexplained about the business of being a musician. I also want to help you preserve your sanity, dignity, and self-respect along your journey toward success.

Systematically going through this book will help you understand what it takes to succeed as an independent musician and will clarify the most common misconceptions. When you clearly know what your mission is, are able to identify the steps necessary to reach it, and are willing to do what's required, your chances of success will increase exponentially.

> *If you don't know where you are going, you will*
> *probably end up somewhere else.*
>
> —Lawrence J. Peter

Keep in mind that the music industry isn't all sunshine and roses, so together we will explore the good, the bad, and the ugly sides of a musician's life. I will share some of the joys to be garnered from expressing yourself on an instrument and many of the frustrations musicians encounter along the way.

To be brutally honest, playing music for a living seldom pays well, and rewards in the form of acceptance, praise, and notoriety can seem even more elusive. For every brightly lit bulb on the Las Vegas strip, there are countless broken ones in dumpsters behind the opulent buildings that shimmer in the night. The shattered bulbs represent those whose dreams of making it as musicians came to a screeching halt after they realized how hard it actually is. Those who have the guts and tenacity to stick it out are few and far between.

You have no right to anything you have not pursued, for
the proof of desire is in the pursuit.

—Mike Murdock

Music and business are two totally different things, yet one's success is dependent upon the other. From the moment I grasped that revelation, I divided my time equally between the music and business aspects of my career; an approach that has served me very well.

Now, a word about some of the most frequent terminology I use throughout the book. The two main characters of our story are inseparable: the artist and the player. Even though they usually share the common goal of giving the best performance possible, their roles, functions, and responsibilities are completely different—and so is their financial compensation.

When I use the term "artist," I'm referring to the recording artists from whom players seek employment. They may not always be signed recording artists with record deals, but they are the people who are in need of our services and are hopefully able to compensate us for our time and effort. The artist can be one person, a band with many members, or a producer, contractor, or musical director. These are the employers and the ones doing the hiring.

The terms I most frequently use to describe the employee are: "player," "musician," "sideman," "hired gun," "freelance musician," or "independent musician." They are all one and the same. Players are the hired guns who rent out their musical services to those who will pay for them.

This book will introduce you to many principles of success, but you must supply the desire, faith, and action. You, alone, must pursue your dream with all your heart. Through pure instinct, hard work, the help of family and friends, and an unquenchable desire to succeed—as well as God's undeniable favor—I managed to break the unbreakable code and accomplish what I set out to do. The success I have enjoyed in my life has not been because of my own brilliance. My accomplishments are the result of a burning passion and clear vision, combined with sheer determination and persistence...and, oh yeah, and a little luck and some God-given talent thrown in as well.

Like many other books, this one has evolved over the years. It is literally a result of more than thirty years of experience and research. My goal was to write the most comprehensive and in-depth manuscript ever written on the subject of becoming a successful independent working musician. My objective throughout the upcoming text is to inform, warn, direct, inspire, and motivate you. Anyone who reads it should come away with a thorough sense of the way the music industry works from a player's point of view.

An incredible amount of hard work, love, and passion have gone into this project. I hope it will prove to be one of the most useful and inspirational tools you use on your journey to landing a big gig—and to becoming a better musician and person in the process. One vital piece of information could mean the difference between success and failure, but remember that reaching your goals hinges on your ability to apply what you've learned.

It is with great pleasure that I present to you *The Big Gig: Big-Picture Thinking for Success.*

There is no happiness except in the realization that we have accomplished something.
—Henry Ford

HOW MY DREAM GOT STARTED

*Cherish your visions and your dreams as they are
the children of your soul; the blue prints of your
ultimate achievements.*

—Napoleon Hill

For as long as I can remember, I've had an incredible passion for music. I love to listen to it, read about it, talk about it, think about it, and ultimately express my creativity by playing it. Between my enormous CD collection and massive number of digital downloads, I have nearly one hundred thousand songs in my music library, and my passion for music shows no signs of slowing down any time soon.

My deep love affair with music began when I was a young boy growing up in Los Angeles. Everyone in my family loved music immensely and I grew up listening to every style imaginable. My mother was an incredibly passionate woman and a voracious music lover who always did her best to make sure her seven children were exposed to a variety of music. She was a dreamer with a lust for life, and she intentionally filled my little head with the notion that dreams really can come true if you're young at heart and truly believe.

Mom raised all seven of us on her own, and together we endured some pretty tough and unstable times. Through it all, we stuck to each other like glue; our love for music was one of the things that bonded us together as family.

We didn't have any fancy things around our house, but we did have a record player and plenty of great records by artists like Frank Sinatra, Nat King Cole, Elvis Presley, Dean Martin, Bing Crosby, Tony Bennett, Doris Day, Harry Belafonte, Mantovani, Henry Mancini, Percy Faith, and Glenn Miller. We also had Mom's mariachi music, the traditional music of her native Mexico, and legendary singers such as Jorge Negrete and Pedro Infante got plenty of rotation time on the turntables at our home. The festive sounds always gave us cause to celebrate.

We lived in an area of south central Los Angeles known as Compton for a long time. Growing up in that

http://4wrd.it/A.BGDream

neighborhood in my formative years throughout the 1960s exposed me to intoxicating doses of soul music. That sound had a profound influence on me, and as a result, rhythm and blues music became my life's blood.

My older siblings were big record collectors. Ricardo dug a lot of the Memphis soul artists like Al Green and Otis Redding and had a strong love for jazz and big band. Patricia loved Diana Ross & the Supremes, The Temptations, and all the Motown artists who came out of Detroit and many of the other great rhythm and blues singers of the era. Mary was a bona fide flower child in the midst of the hippie revolution and loved all the classic psychedelic rock of the day: The Doors, Janis Joplin, and Jimi Hendrix. Armando loved Elvis Presley and what we refer to today as "oldies but goodies." Only back then they weren't oldies, they were current radio hits.

A potpourri of musical sounds emanated from every bedroom of our red and white post-World War II stucco home. Armando and Mary hosted dance parties at the house for their friends from high school, and when my younger brother Bobby and my little sister Lisa and I heard them playing all their great 45 rpm records all night long, we loved every minute of it!

Back in 1969 at the ripe old age of seven, I can specifically remember listening to "Twenty-Five Miles" by Edwin Starr and "Grazing in the Grass" by Friends of Distinction. Both songs had these really funky drumbeats that seemed to beckon me to follow.

Funk is an infectious force to be reckoned with so I naturally gave in to the force. Inspired by the countless songs that were birthed during this incredibly vibrant era in music history, I built a makeshift drum set out of an array of leftover garbage—everything from empty Folgers Coffee and Almond Roca cans to oatmeal canisters.

> *The poor man is not he who is without a cent, but he*
> *who is without a dream.*
>
> —Harry Kemp

With a portable radio and my junkyard drum set straight off the set of *Sanford and Son*, I was ready to hit the big time. As palm trees swayed in the hot California summer breeze, I sat on the street corner and jammed along with anything funky that came on the radio. It was my street version of a lemonade stand, but instead of lemons, sugar, and ice, I was peddling music, and the people were literally dancing in the streets.

My fate was sealed early on when I was fortunate enough to attend a life-changing concert. It was none other than Diana Ross & the Supremes with The Temptations—two of my family's all-time favorite groups—live at the Long Beach Municipal Auditorium. My mom's friend, Bertha, was kind enough to buy us the tickets, and she even picked us up and drove us to and from the concert in her Cadillac.

I'm sure Bertha had no idea how much that concert impacted my life. Watching the performances and hearing these famous artists sing all my favorite songs made for an evening of magic. It was a mesmerizing night, and better than a trip to Disneyland!

That evening will forever be etched in my memory. Looking back, I know it was one of the biggest inspirations for me stepping into my destiny as a musician. My fate was further cemented when my mother scrounged up enough money to take us to see Frank Sinatra. All I could say was wow!!! Hearing Frank doing it "his way" certainly made me want to do it my way, and my way was the way of rhythm.

Thus, my dream of being a musician was born, and against all odds, it has stayed alive in my heart all these years. My mother was right; dreams really can come true if you're young at heart, and I am excited to share with you exactly how mine became a reality!

> *If a man for whatever reason has the opportunity*
> *to lead an extraordinary life, he has no reason to*
> *keep it to himself.*
> —Jacques-Yves Cousteau

1

The Art of Accompaniment
THE PROS AND CONS OF BEING A FREELANCE MUSICIAN

*Don't make music for some vast, unseen audience
or market or ratings share or even for something as
tangible as money. Though it's crucial to make a living
that shouldn't be your inspiration. Do it for yourself.*

—Billy Joel

Like most musicians who started out during my era, I spent a lot of time in cover bands playing the top hit songs of the day. I also spent plenty of time playing "casuals," a West Coast term for weddings, parties, and corporate gigs.

Like most other musicians who dreamed of making it big, I put forth significant effort into playing in original bands—nobody has ever made it big playing cover tunes or doing casuals. I assumed that being a member of some kind of original band would be my ticket to fame and fortune. All the musicians in those bands had high hopes for success; we spent hours talking about what it would be like when we made it big.

Unfortunately, I learned early on that I had very little control over the destinies of the other people in a band, and that I was only one voice in the decision-making process. Being in a band can be very frustrating. You invest all your time, energy, and money in the group and then all of a sudden someone less ambitious decides to up and quit and you find yourself having to start all over again with another musician. It happens so frequently that you soon find yourself standing on shaky ground and your dream of making it big goes up in flames.

There are a zillion and one reasons why bands break up before they ever get off the ground, most of which are completely out of your hands. Things like band morale, camaraderie and chemistry, record label support and politics, radio airplay, tour support, management, public appeal, marketing savvy, originality, talent, and a plethora of other critical concerns determine if you "make it." After years of hard work, many groups break up just when they finally start to experience a little taste of success—all because of greed, ego, and jealousy. Being in a band can be like one big soap opera. Before you know it, years of your life have gone right out the window.

> *I learned early on that I had very little control over the destinies of the other people in a band, and that I was only one voice in the decision-making process.*

Eventually, the drama of being in a band became way too much for me, and I realized I was wasting my time with groups that clearly didn't have what it took to make it. I learned that the only thing I could control was how hard I was willing to work for my own success, and I decided to put my efforts into becoming a freelance musician. I knew that changing my direction required a focused and deliberate course of action, and I was willing to take the next step.

With so many critical success factors to contend with, making it in a band seemed to be the equivalent of hitting the Lotto. Not that making it as an independent musician was any easier, but at least there were far fewer variables completely out of my hands. If I didn't make it, there could be no finger pointing on my part—I would only have myself to blame, and I could live with that. Besides, I figured I could always be in a band again if the right situation presented itself.

LIFE AS A SIDEMAN: A CLOSER LOOK AT THE WORLD OF THE FREELANCE MUSICIAN

YOU DON'T HAVE TO BE A STAR (TO BE IN MY SHOW)

Now, before I can give you some reasons for becoming a sideman, I should first explain exactly what sidemen are and describe their role in the music industry. "Sideman" is a music industry term for a musician or vocalist who performs behind recording artists. There are many other terms that describe this select group of musicians, all of which have identical meaning: freelance musician, back-up musician, singer or vocalist, independent musician, independent contractor, hired gun, player, session musician, and studio musician. A sideman can be a studio musician who plays mostly recording sessions, a touring musician who plays mostly live dates, or both.

What mainly distinguishes sidemen is that they are not full-fledged, contractual members of the bands with whom they play. Subsequently, if the band is signed to a record label, a sideman doesn't receive royalties from record sales. Drumming legend Steve Gadd was a well-paid sideman when he toured with Paul Simon, James Taylor, and Eric Clapton. So is bassist Daryl Jones when he tours with The Rolling Stones. The Stones first hired him to go on the road with them in 1993 when their original bassist, Bill Wyman, retired.

In contrast, Ringo Starr, who was the drummer for The Beatles, and Charlie Watts, who has been with The Rolling Stones since 1962, are not sidemen. They are royalty-earning musicians signed to the record label with the rest of their band mates. This entitles them to a piece of merchandising and concert revenue, licensing agreements, and any other form of monetary compensation the band is able to generate from newer technologies that consistently hit the market.

> *A sideman is like a chameleon; the good ones often wear many different musical hats.*

Think of signed band members as corporate shareholders, but in this case the company is a rock 'n' roll band. The stock is divvied up between the band members based on the percentages that were set forth in the band's original agreement. Songwriting royalties, which go to whomever penned individual tunes, are separate.

Sidemen, on the other hand, are only entitled to an agreed-upon amount of money for their services. For recording work, their compensation can be a one-time fee, a per-song or per-day fee, or some other form of union scale as set forth by the American Federation of Musicians (AFM), fondly referred to as the Musician's Union. If you are a vocalist, your union scale is set forth by the

American Federation of Television and Radio Artists (AFTRA). For live dates and touring work, compensation can be in the form of a per-gig or weekly salary, a flat rate for an entire tour, or any number of other financial arrangements. Sidemen are not shareholders who are entitled to a piece of company profits; they are strictly hired guns.

If you are playing in a band and are not actually part of the contract the band signed with the record label, you are considered a sideman, a back-up musician, a hired hand, or an independent contractor. In other words, you are your own entity. With the exception of signed bands and individual solo recording artists, sidemen represent the majority of musicians around the world who are in the so-called "limelight" of the music industry. From recording sessions to live events and television—and everything in between—sidemen are used in just about every imaginable musical situation.

> *Firmness of purpose is one of the most necessary sinews
> of character and one of the best instruments
> of success. Without it, genius wastes its efforts in a maze
> of inconsistencies.*
> —Lord Chesterfield

When I was a kid growing up, I was more fascinated by the musicians playing behind the big stars than I was by the artists. To me, the world of the sideman was far more intriguing. A sideman could play for countless recording artists as opposed to the recording artist who could only be themselves. A sideman is like a chameleon; the good ones often wear many different musical hats.

There are a number of reasons why being a sideman is the best gig in the music business. First and foremost, there is the matter of control. As an independent musician, you have complete control over your own destiny, or at least more control than musicians who are locked into band situations.

Second, you will enjoy far more musical variety as a sideman than you will as a solo artist or with a band. One of the downsides of being an established superstar recording artist is that for the rest of your life you will be expected to play your hit songs wherever you go. It's almost like being handed a life sentence of repetition.

Sidemen, on the other hand, lead far more musically exciting lives, at least creatively speaking, and variety is the spice of life! One of the biggest complaints I hear from the recording stars I know is how bored to death they are with their own music, especially those who have been around for a while. Believe it or not, I have been around some world-class recording artists who were actually envious of their sidemen. Their musicians had ample opportunities to be employed by a variety of notable recording artists, and they were a bit jealous that others were seeking the services of their players.

No matter what you do to earn a living, there are pros and cons. I would like to share with you both sides of that story from a sideman's perspective.

ADVANTAGES OF BEING A SIDEMAN

ON THE SUNNY SIDE OF THE STREET

Too many people in the world spend the better part of their lives working at jobs they don't really enjoy. Perhaps the greatest thing about being a sideman is that you get to love what you do, which is to play music for a living.

Realizing how quickly life goes by, I would rather spend the majority of my life doing what brings me the most joy and what I feel I was put on the planet to do.

> *Success is not the key to happiness. Happiness is the key to success. If you love what you are doing, you will be successful.*
> —Albert Schweitzer

As a musician, I have traveled all over the world to some of the most interesting and exotic places on our planet—and I get paid for it. Now *that's* living!

The amount of actual work you do while gigging is small in comparison to the average eight-hours-a-day workload. If you are playing club dates or casuals, your total playing time for the average four sets a night is somewhere between three and four hours, tops. In all of the concerts I've played, I've rarely performed more than a two-and-a-half-hour show. Of course, we can't forget to take into account the countless hours of practice it took to get there, but the hard work you put in early-on allows you the luxury of not having to punch the time clock later in life.

Playing concerts behind most "name" recording artists is usually the least amount of physical work because you don't have to set up any of your gear or drive yourself to the gig. If it's a major act, all of that is usually taken care of for you. There are always exceptions; the decisions about travel arrangements and whether or not technicians are hired to set up your gear are based on economic factors and the generosity of the artist. I know several famous jazz musicians who set up their own gear and drive great distances to get to their engagements simply for economic reasons.

A QUICK GLANCE AT THE ADVANTAGES OF BEING A SIDEMAN

FOLLOW THAT DREAM

- **SELF-EXPRESSION:** The sense of fulfillment that comes from knowing you are doing what you love to do and what you were uniquely created to do.

- **PURPOSE:** The satisfaction of knowing that what you do musically brings joy to so many around the world and profoundly touches upon the hearts of those who listen.

- **VARIETY:** Work with different people and in different settings on a regular basis. Work is not mundane or routine.

- **NOTORIETY:** Respect, admiration, and adoration often accompany a successful sideman.

- **FRIENDSHIPS:** The opportunity to develop relationships with interesting people from all walks of life around the world.

- **OFF-PEAK HOURS:** No need to drive and run errands during peak hours or on weekends.

- **WORLD TRAVEL:** Exposure to a vast array of cultures and cuisine throughout the world.

- **PREFERENTIAL TREATMENT:** Many people are star struck or fascinated by anyone in the entertainment business. As a result, you are often given special treatment.

- **COMPLIMENTARY MEALS:** Frequent meals paid for by the artist, fans, record companies, promoters, agents, and equipment manufacturers.

- **QUALITY TIME:** Because of your unpredictable schedule, you often have greater periods of time available to spend with family and friends than do nine-to-fivers.

- **FAMILY VACATIONS:** Sometimes you can take your family along to exotic places while you're there on a gig. The hotel is already paid for and you can use your frequent flyer miles for additional plane tickets, if necessary.

- **LEVERAGE:** The opportunity to use your position as a springboard to another side of the industry, such as becoming a songwriter, producer, record company executive, etc.

DISADVANTAGES OF BEING A SIDEMAN

DON'T LET THE GREEN GRASS FOOL YOU

It wouldn't be fair to share only the pluses of being a sideman without at least shedding a little light on some of the minuses. Before you can even consider pursuing a career as a sideman, there are a few hard, cold facts you must come to terms with in order to make an informed decision.

Perhaps the first thing to understand is the public's perception of a famous sideman. Most people assume that if they hear you on records, see you on television, in an advertisement, or in front of thousands of screaming fans, you are rolling in millions and living the high life. For the vast majority of sidemen, nothing could be further from the truth.

It's true that you can earn a good living if you are a successful sideman—a better than average living, in fact—but it's no easy task. Please don't get me wrong; in the best of circumstances, this is an incredibly rewarding and fulfilling job. Part of the job is being in the limelight, and one of the perks is incidental fame.

Unfortunately, though, unless incidental fame somehow translates into money, it doesn't mean much in terms of being able to make a living. In other words, if it can't help pay your bills, it's really not that beneficial—other than for stroking your ego and impressing people. Don't mistake notoriety for financial fortune. In some instances, incidental fame can actually become a burden, because it puts undue pressure on musicians to live up to that inaccurate financial picture others have of them. I have seen plenty of sidemen succumb to that pressure and live a total facade only to end in financial ruin by living way above their means.

The public at large does not understand how money is distributed in the music business; there is a great divide between a hired sideman and a musician who is a part of the recording contract, earns artist royalties, and has other streams of residual income.

> *Success follows doing what you want to do. There is no other way to be successful.*
> —Malcolm Forbes

Very few sidemen in the history of the profession have earned seven figures. The best way to earn that kind of money in the music industry as a creative artist is to make it big in a band or become a successful songwriter, publisher, or producer and get royalties on hit recordings. Most of the serious wealth in this industry comes through the ownership of intellectual properties, which in our business refers to the legal rights of the artist who owns the copyright of a particular work, or by earning a percentage of the artist's income as in the case of managers, agents, and concert promoters. It doesn't come from the recording or performing of the music by sidemen.

Of course, there are always exceptions, but much of that depends on your status and who is employing you. In that respect, our industry is just as varied as any other. Some companies take care of their employees and some don't. Some bosses are totally fair and cool while others are completely selfish jerks. If you can accept the reality and challenges of these working conditions, then you can at least pursue this career without being disillusioned.

There is virtually no real wealth to be made as a sideman, so if your ambition is to get a huge paycheck, this may be the wrong career for you. Like Billy Joel said in the quote at the beginning of this chapter, the desire to express yourself on your instrument has to be your driving force.

> *The road to happiness lies in two simple principles: find what it is that interests you and that you can do well, and when you find it, put your whole soul into it—every bit of energy and ambition and natural ability you have.*
> —John D. Rockefeller III

Despite all the difficulties associated with the life of a sideman, there are also moments of inexplicable joy that come from expressing yourself creatively as an artist. I have come to the conclusion that there is just no utopian situation here on the earth, and I have learned the art of compromise in order that I might still fulfill my purpose. My career has been a series of trade-offs and sacrifices; I gave up certain things in order to make gains in other areas I felt were more important. You will have to decide what you are willing to forego in order to emotionally deal with the challenges that will come down the pipeline.

There are surely more financially profitable professions you can choose than music, and there are many that are far less monetarily rewarding, too. What it really comes down to is this: What do you feel you're on the earth to do? What are you compelled to do? What are you driven to do? What do you have a deep passion to do? When you can answer these questions honestly, you must then follow your heart and go after it, whatever that might be.

A Quick Glance at the Disadvantages of Being a Sideman

YOU CAN'T ALWAYS GET WHAT YOU WANT

The situations described below can vary greatly depending on whether most of your work is from recording or touring, and how successful you become at either. If it's something I feel can apply to both the studio and the touring musician, I simply put the word "both" in parentheses. If it's a disadvantage commonly associated more with one than the other, I simply put the word "studio" or "touring" in parentheses.

In addition to the cons I have already stated, there are some other disadvantages you should keep in mind when thinking about becoming a sideman.

- **Financial Hardship:** Inconsistent money flow, particularly because of waiting on previously earned money to come in. Vacation pay is also a rarity, as are job perks that would come with most forms of corporate employment (both).

- **Inconsistency:** Frequently unpredictable work schedule (both).

- **Personal Challenges:** A large amount of time is spent away from home, often putting a strain on personal relationships (touring).

- **Scheduling Challenges:** Your time is not your own, and you are often at the beck and call of whomever is employing you. Making personal plans can often be difficult (both).

- **Infrequent Promotions:** Advancement is extremely rare. Usually the only possible promotion is to go from being a sideman in a band to being the musical director on tour. After that, you reach a financial plateau unless you produce or write songs for the artist or are invited to be a part of the recording contract (touring).

- **Adverse Challenges:** Little to no room to call in sick. You have to learn to function even in the worst of physical conditions (both).

- **Holiday Obligations:** Holiday gigs can be lucrative for the recording artist, so having to forgo spending time with family or friends on those special occasions is a common occurrence (touring).

- **Sudden Cancelations:** It's not uncommon for live dates or sessions to be canceled with little notice. In many cases, there is no compensation for the cancelation (both).

- **PHYSICAL STRESS:** Frequent late-night meals, lack of sleep and exercise, and poor nutrition are common pitfalls that can come with the job. Of course, these challenges occur by personal choice and are universal issues that can happen in any occupation (both).

- **EXHAUSTION:** Long hours traveling on planes, buses, cars, and in transit from one gig to the next (touring).

- **SELF-EMPLOYMENT:** For most working situations, you are considered an independent contractor, which means you must allot money for taxes as well as your own retirement benefits and medical insurance (both).

THE SHOW MUST GO ON

As I mentioned earlier, being a sideman in the music industry is not a nine-to-five job, and as much as that is a good thing for us creative types, it does have some drawbacks. In most occupations, if you don't feel like going into work, you can just call in sick. If I did that just before a concert where 25 thousand people were waiting to see a big-name recording artist, there would be a major riot. I have seen that happen before, but fortunately it wasn't caused by one of the sidemen missing the gig—it was actually the artist who blew it off.

There's another golden rule: "He who has the gold makes the rules." There are many double standards you must accept as a sideman until you're the star forking out the cash. There would be serious ramifications if you did some of the things artists get away with. Reliability is the name of the game for a back-up musician; you are expected to show up no matter what your circumstances.

I once broke my right pinkie toe the day before I had a big gig in Las Vegas, and I dreaded the thought of having to play the bass drum with that sore toe. As I was backing out of my driveway

> *There's another golden rule: "He who has the gold makes the rules."*

the next day to make the five-hour drive from Los Angeles to Las Vegas for the show, a yellow jacket swooped in my car window like a Japanese kamikaze pilot and stung me on the arm—not a good scenario for a drummer! I immediately stopped and got something from my medicine cabinet to lessen the long-term effects of the sting, and 10 minutes later I was back in the car heading to Vegas.

Let me tell you, that was the most uncomfortable drive of my life! It was well over 100 degrees traveling through the desert, and I was hot, itchy, and miserable because my air conditioner was broken. By show time, which was around 9:00 p.m., my arm had swollen up like a hot air balloon. It was the size of an elephant's trunk—only instead of being flexible, it was as tight as a drum. Every time I hit my drums, I felt excruciating pain.

In addition to my arm feeling like it was going to explode, my right foot was killing me because of the broken pinkie toe. Every time I hit the bass drum pedal, I thought it was the end of the world! When you play a physical instrument like drums, absolutely any pain, anywhere, affects your playing because you use your entire body. I was a total mess; if there were ever a time I would have loved to call in sick, it surely would have been that evening. Yet, I still had to go on and perform that night because I didn't have any other choice.

There have been many occasions throughout my career where I was forced to perform despite ailments and illnesses because the artist was counting on me. From horrible cases of the flu and fevers that ran over 105 degrees, to a broken thumb, dislocated knee, and sprained ankle, I've endured it all. It's no easy thing to perform under those conditions. Unlike in the sports field, there was nobody waiting on the sidelines ready to cover for me. I had to be resourceful and find ways to play in pain while simultaneously trying my best to recover.

The most common trait I have found in all successful
people is that they have conquered the temptation
to give up.

—Peter Lowe

2

THE ART OF VISION
DEFINING THE DREAM

*Just because a man lacks the use of his eyes doesn't
mean he lacks vision.*

—Stevie Wonder

My mom gave me my first drum set as a Christmas gift in 1971 when I was nine years old. I think she got me those drums in an effort to soften the blow of just having moved from massive Los Angeles, California, to puny Grants Pass, Oregon—population 13 thousand. I missed my old friends and sunny California, and I was still in culture shock from the enormous lifestyle change. It felt like we had left the set of the sitcom *Sanford and Son* and went on location to shoot *The Waltons*—only we stayed!

After savagely tearing the wrapping paper from a fantastically large box on that first Christmas morning in Grants Pass, I was blown away to discover that it was the Disney Rocket drum set I had wanted so badly. "You knew that I always wanted a drum set so bad Mommy, thank you so much. I love it! Thank you, thank you, thank you Mommy!"

My mother couldn't have been happier for her little boy. She smiled at me over the wood burning stove with such love and happiness—it is a memory I will cherish all the days of my life.

Several of the most popular Disney characters were on the front of the bass drum. Goofy was playing a banjo that looked more like a bass guitar, Donald Duck was on drums, and Mickey and Minnie were jamming out on lead and rhythm guitars—all in glorious color. It was a legendary rock 'n' roll line up if there ever was one, and the cost of the kit was only $9.99 since it was made of all paper heads.

http://4wrd.it/A.BG2

I was so excited to unleash the groove buried deep within me that I destroyed the kit by the end of Christmas evening. Sadly, that put an end to my drumming endeavors for several years—but not to my dreams. It wasn't a complete waste because that little toy drum set ignited a fire inside of me. Luckily, my mom lived to see her son's dreams come true; dreams that all began one very special Christmas day.

Eight years later, I finally bought my first real drum set for $100 from John Perkins, a drummer pal at my school. As I played those drums, I often visualized myself being a successful drummer and meeting all my favorite musicians. I imagined myself on an airplane bound for an important event sitting next to members of the groups with whom I wanted to play. I saw myself recording at famous Hollywood recording studios, going on world tours, and being interviewed by my favorite music magazines. I envisioned myself in an advertisement or on a poster endorsing my favorite equipment. I daydreamed for hours on end about what my life was going to be like. It was then I first began to understand the power of vision; those thoughts consumed me and awakened senses I had never known before.

WHAT IS SUCCESS?

THIS ONE'S FROM THE HEART

When my musical journey began, I had no idea what it really meant to be successful. As time went on, I realized that the term "success" means different things to different people, so I had to figure out what that was going to mean in its entirety.

To make sure we are on the same page, let me start off by giving you my full definition of the word "success":

Success: To experience fulfillment in the personal,
spiritual, and vocational aspects of life, while fulfilling
your divine purpose for your time on the earth.

This kind of complete success is purpose driven, and it requires seeing life not as a vehicle for self-indulgence and glorification, but rather as a divine opportunity to serve people with your unique gifts.

True success is not measured by how much we have acquired, but by how much we have given of ourselves. In essence, this kind of success is service oriented as opposed to the self-centered substitute that permeates our society today and lacks the depth we all long for.

If you make your life entirely about self-gratification, you will surely self-destruct. There are countless examples of men and women throughout history who did just that, including many people in the entertainment industry. But if you make your life about serving others with your gifts, you will experience the fulfillment you were intended to experience. That will give your life what so many people today lack—purpose!

THE FOUNDATION: THE ESSENTIAL COMPONENTS OF TRUE SUCCESS

THESE THREE WORDS

A successful life is not just having a thriving career; that's only one aspect of success. True and meaningful success encompasses the spiritual, personal, and vocational aspects of life and includes the person as a whole. If you neglect to plan for success in all three areas, you will fail to find genuine contentment in your soul.

SPIRITUAL SUCCESS

To live life and play music without making the spiritual connection is no more possible than living without blood running through your veins and air flowing through your lungs. Spiritual revelation enables you to see music as a divine gift from above and will inspire you to play from that deep place within your soul that connects you directly to God. In doing so, you will find meaningful purpose in your music and all that you do.

True spiritual success is more eternal than temporal, and it is measured by your effectiveness to inspire, encourage, motivate, and uplift others as your talents flow through you. This mindset enables you to make a lasting impact with your art that far surpasses your own lifetime and ripples into eternity.

And now here is my secret, a very simple secret; it is
only with the heart that one can see rightly, what is
essential is invisible to the eye.

—Antoine de Saint-Exupéry

PERSONAL SUCCESS

Personal success is reflected through the development of fruitful relationships with family, friends, and colleagues in the workplace. To thrive in mutually beneficial relationships is the crowning achievement of the human experience, and it satisfies the deeper longings of the heart.

My goal is to live the truly religious life, and express
it in my music. If you live it, when you play there's no
problem because the music is part of the whole thing.
To be a musician is really something. It goes very, very
deep. My music is the spiritual expression of what I
am—my faith, my knowledge, my being.

—John Coltrane

In order to prosper in a personal way, genuine love must be the dominant force in all your relationships—whether platonic friendships or romantic love. Another hallmark of personal success is being able to walk in freedom from various addictions and destructive behaviors that will stifle your growth, destroy your valued relationships, and keep you from living a healthy and productive life. You become a slave to anything you allow to imprison you. True liberty is being *unable* to indulge in destructive vices to your heart's content but *able* to run the race of life unshackled, in order that you might accomplish incredible achievements.

VOCATIONAL SUCCESS

In order to experience vocational success, you must be doing what you were created to do. With that naturally comes some form of employment opportunity that will make use of your gifts and talents. A demand for your skills is certainly proof of one aspect of vocational achievement, but the sense of satisfaction that comes from doing what you love to do as a creative being is the real reward of your vocation.

Jonas Salk, who is best known for his discovery and development of the first safe and effective polio vaccine, said, "The reward for work well done is the opportunity to do more." However, of no less importance is the privilege of being able to prosper financially from the fruits of your labor. That monetary resource is vital to the business of your craft and is what allows you to keep on producing fruit. Notoriety, as well as acceptance and respect from your peers, is the secret desire of every artist and another significant component of vocational success.

THE COMPLETE PICTURE OF SUCCESS: A QUICK SUMMARY

- Spiritual Success = Knowing God, fulfilling your purpose, and inspiring others

- Personal Success = Having loving, meaningful, and fruitful relationships with others

- Vocational Success = Excelling with your gift and being rewarded for it

---

I believe the earnest desire of every human being is to flourish in the spiritual, personal, and vocational aspects of life. Experiencing success in only one or two of these areas will leave you dissatisfied, because as a human being you are pre-wired with the need to experience fruitfulness in all areas. True fulfillment in each of these dimensions is the only real measurement of success.

You will be glad to know that by the time you finish this book, you will know exactly how to achieve this kind of three-pronged success. You will be armed with the knowledge and insight necessary to create an even greater you—a more purpose-driven, directed, and inspired you. You will be equipped with the master plan.

You don't have to see the whole staircase,
just take the first step.
—Martin Luther King Jr.

25

PYRAMID POWER
ONCE YOU GET STARTED

Now that you have an accurate picture of what true and meaningful success looks like, let's explore what it takes to achieve it. We'll start by examining the following diagram:

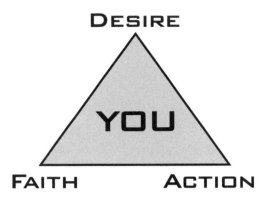

In the center of the pyramid is the word "You." Yeah, you got it, everything revolves around you. Fulfilling your musical purpose hinges entirely on your actions, and what you do every step of the way will ultimately determine the outcome of your career goals.

Along with "You" being center stage, there are a few other important words that must share equal billing if you hope to reach that higher ground. Each side of this "pyramid of success" triangle represents another key element that's necessary to achieve any kind of success: desire, faith, and action.

Success stems first and foremost from your heartfelt desire to pursue a vision with all you've got. What this really means is that you want something so bad you're willing to do whatever is necessary to obtain it. This genuine longing comes from within; only you can activate the internal craving that will then drive your efforts.

> *Desire is the starting point of all achievement, not a hope, not a wish, but a keen pulsating desire which transcends everything.*
>
> —Napoleon Hill

Once your desire is full-blown, it takes faith to believe that the dreams you dare to dream really can come true. Faith is the ability to believe in yourself and your dream when no one else does. It is the invisible force that allows you to withstand the many obstacles that will surely cross your path. How far you go toward fulfilling your dream will be determined largely by the extent to which you develop this invaluable substance we call "faith."

As important as faith is, however, it's devoid of power if it is not backed up by real-life action. You could be extremely talented and have the desire to be the world's greatest jazz guitarist all day and night, but if you don't take action, it will never happen. Action is another word for hard work; it puts you in the game of life instead of in the bleachers where most people are seated. You can't sit on the sidelines and wait for your dreams to come true—you have to do something!

At the beginning of my career, I had an unquenchable desire to become a great drummer. But if I'd only had that desire and never investigated what steps would be required to satisfy that desire, I would still be sitting in Grants Pass. It would have been impossible to accomplish what I wanted to do musically without leaving that wonderful little town. It took a step of faith and a plan of attack to transform my desire into something more than just wishful thinking. Faith and action must be developed, because they give legs to your dream and set you on the course toward your destiny. Remember, though, that neither faith nor action is automatic or a one-time investment. They are ongoing works in progress and must consistently be cultivated throughout the course of your life.

Faith is to believe
what you do not yet see; the reward for this faith
is to see what you believe.

—St. Augustine

VISION

DREAM ON

At some point in our lives, we have all heard the adage, "Seeing is believing." I have always believed the opposite to be true: "Believing is seeing." In other words, before something can come to pass in your life, you must first see it in your own heart, mind, and soul. You must believe in the vision before you can confidently take the steps necessary to bring it to life. Embracing the dream is critical, or it will be impossible to make believers out of those you want to come along beside you. It all begins by visualizing yourself doing exactly what it is you really want to do and enjoying the fruits of your success. Close your eyes and envision yourself walking up to the podium to accept your Grammy award, receiving a gold or platinum album, or playing on a big tour behind an artist you've always admired.

Acting these things out in your mind may seem childish at first, but believe me—visualization is crucial to establishing the dream in your heart. Dreaming is healthy provided you eventually act on those dreams in an effort to turn them into realities. But before you can develop a strategic plan, you need to have a clear vision of what it is you are striving for in the first place. Visualizing in this way will enable you to accomplish seemingly impossible things.

> *Vision without action is merely a dream. Action without vision just passes the time. Vision with action can change the world.*
>
> —Joel A. Barker

You are truly a one-of-a-kind individual with the capacity to dream never-before-realized dreams, so it does you no good at all if your vision originates from anyone other than you. It can't be the dream your spouse, family, friends, or teachers have for you. It isn't their dream, it is yours; do what you must to keep the vision burning brightly in your mind. Most importantly, keep hope alive in your heart—this is one area in which you ride solo, and it is where most dreams die.

No matter how crazy or ridiculous your vision may seem to others, it takes courage to hold onto it and truly believe it's possible. So go ahead—dream big. People seldom rise above their own expectations, and, sadly, most of the time they shoot far too low. What you think of yourself deep inside can often become a self-fulfilled prophecy. Thinking positively in the face of negativity is critical to the success of your mission.

Your dream must be anchored in faith, hope, and love, because without them you will drift and retract when the strong winds of opposition blow. You must know your dreams could take years to realize, but my thought has always been, "Hey, the years are going to go by anyway, so they may as well go by while I am at least in pursuit of the dream." With each passing year, I may get a little closer to living it; and besides, I'd much rather die while in pursuit of my dream than live my whole life having never gone after it.

Anybody who has ever accomplished something notable did so by first entertaining dreams no one else could see. The next logical step was to take a giant leap of faith. By following their hearts and doing what was required, their dreams eventually came to pass.

> *Formulate and stamp indelibly on your mind a mental picture of yourself as succeeding. Hold this picture tenaciously. Never permit it to fade. Your mind will seek to develop the picture.*
>
> —Norman Vincent Peale

The other aspect of vision is to make sure you think it all the way through—a concept that is totally foreign to most musicians. Very few can tell you anything more specific than "I want to be a musician." It takes a much more detailed vision to design a master plan and a strategy for seeing it to fruition.

Think like an architect instead of a musician. When an architect designs a building, he has to draft out every detail of the structure before he can submit the plans to the contractor to begin construction. Most of the work is preparation, planning, and designing. When the contractor finally begins the physical work of building, he simply follows the architect's blueprints that have already been well laid out.

The same type of advanced preparation is required in countless other professions: screenwriters, doctors, city planners, authors, clothing designers, engineers, movie directors and producers, and military commanders, just to name a few. In order for you to become an in-demand independent musician, you need to think along these lines of advanced preparation.

Of course, there are particulars about what we do as musicians that are unique to our profession. But if you approach your career with the end in mind, you will be forced to devise a plan. By doing so, you will greatly increase your chances for success. Once the plan is in place, you can begin to assemble a dynamic course of action, keeping in mind that throughout your career it will be necessary to refocus your vision by periodically retooling, recalibrating, and reassessing your current state of mind and progress.

> *It is always wise to look ahead, but difficult to look*
> *farther than you can see.*
> —Winston Churchill

Vision is so important that I believe every college, especially music schools, should require a course that teaches students how to develop a vision and shows them the strategic process for bringing it to life. After all, what good is it to master your instrument and incur huge college debt if you have no idea how to turn that skill into a viable career from which you can make a living?

WRITING A MISSION STATEMENT

DO YOU KNOW WHERE YOU'RE GOING TO?

When I first starting playing the drums at age 17, my mission was to become a successful drummer and make a living at it. The love for music that had been lying dormant inside of me had finally been ignited, and the timing felt right to pursue my dreams.

In order to achieve my dreams, I wrote out some specific goals that would help direct my daily efforts. This was a great starting place, but I soon realized I needed something much more in depth that would reflect the broader scope of my core values and ideologies with a definitive purpose. What I needed was a mission statement. Writing a mission statement has proven to be an invaluable tool for me over the years, helping me accomplish all I had envisioned for my spiritual, personal, and vocational success.

In essence, a mission statement is just a short written declaration of the purpose of an individual or organization. Most successful companies have a mission statement of some kind that clearly states something about their products or services, what they believe in, what they are working toward, and what they stand for as an organization. A nation, state, city, or company without a vision goes nowhere and fails to accomplish anything significant. The same goes for an individual. Having a clearly defined mission statement kept me on the right path and set me apart from the countless musicians who were plagued by a loss of direction and devoid of any sense of conviction for what they believed in and stood for.

> *Where there is no vision, people perish.*
> —Proverbs 29:18, KJV

The road to fame and fortune is paved with many casualties. A mission statement can help direct your steps in an orderly fashion and greatly reduce your chances of defeat. Most mission statements for organizations are written in paragraph form, but since there's no law here, I opted to write mine using bullet points. Doing so helps me remember the key points with a quick glance.

ZORO'S MISSION STATEMENT

IF I CAN DREAM

- To serve God, my wife, children, family, friends, and my fellow brothers and sisters on planet Earth by making a positive personal impact into each and every life possible.

- To live life with passion, fire, and zeal, and fulfill my purpose by maintaining a healthy balance between God, family, friends, and career.

- To strive for a spirit of excellence in all that I do and to reach my full potential with my gifts, talents, and skills.

- To intentionally use every platform, opportunity, and medium I am given to inspire, motivate, educate, and encourage all who cross my path.

- To be an asset wherever life takes me with whatever I am called upon to do.

- To experience consistent growth in the spiritual, personal, and vocational aspects of life and overcome the fear of learning new things.

- To consistently renew my mind and spirit through positive influences and by carefully guarding what I listen to, read, and watch.

- To leave behind a lasting legacy through my life's work for subsequent generations to build upon.

This mission statement has helped me stay the course and remain true to who I am in a world that is often fickle and uncommitted to anything; a world that so desperately wants to mold us into something other than who we were uniquely created to be. The words I wrote inspired me to stand firm and remain uncompromising in my purpose.

Author Robert Byrne asserted, "The purpose of life is a life of purpose." Living a purposeful life has always been of great importance to me, and the purpose of my talents has always been to use my platform to live out the principles expressed in my mission statement. This helped me remain humble when success finally came and kept me focused on positively impacting others rather than getting caught up in the destructive forces of self-idolatry.

The soul that has no established aim loses itself.

—Michel de Montaigne

It's not that I'm not proud of my accomplishments, it's just that, more importantly, I view them as divine opportunities to bring joy, inspiration, motivation, and encouragement to all who hunger for such things. My creative platforms are merely means for refreshing the souls of the weary, lost, discouraged, and downtrodden. This purpose has given my work more depth and meaning, and it continues to push me to even greater heights in an effort to touch more people during the time I am allotted here on the earth.

IMPORTANT QUESTIONS TO ANSWER

IT'S NOW OR NEVER

There are many things to contemplate when it comes to envisioning your life, but a well-constructed mission statement should answer questions like these:

- What is your vision for your future?

- What are your key values?

- What do you aspire to be spiritually, personally, and vocationally?

- What are some of your major goals?

- What would you specifically like to achieve in your career?

- What kind of impact do you want to make with your craft?

- What is the purpose of your life's work?

- What do you want your life to stand for and represent?

- What are you most committed to?

- What would you do if you knew you couldn't fail?

- What do you hold as most precious in your heart?

- How do you want to be remembered when you're gone?

Don't wait until you have perfected your mission statement or have the answers to every one of these questions before you think about drafting it out. You can constantly revamp and update it as you get a clearer picture of what you would like to become. The point is, by at least initially drafting one up, you force yourself to think about these things in a deeper sense, which will help you in all aspects of your life.

Like any other muscle in your body, your brain must be exercised in order to get the most out of it. Deep thinking is like calisthenics for the mind.

> *Few people think more than two or three times a year;*
> *I have made an international reputation for myself by*
> *thinking once or twice a week.*
>
> —George Bernard Shaw

DEFINING YOUR OBJECTIVE

AIN'T NO STOPPIN' US NOW

An important step in drafting your mission statement is to define your objective. What is an "objective," you ask? It is a more detailed, multi-dimensional version of your goal. If someone were to ask you what your career objective is, you need to be able to clearly define your intentions and answer the question in a succinct and concise manner. The only way you will be able to do that is to give your objective some serious thought.

Writing an objective is a discipline few musicians take the time to do. But there is something very powerful about taking a thought and releasing it on paper for all to see in order to keep you accountable. A study conducted by Gail Matthews, PhD at Dominican University concluded that those who wrote down their goals accomplished significantly more than those who did not. The study also reported that accountability and commitment were key factors to bringing your goals to life.

I have met many musicians who said they were just too busy to write out their goals. Honestly, people, if you won't make the time to write your goals, how in the world will you find time to accomplish any of them?

In the long run, men hit only what they aim at.
—Henry David Thoreau

So, let's stop jiving and get down to business. To write your own mission statement, start by creating a document on your computer, date it, and save it as version one. As time goes by, you'll create subsequent drafts and you can date and title them accordingly. This way, you can always go back and see what the initial objective was on your first pass. The best part of saving it on your computer like this is that it becomes an incredible tool to document your progress, and it will allow you to see how your objective may have evolved as you gained more insight into the music business.

Now that you have created a document, what do you write? As an independent musician, there are several different possibilities for your objective. Here are a few questions to get you thinking.

- Which musical genres are you most interested in playing: rock 'n' roll, jazz, country, fusion, blues, Latin, R&B, classical, or symphonic music?
- Do you want to specialize in one particular style or be a great all-around player who is equally proficient in a wide variety of styles?
- Are you primarily interested in being a working club musician?
- Are you interested in achieving notoriety as a great soloist?
- Do you want to be a studio musician and play record dates, jingles, and work on movie soundtracks?
- Do you want to be a touring musician and spend most of your time traveling around the world?
- How important is gaining the respect of your peers and musical heroes?

There are many more questions you should ask yourself, but somewhere early on in the course of your development as a musician, you will have to come to terms with these types of questions. In the end, how you answer them will determine the kind of musician you will become, which will naturally lead you down the roads you must travel in order to reach your destination.

> *There are many things that will catch my eye, but there are only a few that catch my heart....It is those I consider to pursue.*
> —Tim Redmond

As you can see, there are many different paths you can choose, which is precisely the reason you need to sit down and give your objective some serious thought. For most people, pondering their future is something they wish to avoid, but doing so could only be to your own detriment.

Identifying your objective may take some time, but trust me—it's time well spent. Once you do your homework, you'll stop wasting time and energy going in the wrong direction or in no direction at all. A clearly defined objective will help you focus your efforts much more efficiently.

> *The indispensable first step to getting the things you want out of your life is this: decide what you want.*
> —Ben Stein

Imagine if the leaders of Apple Computer, Inc. had said, "We just want to make good computers," but had no specific objective for the Macintosh brand? Who would buy products from a company that put no real thought or effort into their product development? People don't purchase products based on good intentions; they part with precious money on quality products that fulfill a need. Remember that you are the product, and if you want someone to eat from your tree, you'd better make sure the apples you produce taste good.

In order to experience the complete picture of success, you should also identify your spiritual and personal objectives as well. I am a drummer by profession, but as we discussed earlier, my life does not consist solely of my career. Being a drummer is a big part of who I am, but I am also a husband, father, brother, friend, mentor, motivator, writer, and a child of God. If relationships are important to you—which I hope they are—you'll need to make room for them in your life when mapping out your master plan.

Considering the three facets of your life, try answering the following questions as you put together your personal objective:

- Do you want to be single or married?
- Do you want to raise a family?
- How many children do you want?
- In what city would you like to live?
- Do you want to live in the country or city?
- How important are material possessions?
- How do you feel about spending a lot of time traveling?
- How flexible are you?
- Can you deal with constant change?
- How important are friendships to you?

If your only desire is to become one of the world's greatest classical pianists, there are certain studies you won't need to undertake, such as learning to play rock 'n' roll. There would be no sense wasting time on that style of music. On the other hand, if you prefer a more diverse career with a broader base, you will need to develop more diversified skills. Each objective requires a unique set of priorities.

It's not enough to know that you want to become a successful musician; more specifically, you must define what you want your career to do for you. Personally, I want my career to fulfill my need for self-expression as an artist. It is also essential that my profession rewards me financially in order to support my family.

> *It's not enough to know that you want to become a successful musician...*

What about you? Do you want to play music merely to supplement your income and have a good time rather than to be your full-time occupation? There are many benefits to doing music part time. For starters, you won't have to deal with as many negative things as someone who is completely dependent on music to make a living. You would be free to play what you want with whomever you want, allowing you to express your full artistic creativity without the pressure of having to make money at it.

There are plenty of great musicians who make a living doing something other than music as a full-time gig. By choosing that path, they play their music without sacrificing their artistic integrity. There is something truly beautiful and freeing about that.

THE BIG PICTURE

I CAN SEE CLEARLY NOW

For a moment, envision a puzzle of the United States. Each of the 50 states is vital to the nation as a whole. If you take away California, there goes the movie industry and much of the world's entertainment. Without New York, there goes the stock market and a strong part of the financial infrastructure of our country. If you take away one of the Midwestern states like Iowa, there goes a huge part of our food supply, since they are major producers of corn, beans, and wheat. Individually, each state is a unique and separate entity, but collectively they are all part of a greater unified purpose that makes the United States of America what it is today.

I think of achieving success in the music business much like the task of putting together a puzzle. Each step of the process is critical to mapping out the entire picture. If you are not currently experiencing the success you envision, I guarantee there are pieces missing from your puzzle. The most important thing is to become acquainted with the big picture so you can identify those missing pieces.

The problem many musicians experience is that the picture they see is often much too small. They tend to see only a portion of the ingredients needed for success and miss other key components in the process, preventing them from experiencing the success they hope for.

*Nothing is particularly hard if you divide it
into small jobs.*

—Henry Ford

Take a look at the following diagram. As you can see, some of the
pieces are already in place. The corners are labeled with words:
goals, talent, experience, and attitude. They are the obvious starting
point for completing any puzzle, but the missing center pieces that
comprise most of the picture are far more difficult to complete. My
goal throughout this book is to help you understand and identify
each piece and inspire you to put the rest of the puzzle together, one
piece at a time.

PIECING TOGETHER THE
PUZZLE FOR SUCCESS

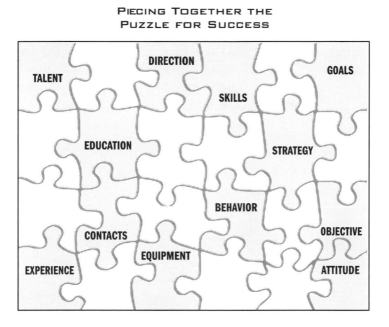

SCORING POINTS

PICK UP THE PIECES

The music business as a whole is very different from most other
businesses. Unorthodox, there are no set rules on how one makes
it in this industry, no exact steps etched in stone or delineated in a
formal document like one would find when pursuing a career as a

teacher, lawyer, or architect. For example, if you want to become a doctor you must follow this course:

1. Get a good grade point average and score high enough on your entrance exams to be accepted into college.
2. Earn an undergraduate degree at a four-year college or university.
3. Pass the MCAT (Medical College Admission Test) and get accepted at an accredited medical school.
4. Choose an area of specialty and complete medical school.
5. Complete a residency training program.

All of the steps are laid out for you; you simply follow the formula without deviating from the plan. It is only after completing each step and passing crucial exams that you have the privilege of entering the medical profession—not one minute before.

Conversely, in the music business there is no singular golden path. You can skip straight to Step 5 if the right situation presents itself. You might know somebody who is in a prominent position in the industry, and all of a sudden, voilà! You are suddenly connected.

What if you really didn't have to learn the skills necessary to work as an airline pilot or at a nuclear power plant? What if you were a defense attorney handling a capital murder case and you didn't know jack about the law, but you were able to jive your way in? What if you were a food chemist charged with designing a new diet pill and you were able to schmooze your way into the laboratory without having to study science?

Imagine what it would be like if someone could say, "Hey, my uncle's a brain surgeon at 'so and so' hospital and he totally hooked me up, so dude I'm doing brain surgery now. Isn't that totally awesome, bro?" If that were the case, lobotomies would be commonplace, and there'd be even more crazos walking around our planet than there are now.

> *Your career as a musician should be approached with the same seriousness demanded of other professions.*

Fortunately, our society still demands substantial credentials before handing over the mantle of authority in areas where critical expertise is a must. But since there are no set rules or rigid standards to abide by in the music business as in these other professions, there are a lot of musicians who don't know what they're doing.

Your career as a musician should be approached with the same seriousness demanded of other professions. The musicians in high demand as sidemen are extremely proficient at what they do. Of course, there are always a few individuals who luck out and make it without much effort, but without true skill, the chances of having an enduring career as a back-up musician are very slim.

There are as many diverse ways to make it in this business as there are musicians in it. In spite of that, I do believe there are specific strategies you can employ to stack the odds in your favor and increase your chances. To help guide you through the steps, I've devised something I call "finger pointing."

Let's say, for example, that it takes 100 points to achieve success in the music business. Now, imagine each piece of the puzzle having a point value. You would receive x number of points for having raw talent, x number of points for having a strategy, and a certain number of points for setting short-term and long-range goals, your skills, education, equipment, experience, contacts, reliability, and so on. As you point out these pieces and get more and more of them together, your score gets higher and you narrow the margin for failure and increase your odds of success.

> There are as many diverse ways to make it in this business as there are musicians in it.

In the next chapter, we will explore what some of those pieces are and what it takes to prepare them for legitimate placement onto the puzzle.

Champions know there are no shortcuts to the top.
They climb the mountain one step at a time. They have
no use for helicopters!

—Judi Adler

THE ART OF STRATEGY
IMPLEMENTING YOUR PLANS FOR SUCCESS

What do you want to achieve or avoid? The answers to this question are objectives. How will you go about achieving your desire results? The answer to this you can call strategy.

—William E Rothschild

I went to school with a guy we'll call Joe Schmoe. Joe was a multi-talented musician with incredible natural talent and an unbelievable ear; he could play anything he heard. I felt my own talent was narrow in comparison. I played the drums, but Joe played everything. Everyone expected him to make it big—everyone except him. Sadly, Joe got involved with drugs and never reached his full musical potential.

The outcome of our lives has less to do with public expectation and more to do with belief in oneself. Joe failed, in part, because he lacked a strategy for taking his gift to the marketplace. I am a living example of how one with less talent can achieve more than those who are favored to win—all because I had vision. My journey in music started so late in the game that I had to formulate an effective strategy quickly in order to be a contender. My goal was to make it as easy as possible for someone to hire me.

THE IMPORTANCE OF STRATEGY
DON'T YOU (FORGET ABOUT ME)

The most important building block for any kind of achievement is your strategy. No matter how sincere, noble, and honest your intentions may be, without a strategy, they will be aimless and unfruitful.

The New Oxford American Dictionary defines strategy this way: "A plan of action or policy designed to achieve

http://4wrd.it/A.BG3

a major or overall aim." In other words, a strategy signifies having a game plan of how you are going to get to a specific destination.

Pretend for a moment that I am a high school band director planning to take my entire stage band on a trip from Chicago to New Orleans. Obviously, there are several different means of travel I could choose—we could go by bus, take a train, fly, or rent cars and drive ourselves. I could even recommend we take bicycles if I am crazy enough and want to get fired.

If I exercise wisdom, I will base my decision on a number of factors—my goals, the budget I have to work with, our schedule, and the number of travelers—and then determine which means of travel would be the best fit. Beyond that, there are several details that would have to be well thought out in order for the trip to run smoothly and be considered a successful experience.

Formulating a plan, or a strategy, is crucial to reaching your goals. So many people get up every morning without the slightest clue as to where they are headed. Most have more than enough talent to achieve some kind of success, but they rarely develop and adhere to a game plan. They wander aimlessly, much like a carefree hitchhiker, and go in whatever direction the wind may blow. Because they refuse to give much thought to what they want to achieve, the long and winding road upon which they travel is filled with uncertainty.

Weeds grow easily in the soil of indecision.
—Harry Cox

There is, of course, another road, a better road, one paved by those who know exactly where they are going and have calculated precisely what it   will take to get there. This road requires vision, foresight, and tenacity. It is the road to self-fulfilled prophecies; a place where what you think about yourself and what you plan come to pass.

Alan Lakein, a well-known expert in personal time management, said, "Failing to plan is planning to fail." Those who invest the time to map out and adhere to a game plan will, more often than not, arrive at their destination; failing to plan will sidetrack you every time.

Most of us have one thing in common—we all want to be winners! No one wakes up hoping to fail miserably in life. I don't believe for one minute that anyone dreams of working at a job day in and day out that they absolutely hate and living an unfulfilled life.

Due to an unfortunate lack of planning, many people never achieve their goals. By neglecting to plan and formulate some kind of strategy, you too will most likely fail to reach your desired destination. Developing a strategic plan for your life is crucial for the manifestation of your dreams and the realization of your potential.

Let me make one thing clear, however: having a strategy is not going to lessen the hardships, barriers, and discouragement that visit us all. No matter who you are, adversity always finds your home address, especially after you set a plan in motion and are determined to see it through.

Just because you have a strategy does not mean your train won't get derailed from time to time, but having one compels you to get back on the tracks no matter what happens. The reason they are called "detours" is because they make you go out of your way, insinuating you were going in a specific direction in the first place. It took Albert Einstein more than 15 years to prove his theory of relativity, and during that time he ran into horrendous obstacles, grave setbacks, and unimaginable disappointments. Even though he was greatly challenged on all sides, he was victorious because he stuck to his plan and, in the process, changed the world forever.

It is those who have this imperative demand for the
best in their natures and those who will accept nothing
short of it, that hold the banners of progress, that set the
standards, the ideals for others.
—Orison Swett Marden

While most great opportunities are the result of strategic efforts, there are, of course, cases in which circumstances just happen to fall into place. Unfortunately, you can't bank on that happening. Luck. Karma. Kismet. Serendipity. Call it what you want, it cannot be manipulated. You need only concern yourself with the things you do have control over such as preparation, persistence, perseverance, and patience.

SETTING SHORT-TERM GOALS

I ONLY HAVE EYES FOR YOU

Once you have defined your objective and finished drawing up a basic personal mission statement, the next step is to map out some short-range goals to help you achieve it. When I was a teenager, I had four important short-term goals:

- To take private drumming lessons and develop some basic skills
- To get into the high-school stage band, swing choir, and concert bands
- To earn enough money to buy a new drum set
- To acquire some kind of motor vehicle for transportation

In order to achieve the financial goals that would allow me to purchase a new drum set and pay for my private lessons, I found it necessary to work two jobs. During the summer before my junior year in high school, I worked 16 hours a day. From 7:30 a.m. to 3:30 p.m. I worked at Rogue Community College in Grants Pass, Oregon, as a maintenance man and groundskeeper. My responsibilities included watering the plants, mowing the lawn, weeding, sweeping, and whatever else I was asked to do. Needless to say, this job was purely physical labor and was humbling for a teenage boy, but every morning, come rain or shine, I rode my white 10-speed bike to work, showed up on time, and was grateful for the opportunity.

My second job, which was from 4:30 p.m. to 12:30 a.m., was at Hellgate Jet Boat Excursions, a tourist attraction on the wild and scenic Rogue River. The tour included a dinner stopover at the OK Corral, a restaurant situated along the bank of the river, where hungry rafters were served greasy chicken and barbecued ribs. My friend Paul Baker and I set the tables, cooked the food, and then washed all the dishes by hand—this fine dining establishment didn't have a dishwasher.

> *Opportunity is missed by most people because it is dressed in overalls, and looks like work.*
>
> —Thomas Edison

Pulling double duty was exhausting, and by the end of each night I was beat, but my hard work paid off. At the end of the summer, I achieved three of my short-range goals. First, I bought a brand-new, five-piece Slingerland maple drum set. Second, I started taking private drum lessons from a really cool senior at my high school named Eric Christianson; he gave me a solid foundation upon which to build. Then came goal number three. My older brother, Ricardo, left his 1968 Chevy Malibu Super Sport 396 behind for the family to use when he went into the military. For the first time, I had reliable—as well as fast—transportation and was no longer dependent on my bicycle or the school bus.

I was ready to take on the world! It was an incredible feeling of accomplishment to be able to pay for the drum set and lessons with my own hard-earned money, and I felt blessed that my brother allowed me to use his car.

If you want to be happy, set a goal that commands your thoughts, liberates your energy and inspires your hopes.
—Andrew Carnegie

The importance of setting short-term goals cannot be overemphasized. Without them, most people drift, unable to accomplish anything of value. Setting my goals allowed me to chip away at my big dreams with forward momentum. Most people prefer to achieve success in one single swoop. In reality, it is a series of faithful little steps that lead you to big things. Rather than trying to jump your way to the top of the castle, which seldom works, build it yourself, brick by brick, and give each layer your absolute best. When you get to the top, you will appreciate just how much hard work goes into building anything of worth.

SETTING LONG-TERM GOALS

YOU'RE IN MY HEART

When I was a young boy, my mom taught me to value and preserve family history. As a result, I've become a very sentimental man who holds on to the precious memories of my past. I have a collection of mementos that would astound you—everything from junior-high and high school homework to a sampling of every hobby I was ever into. My stamp collection, ceramic projects, drawings from art class, a cheesy jewelry collection, my nasty extracted wisdom teeth, 4-H Club prize ribbons, my diary, and all my report cards are just a few examples of things I kept.

I actually have separate trunks for each era of my life, from childhood through the present. They contain an incredible collection of photos, clippings of every magazine interview I have ever done, old fan mail, and any semblance of recognition I have ever received. I guess I've saved it all as a reminder of where I came from and how far I have traveled from the start of my incredible journey. These trunks contain the legacy I hope to preserve for my children and generations to come.

One day when I was in a particularly reflective and nostalgic mood, I riffled through my trunks one by one and reminisced. As I looked through the pages of my life, so many memories raced through my mind. I could actually remember how I was thinking and what I was feeling at different points in my life. As I browsed, I stumbled across two pieces of archaic-looking paper. Written in absolutely shameful handwriting were the original goals I had set for myself at the age of 15 and some additional ones I had written just a short time after high school. They had been taped to the refrigerator, and every morning when I awoke, I had read them to remind myself of my mission and my dreams. That sense of purpose kept me going during some difficult days.

You must have long-range goals to keep you from being frustrated by the short-range failures.
—Charles C. Noble

These were my goals:

- To move to Los Angeles and seriously pursue a career in the music industry
- To study with a great drum instructor who was a successful freelance musician, someone who could take me under his wing and show me the ropes
- To make contacts and develop strong relationships with other serious young musicians
- To get into a variety of working bands and play in as many different musical settings as possible
- To become an accomplished player and express myself on a high musical level
- To make a name for myself and develop an image and identity
- To score the dream gig, the big kahuna, that vehicle that was necessary to establish a world-class reputation as a player
- To earn the respect and friendship of my musical heroes
- To travel around the world to exotic locations
- To prosper financially through my craft
- To be happily married, raise a family, and experience the joys of fatherhood

I was shocked when I looked in the trunks that day and realized I had achieved all my goals. Those handwritten pieces of paper helped me discipline myself to do the things I didn't always want to do, and I honestly felt motivated each time I read them. They represented why I was working so hard at jobs I didn't like.

Many people achieve success in the music business for just a very brief time, like a sideman who lands one big gig backing up a major artist but is never able to parlay that into a thriving career. One year, some one-hit wonders make incredible amounts of money with a chart-topping record, and three years later they're broke, down and out, and working at a convenience store.

This flash-in-the-pan scenario happens for several reasons. Sometimes it is sheer ignorance on the part of the musicians, but in other cases, their demise is due to industry factors beyond their control, such as a lack of label, radio, and management support, or a sudden loss of interest by the public. Audiences can be very fickle, and their musical tastes can change as often as the weather. You may have been the flavor of the month, or the year—but suddenly there's a new kid on the block, and you're yesterday's news. That's just the nature of the biz.

There's not much you can do to prevent this kind of regime change, but being aware of these eventualities and capitalizing on every opportunity that comes your way can make a huge difference. Ignorance may sometimes be bliss, but sticking your head in the sand like an ostrich will be your doom.

> *You cannot escape the responsibility of tomorrow*
> *by evading it today.*
>
> —Abraham Lincoln

While short-term success often centers on being in the right place at the right time, long-term success is the result of a deliberate course of action that cultivates your talent and elevates it to the highest possible level. To attain long-term success requires serious foresight. Forging out a long-term career in this business is nothing short of strategic military warfare; if you are not prepared for battle, you will eventually run into land mines and unwittingly succumb to defeat.

A power is released deep inside when you forge out your goals and commit yourself to attaining them. The process worked for me, so I know it can work for you.

PRIORITIZE YOUR GOALS

EVERY LITTLE STEP

Once you have set all your short-term and long-range goals, it's time to prioritize them in order of importance and begin implementing strategic steps toward their achievement. Let's say, for example, that one of your long-range goals is to play with a famous jazz artist. To make that possible, you need to acquire a certain set of skills. Every style of music has its own unique language, so you'd have to master the language of jazz to be considered by any great jazz artist.

To do that, you would immerse yourself in the art form and study privately with a jazz master who could teach you all of the underlying musical principles that constitute the genre. One of the major requirements would be to know a vast number of jazz standards and become fluent in the dialect. You would also need to be able to confidently solo over a variety of jazz-oriented chord progressions and in the time feels most commonly associated with jazz, such as 4/4 swing, 3/4 swing, samba, bossa nova, and 6/8 Afro Cuban.

> *The secret of getting ahead is getting started. The secret of getting started is breaking your complex, overwhelming tasks into small manageable tasks, and then starting on the first one.*
>
> —Mark Twain

It's all very systematic and logical. If you want to get to Step B, you must first take care of Step A. To reach Step C, you have to blow through Step B. You have to learn to walk before you can run. Once your priorities are in the proper chronological order, approaching your goals is far less daunting. Adhering to the plan keeps you from going around and around the same mole hills, when what you really need to do is scale some rather large mountains.

ACCOUNTABILITY

WIND BENEATH MY WINGS

My sister, Patricia, invited me to visit her in New York City when I was 18. I was totally thrilled when I walked down 48th Street, the home of many legendary music stores I had read about and seen in magazines. The Big Apple had energy like I had never experienced before. For a wannabe musician, this was the place to be!

When my younger brother, Bobby, and I visited Drummers World, I remember looking around in utter amazement at all of the gear. There was more equipment there than I had ever seen in my life. While browsing, I met the owner, a very nice man named Barry. After making my purchase, I confidently told him, "Hey Barry, I want you to remember my name. Someday I'm going to make it big and be a famous drummer, and when I do, you'll remember this day."

In his thick New York accent, I'm sure Barry must have mumbled something like, "Yeah sure kid, everyone thinks he's gonna make it, brother, have I heard that one before, yadda yadda yadda!" It wasn't with an arrogant spirit that I shared those words, but with a sincere heart and an earnest desire to do something great with my life. Amazingly, in five year's time Barry began to see my name appear in all of the drum magazines he carried on his store shelves.

> *A man can succeed at almost anything for which he has*
> *unlimited enthusiasm.*
>
> —Charles M. Schwab

I made my triumphant return to the city performing at Madison Square Garden with The New Edition, a wildly popular group at the time. The day before my concert, I stopped in to see Barry. The shop owner remembered me as the enthusiastic kid who'd spoken so confidently about the future, and he seemed genuinely thrilled to see me. I was equally thrilled to share my accomplishments.

Throughout the years, I ran into Barry at various music retailer trade shows, and with a big smile he'd tell my story to those who gathered around us. It always deeply touched my heart.

When I first started playing music, I told all my friends that I believed I had a gift for playing the drums and that I would someday make it big as a drummer. I didn't say it in a braggadocios way; I merely shared my dream in an enthusiastic manner. I knew if I went public with my goals that I would eventually have to answer to those bold claims or risk looking like an idiot—just the incentive I needed to keep pushing hard. He didn't know it, but Barry from Drummer's World was one of my accountability partners.

If you're serious about making it in music, it's time for you to step out and make a public confession of your intentions and share your plans and goals with others. After writing your mission statement, determining your specific goals, and prioritizing them, you should build in an accountability mechanism to ensure success. That could be a friend, family member, or fellow musician, but it's important to find someone who wants you to succeed and who will keep you accountable to the goals you have set for yourself.

Accountability is one of the most important steps in making your dreams come true. If your goal is to lose 25 pounds but you don't tell anyone about it, there would be no accountability and no one to encourage you to work out or stick to your diet. No one would put you in check for eating 16 gallons of Ben & Jerry's Chunky Monkey ice cream, or scarfing down a 72-ounce steak with mushrooms, or frequenting all-you-can-eat buffets.

> *Our greatest weakness lies in giving up. The most*
> *certain way to succeed is always to try one more time.*
> —Thomas Edison

It's far too easy to quit when the going gets tough if you don't have someone to keep you on track. I always work out harder at the gym when I train with a partner because of the synergy that you cannot experience alone. Left to myself, I don't push as hard as I do with someone to spur me on. Each one of us needs people who will challenge us to demand more from ourselves. Telling trusted people about your goals will help to affirm and clarify your intentions and apply the pressure you need to make good on your promise.

TENACITY

AGAINST ALL ODDS

From the time I decided to pursue music as a full-time occupation, I was like a horse with blinders on. I could see nothing else and focused solely on developing my music skills. Because I had made a public confession of my goals, I had no escape. I didn't allow myself to even contemplate a Plan B, because I knew that kind of thinking would make room for the possibility of defeat.

There was nothing else I could fall back on because nothing else impacted my soul like music did. I still had to work day jobs along the way to make a buck, but I didn't devote my free time to studying something I had no intention of pursuing. Why would a pre-law student concentrate on something other than law if he wanted to become a lawyer? Would a medical student study drums on the side just in case he didn't make it through medical school? How could becoming a musician be any different?

> *Once you say you're going to settle for second, that's*
> *what happens to you in life, I find.*
>
> —John F. Kennedy

When you focus on two things at once, one of two things will happen: either one of them will end up playing second fiddle, or both will be compromised and you won't be great at either one. By dividing yourself in this manner, you greatly reduce your chances of success. If you do have a Plan B, there is a strong likelihood you will change directions when facing adversity and head there instead of where you really want to go. Most of us will choose the path of least resistance every time. In other words, we settle.

I was not willing to settle for second best. Because I intentionally left myself with no back-up plan, there was no room for failure. Music was an all-or-nothing proposition for me, and there was no turning back. To maintain my focus, it was mental warfare all the way. I realize this seems like pretty hardcore militant thinking, but you need to accept that the world is one big battle zone with hidden land mines everywhere. Your job is to take them out one by one and defuse them ahead of time.

> *It is fatal to enter any war without the will to win it.*
>
> —General Douglas MacArthur

Being left with no alternative will force you to get on the ball and stay there. When your existence depends upon it, you'll learn to give your dreams all you've got. Being under pressure is often the best place to be, because it forces us to give our personal best. The whole concept of bodybuilding is built upon this premise; it takes resistance to build muscle. The purpose of that resistance is not to destroy you, but to build something that could not come any other way—strength!

The process of refining silver involves holding a piece of silver in the middle of a fire where the flames are hottest so the impurities can be burned away. The silversmith has to keep an eye on the metal the entire time it is in the fire; if the silver is in the flames for a moment too long, it will be destroyed. The silver is fully refined when the smith's own image can be seen in it.

Although we all love times of prosperity, the truth is that we only grow in times of great opposition. Sometimes life has a way of taking us through the furnace in order to bring about something greater that lies within us. The real point in forging through the great difficulties of life is that it will bring about your greatest strengths and purest of intentions if you allow yourself to go through the fiery process. Don't always view hardship as a negative thing—without it, you will never reach your full potential.

FOCUS

I CONCENTRATE ON YOU

My in-laws would invite my wife and me over for dinner fairly regularly when we lived across the street from them. On one occasion, there was something really interesting on television, so we opted to set up TV trays in the family room and eat in front of the big screen.

Their German shepherd, Dillon, decided to plop himself right in front of me for the entire meal. You should have seen him; he sat upright like a statue with his eyes glued on my plate. His head remained straight forward, and his eyes didn't move for a split second. The dog was so focused on my plate that I couldn't enjoy my food without feeling guilty.

Dillon's goal was to eat everyone's leftovers, a worthwhile objective if you're a dog. He patiently sat in a trance for as long as it took to get what he wanted. Nothing distracted him. The house could have been burning down, but that pooch didn't move until someone put a plate down for him to lick. I eventually caved in and offered mine, and the moment he was done licking it, he moved to the next person who was still eating and commenced the killer stare all over again.

Although my family had several German shepherds while I was growing up, over the years I had forgotten that dogs dwell constantly on their stomachs. I was so taken by Dillon's total immersion in the food on the table that I grabbed a little piece of roast beef from another plate and waved it in front of his face. If I were a hypnotist, Dillon would have spilled his guts about the emotional pain he'd experienced as a puppy and how his parents had left him. He was totally in the palm of my hand.

Not being one to practice animal cruelty, I finally gave him the piece of meat after conducting my experiment. My father-in-law, Wil, uttered something profound: "If we could all learn to be as focused as Dillon was on that food, we could be giants of accomplishment." He was right on target, and the truth of his statement hit me hard. I thought, "Man, if I could approach every goal in my life with that kind of focus, there would be nothing I couldn't accomplish!"

The dog's simple act of concentration and laser-sharp focus amazed me. I have often found myself thinking of Dillon when trying to achieve one of my goals—including finishing this book. He was a profound example of diligence.

SELF-MOTIVATION

THE BIGGEST PART OF ME

The difference between successful people and those who are not is often just a matter of desire. The innate abilities of those who fail are usually not any less than those who succeed; what they most often lack is vision, passion, and drive.

It's important to have dreams, but none of them will ever come true unless you learn the art of self-motivation. If you are unable to discipline yourself, writing down your goals will become nothing more than a useless mental exercise. It takes good old-fashioned hard work to succeed.

Working hard is merely a choice one makes. To some degree, your work ethic was modeled for you by those who influenced you in your formative years. Some parents teach their children the importance of hard work and personally demonstrate it, while others do nothing to foster that mindset because they are lazy and lack drive.

Whether you had hardworking role models who encouraged you, or you were surrounded by people who belittled you, put down your aspirations, or laughed at your dreams, there is no excuse for being unmotivated. In the end it will always remain a question of will.

If you learn to embrace hard work rather than avoid it, your life will yield far more positive results. Practice when you don't feel like it, and go out and meet people when you feel like lying on the couch. Music is one of the most competitive careers you could possibly choose, so you must do everything possible to stack the odds in your favor. Self-motivation is the cornerstone of all true accomplishment.

> *The secret of discipline is motivation. When a man is sufficiently motivated, discipline will take care of itself.*
>
> —Sir Alexander Paterson

To remain positive, surround yourself with people who are motivated and inspiring. We all run out of steam eventually and need to get recharged by those who can encourage us. Being around people who are driven and ambitious always forces us to pull ourselves up by our bootstraps and get back in the race. Motivation is infectious!

We all need people on the sidelines who are willing to cheer us on. If you don't have any yet, don't worry. Many of the world's most successful people found themselves alone in the cheering squad at some point in their lives, but they refused to let that stop them.

Deafening crowds root for winners. Just go to a rock concert or any major sporting event and you'll see what I mean. Where were all those fans when the artists and athletes were just starting out? The answer is nowhere—they didn't show up until their talent became obvious and attracted everyone's attention. Believe in yourself enough to cheer like a maniac even when no one else is there! Enthusiasm is contagious; eventually, others will join in and sing a chorus of your fight song along with you. Once you break certain barriers and reach introductory levels of success, more and more cheerleaders will show up. Soon, everyone in attendance will be screaming your name!

> *People often say that motivation doesn't last. Well,*
> *neither does bathing—that's why we*
> *recommend it daily.*
>
> —Zig Ziglar

CONSTRUCTIVE CRITICISM

GOT TO BE REAL

Back in 1983, I played with Philip Bailey, the lead singer of the Grammy Award-winning group Earth, Wind & Fire. I felt completely out of my league on that gig; I was just an up-and-coming young musician playing with some of the top studio pros of the time. The all-star lineup included James Jamerson Jr., son of legendary Motown bassist James Jamerson Sr., on bass, and celebrated Los Angeles studio guitarist Paul Jackson Jr. Much to my surprise, they seemed to like my drumming, personality, and enthusiasm and decided to work with me.

On a flight to one of our shows, I asked Paul for his advice on what I could do to increase my chances of becoming a successful musician. He told me that the most important thing I could learn as a drummer was to play a groove, any groove, no matter how simple it was, and make it feel great.

He urged me to play regularly with a metronome. "Don't change the groove—don't alter it, don't do one fill, don't change anything—just play that same groove with the metronome for 10 minutes straight and sit on that groove until it is as smooth as silk, until it's flawless." His keen insight was a turning point for me as a drummer, because it caused a paradigm shift in my thinking.

Expert advice like the kind Paul gave me can drastically shape you if you allow it to. I soaked up that information like an absorbent paper towel on a wet surface, and it has changed my approach to playing music ever since. Asking for criticism certainly isn't easy. Who wants to hear, "Dude—you're not happening," or, "You need an awful lot of work in this area of your playing"? Unfortunately, a combination of fear and pride causes reluctance in musicians of all levels to seek constructive criticism or counsel from others, which is a huge mistake.

It takes humility to seek feedback. It takes wisdom to understand it, analyze it, and appropriately act on it.
—Stephen R. Covey

From the time I first started gigging in clubs, I asked musicians I respected to critique my playing and suggest areas for improvement. I desperately wanted their opinions and sought their advice on what I needed to work on most. By humbling myself, I got it.

I didn't stop asking for advice when I hit the big time and played on major tours with established pop stars. I made it a point to invite prominent professional musicians to my concerts whenever possible. After the show I would ask them to honestly evaluate my musicianship.

Initially, it was awkward for them to be candid with me, because most people are uncomfortable with brutal honesty. People won't want to step out on a limb and tell you how they really feel—for fear of offending you or breaking your heart—unless you are somehow able to make them feel totally comfortable in doing so. In my case, I truly wanted to know what I needed to improve so I could reach the next level and become like them. I was prepared to take their criticism like a man. In most cases, I really had to drag the truth out of them, but the extra effort proved to be worth it.

To make my critics feel at ease, I asked them to level with me without sugarcoating their comments. I made it a point to do what former major league baseball player Don Sutton suggested, "Find the grain of truth in criticism—chew it and swallow it." As I listened to their critiques, I felt like a little kid gulping down some really nasty medicine, all the while knowing good and well that it was the best thing for me.

Taking heed of their instruction helped me improve more than any other previous tactic. No matter where you are in your career, if you truly want to continue to grow and develop as a musician, you must welcome critique from your peers and experts.

The Greek philosopher Socrates once said, "The life which is unexamined is not worth living." If you truly want to reach your potential, you must consistently examine every aspect of your life and realize you can benefit from the wisdom and experience of others.

The truth often hurts, but genuine growth is a painful process that requires the abandonment of ego. In my case, the constructive criticism I regularly received always hurt. But once I got off my self-pity trip and realized their instruction was only helping me, I was inspired to work harder. Ultimately, that made all the difference in my career.

KNOW YOUR STRENGTHS AND BUILD UPON THEM

GET DOWN ON IT

My personal strengths are few. I have an innate musical talent, a creative mind, and the gift of communication, which come in many forms, but that's really it.

On the downside, there are so many things I don't have a natural aptitude for that I sometimes feel like the absent-minded professor. I'm not very handy when it comes to home or car repairs or anything that requires mechanical sensibilities. I'm also pretty technologically challenged, if I'm being brutally honest. But if I were to dwell on what I'm not good at rather than on my talents and abilities, I would be so overcome with self-pity and fear that I wouldn't do anything.

> *Do what you can with what you have, where you are.*
> —Theodore Roosevelt

We were all created with specific gifts that give us the propensity to flourish in certain areas. Thank God no one person has it all, or the rest of us would feel completely incompetent. The good news is that we can focus on developing what comes naturally and stop sweating the stuff that doesn't! I've always felt that if I could excel at the things for which I'm naturally gifted I could hire people to take care of the things in areas where I'm clueless.

To succeed, you must use what you have been given and capitalize on your strengths. Of course, that doesn't mean you can ditch your weaknesses altogether; you must work on developing them little by little so you can become more well-rounded and versatile. But never allow your weaknesses to prevent you from shining in your areas of strength.

> *No man could ideally be successful until he has found his place. Like a locomotive, he is strong on the track, but weak anywhere else.*
> —Orison Swett Marden

THE ART OF ATTITUDE
REALIZING THE POWER OF EXCELLENCE

*Nothing can stop the man with the right mental attitude
from achieving his goal; nothing on earth can help the
man with the wrong mental attitude.*

—Thomas Jefferson

Several years ago I hooked a friend up with an audition for a big-name act. Michael went in and nailed the music, and I was totally thrilled when he landed the gig. I'd raved about this cat, and he made me look good!

Not long after rehearsals for the tour started, Michael began to show signs of a bad attitude. He became increasingly difficult to work with; he was persnickety and inflexible and got on everyone's nerves. I had put my neck out on the line and vouched for this guy because he was an incredible musician, but his attitude made me regret I'd ever recommended him.

Michael only played a couple of warm-up dates with the artist before being fired. Unfortunately, he missed a massive world tour with one of the biggest artists, and he lost out on a lot of money and a golden chance to build his name and credibility in the business. If he'd had a good attitude, he would have easily kept the gig and advanced his career as a result.

In the music business, success is not always based on the obvious attributes of talent or genius. More than anything else, it is attitude combined with behavior that earns respect. Enjoying a good reputation and a credible character can make a huge difference in the opportunities that come your way.

When someone makes a decision whether to recommend me for a gig, it is usually based on what they know about my reputation as a musician and the way I have performed in previous work situations. Character is most clearly evidenced by how we live our lives. Good intentions are great, but the truth becomes crystal clear by our actions alone. Therefore, it is essential to develop a great reputation right from the start—the success of your career depends on it.

> *Tell me who admires you and I will tell you*
> *who you are.*
>
> —Antoine de Saint-Exupéry

Personality goes a long way in the workplace, and yours will either work for you or against you. The music business is very socially oriented—one of personalities, chemistry, and vibes—and how these attributes blend with others can either create magic or chaos. A lack of personality (or an annoying, uncooperative one) is often what holds people back from getting a major gig. A bad attitude is one of the most common reasons musicians get fired—or are never hired in the first place. No one wants to work with a jerk no matter how good he or she may be on an instrument. I've seen many cases in which someone of lesser ability was chosen over a virtuoso because the rookie was easier to work with.

> *Perhaps the greatest discovery of this century is that if*
> *you change your attitude, you can change your life.*
>
> —William James

Despite your best efforts to try and conceal it, the attitude with which you play your instrument will become very transparent. If you think you're the hottest player in the world, your arrogance will surely come out in your playing. If you have a lousy attitude, your chances of success will be greatly diminished because no one will want to be around you. The more amiable you are on a gig, the greater your chances of being recommended down the line.

This may be a good time for you to do some serious self-evaluation and honestly answer a few very important questions about yourself:

- How do you feel about hard work?
- Are you willing to go the extra mile to do a good job?

- Do you have a chip on your shoulder?
- Do you feel the world owes you something?
- Do you think you're the baddest cat in town?
- Would you say you are a humble person?
- Would you consider yourself a team player?
- Are you easy to work with?
- If you were an artist, producer, or musical director, would you hire you?

The answers to these questions are more important than you probably realize. When it comes to landing a big gig, perfecting your work attitude is just as important as practicing your instrument.

For a barometer of truth, get an honest assessment from those closest to you about how you are perceived; they are the ones most likely to see you for who you really are. If they level with you about the flaws in your character, you will know exactly what you need to work on most.

THE MOST IMPORTANT SUCCESS ATTRIBUTES FOR THE MUSIC INDUSTRY

Enthusiasm   Gratitude   Humility

Persistence   Patience

ENTHUSIASM

I'M SO EXCITED

Have you ever noticed the energy that is generated when you hang around with enthusiastic people? Enthusiasm is like a virus that spreads—it's electric! Enthusiastic people are passionate and optimistic about everything they do and cause those around them to get more excited, too. Having a spirit of enthusiasm creates an energy within the room and amongst the players that makes it a joy for everyone to play with you. It will be evident in your playing and it will take you a long way. Believe me, recording artists and producers can tell if you're genuinely excited to play their music.

When you are an enthusiastic person, you approach everything with a positive attitude rather than a negative one. You look at the glass as half full rather than half empty, which makes you an asset and not a liability. William Ward said, "Enthusiasm and persistence can make an average person superior; indifference and lethargy can make a superior person average." Enthusiastic people always look at difficulties through the eyes of optimism and find the good in situations, allowing them to meet challenges head-on. Enthusiasm is undeniably contagious. The question you should ask yourself is, how much of it are you spreading around?

> *Every great and commanding movement in the annals of*
> *the world is the triumph of enthusiasm.*
> —Ralph Waldo Emerson

The drummer is in the driver's seat of the band, and that energy drives the rest of the musicians. That's why we are referred to as the "heartbeat of the band." No matter which instrument you play, it's your responsibility to play with a spirit of enthusiasm. Each instrumentalist has his or her own distinct role in pushing the music forward.

Good music, regardless of the style, is an emotional journey for those listening. Even though an audience can't always identify it, they know instinctively that there is something about the music that touches them. They can feel the chemistry that originates from the stage or studio. It is an invisible force.

People will only feel the vibes you emit, so if you want your audience or employer to get excited about what you are doing, you must be genuinely excited. Whether you are playing an upbeat happy song or one that evokes sorrow, your heart must be emotionally invested in every note in order to connect you to the complex emotional range of your listeners.

GRATITUDE

WE THANK YOU VERY SWEETLY

In advance of one of the European tours I did with Lenny Kravitz, I made arrangements to do interviews with several music magazines that coincided with the concert itinerary. I had an extremely difficult time connecting with the editor of the German drum magazine *Rimshot*, partly because of the language barrier but also because of the time difference between Los Angeles and Berlin. After numerous unsuccessful attempts, I finally gave up on the whole idea of hooking up with him.

After a show in Utrecht, Holland, I did an interview with a magazine called *Slagwerkkrant*, the nation's leading percussion publication. The writer, a delightful chap named Hugo Pinksterboer, conducted the interview, and we had a great time talking with one another.

When I got back to the States at the conclusion of the tour, I sent Hugo a letter thanking him for taking the time to come to my show and for the honor of being featured in the magazine. I was genuinely grateful because he had been so pleasant and knowledgeable.

About six months later, I received a large package in the mail from Hugo. It contained several copies of the issue of *Slagwerkkrant* in which my interview had appeared, but also a few copies of *Rimshot*. I couldn't figure out why in the world he had sent me the German magazine. Sticking out of one of the pages was a Post-it note. When I turned to it, I was shocked to see a two-page feature story on me, complete with some incredible photos. It turned out that Hugo also wrote for *Rimshot*.

Later, when I called to express my gratitude, I asked Hugo what had prompted him to send my interview to the German publication. He told me that it was rare for a musician to make the effort to thank him for an interview, and when I did, he was quite taken by my gesture. He went on to say that he genuinely liked me as both a drummer and as a person, and that he wanted to do everything in his power to help promote me. I was totally blown away.

That experience reaffirmed what I already knew to be true: when you take the time to make people feel appreciated and acknowledge what they have done for you, they are more liable to go out of their way to help you. It is impossible to make it on your own in this business. We need all the help we can get from those who are willing to lend a helping hand. You will always reap what you sow when it comes to how you treat others.

> *Good character is more to be praised than outstanding talent. Most talents are to some extent a gift. Good character, by contrast is not given to us. We have to build it piece by piece—by thought, choice, courage and determination.*
>
> —John Luther

To further drive home the point, let me tell you how the outcome of my first book, *The Commandments of R&B Drumming: A Comprehensive Guide to Soul, Funk & Hip Hop*, changed drastically when I showed a little gratitude.

When Thais Yannes, the graphic artist at Warner Bros. Publications who was assigned to the project, sent me her first draft of the book's interior layout, I sent her an encouraging card to thank her for her good work. She later told me it was the first note she had ever received from an author in all the years she had worked there.

Thais' first draft was very good, but her next version was a masterpiece. After she had received my note, she said she wanted to go back and put some serious effort into the layout. It

> *It's all about practicing the golden rule, "Do unto others, as you would have them do unto you."*

was evident she had taken a personal interest in my project because of my simple gesture of thanks, and I was amazed that one minor display of appreciation could garner so much.

I could fill up the pages of this entire book with similar stories. When people go out of their way for me, I always try to make it a point to let them know how much I appreciate their kindness. I do so via a phone call, text message, e-mail, a thank you card or gift, or with some other gesture that reflects my gratitude. I'm extremely grateful to anyone who lends me a helping hand in an industry that is inundated with extremely busy, and often self-absorbed, people.

It's comforting to know I can call someone and ask them for a personal favor when I really need it, and it's reassuring to know that they are likely to respond because of how I treated them in the past. It's all about practicing the golden rule, "Do unto others, as you would have them do unto you."

> *Don't think for a minute that you can exploit people, use them, and then spit them out when you're done and expect to have any kind of long-term success.*

Don't confuse expressing appreciation with being manipulative. Don't think for a minute that you can exploit people, use them, and then spit them out when you're done and expect to have any kind of long-term success. It's certainly possible to make it big by using people along the way, but you will never remain at the top by doing so. People have very good memories when it comes to being used and abused.

HUMILITY
GOT TO GET YOU INTO MY LIFE

Throughout my career, I've had the opportunity to meet many of the greatest musicians, actors, and entertainers on the planet. I have found that those who have reached a level of true greatness are often very humble people. They no longer find it necessary to go on an ego trip because they are secure within themselves and have nothing left to prove.

For some reason, it's the up-and-comers with half the talent and success who seem to be the ones who are always tripping out. You can feel an attitude of superiority when they walk into a room or when you talk with them. Some of them act like they're doing you a favor just talking to you. Obviously, they're insecure and still have something to prove, and that attitude is reflected in how they deal with people.

> *As the nightingale instinctively flees from the sound of the hawk, so does the beauty of humility vanish in the presence of pride.*
>
> —William Ward

What they fail to realize is that one of the most attractive of all human qualities is humility. It is a rare person who recognizes that their talent is merely a gift. You can do nothing to earn your talents; that's why they are called gifts.

Humility is a beautiful thing because it makes someone approachable, admired, and respected. The person who displays a humble attitude is revered and loved beyond what they can imagine, often because their behavior comes as a total shock and pleasant surprise to others.

> *There's no room for nasty egomaniacs. End of story.*

When someone meets a big-time celebrity actor who is down-to-earth, such as Denzel Washington or Will Ferrell, they go on and on about how great that person is. Celebrities, who are great stewards of their fame, have the uncanny ability to make us feel like it's possible to reach for the stars, because they seem so reachable despite their stardom. Some of the greatest musicians I have met are also some of the most sincerely humble and unassuming people I have ever known.

> *To be humble to superiors is duty, to equals courtesy, to inferiors nobleness.*
>
> —Benjamin Franklin

On the other hand, it's a real letdown when you meet someone whose skill is actually quite average but thinks he or she is the greatest thing since sliced bread. There's no room for nasty egomaniacs. End of story.

Along with a sense of humility, however, it's essential to display an attitude of self-assurance when you're playing if you want someone to hire you. Confidence is built as you gain more experience and immerse yourself in a variety of performing situations. You will become much more confident with each and every new experience and by conquering your hidden fears one by one.

There is a fine line, however, between displaying self-assurance and being arrogant. When you act confidently, you are merely demonstrating that you actually know what you're doing and not getting through the music by chance. You can certainly display your skills without having an attitude of superiority. Arrogance, on the other hand, comes across as a spirit of pride. It's easy for people to sense an inflated ego, and if they sense that in you, fewer of them will want to work with you.

PERSISTENCE

GONNA FLY NOW

Rocky is one of my all-time favorite movies. Although it is a fictional story, it exemplifies the spirits of persistence and determination necessary for achieving success. The film is the story of a smalltime boxer named Rocky Balboa (played by Sylvester Stallone) who dreams of making it to the big time. His dream is a total long shot for a has-been from the streets of Philadelphia who's a little too old to get in the game. But after a great deal of hard work, Rocky works his way up the food chain until he has a chance to fight for the title, Heavyweight Champion of the World, only to lose in the end.

In the sequel, *Rocky 2,* our hero eventually beats his arch nemesis, Apollo Creed, and achieves his lifelong dream of becoming the

> *Success is the fruit of two words we have heard all our lives: persistence and determination.*

champ. Nearly everyone around him said he'd never make it, but his trainer, Mick, saw his potential and taught him how to develop his gift and believe in himself. To do that, he put Rocky on a program of vigorous physical and mental training. Through sheer persistence and dogged determination, Rocky climbed the mountaintop and accomplished the impossible.

Success is the fruit of two words we have heard all our lives: persistence and determination. My own achievements were made manifest in large part because I learned to apply those two words to every dream and goal I ever had.

Like for Rocky, there were plenty of naysayers in my life. Life is full of people who are ready and willing to tell you that you don't stand a chance of making it or that you're never going to amount to anything. Unfortunately, the majority of the population speaks like this because they have programmed themselves for failure and don't want anyone else to succeed either. To them, misery loves company; they want to poison those around them with the same pitiful defeatist mentality.

Life is not easy for any of us. But what of it? We must
have perseverance and above all confidence in ourselves.
We must believe that we are gifted for something, and
that this thing, at whatever cost, must be attained.

—Marie Currie

Movies like *Rocky* affect me in profound ways. Watching him batter his way to victory ignites a flame of hope inside me, fueling my passion to pursue my own dreams. People love movies like *Rocky* because we are all underdogs in some way and can relate to his struggles. Most of us secretly want to defy the odds and prove to everyone we are winners, but we lack the courage to make it happen. Rocky's story gives us the hope that we can overcome the doubt and negativity that surround us.

No matter how much of a long shot your goal appears to be, and regardless of what others say, you must persist. Opposition, adversity, and negativity are unavoidable parts of the journey that we must ram through to make our dreams come true. You must learn to view yourself the way Rocky Balboa eventually did—you are a winner chasing after a goal.

If you need a dose of inspiration, here are some other movies to check out. (Although all these films are inspirational in nature, viewer discretion is advised.)

Akeelah and the Bee	Glory Road
A Beautiful Mind	The Great Debaters
Blind Side	Hoosiers
Chariots of Fire	Hurricane Season
Coach Carter	I Am David
Dreamer	Invincible
Facing the Giants	Miracle
Finding Forrester	October Sky
Flipped	Patch Adams

The Perfect Game	Simon Birch
Pride	Soul Surfer
The Pursuit of Happyness	Under the Same Moon
Radio	Up
Remember the Titans	We Are Marshall
Rudy	The World's Fastest Indian
Secretariat	

Films like these pump me up, build my faith, and cause me to believe my dreams are possible. They strengthen my inner man, the one who ultimately drives my outer man, and the part of me responsible for conquering the challenges life will surely bring.

By ingesting heavy doses of inspiration, whether through books, movies, or television documentaries, I am literally flooding my mind with positive stories of people who eventually beat the odds and live the dream. Through this deliberate strategy, I am accumulating ammunition in my subconscious to draw upon when I run out of fuel and need to reload.

I watch very few television programs because I don't find much on the air that inspires me. I have a limited amount of precious free time; unless a program benefits me on some level, I don't have time for it.

There is, however, one series that adds a lot of positive fuel and motivation to my spirit. It's called *A&E Biography*. I am intrigued by the lives of highly interesting and successful people. Their stories encourage me to keep shooting for the stars. Sometimes in order for us to believe in our own dreams, we need to see others who believed in theirs and attained them.

> *Effort only releases its reward after a person*
> *refuses to quit.*
> —W. Clement Stone

Few of the documentaries I watch are about musicians or artists, but the strategies for success are the same regardless of the profession. Trials, tribulations, and great obstacles come to challenge us to see how much we will endure and sacrifice in order to make our dreams become realities.

Let's face it, we need all the motivation we can get. If we listen to the warped and frustrated world around us, we'll eventually give up. So in the continual face of adversity, I make a conscious decision to program my mind with positive images.

A positive self-image is the single-most important picture you will ever develop. The image you print from the film of your mind is determined by the image the camera captured. Just as a photographer adjusts the solution and chemicals in the darkroom until the print looks exactly the way he wants it to, we must continually make adjustments in our lives until our pictures have the best resolution possible.

The funny thing about our self-image is that, just like the film in a camera, nobody sees what's inside until it is outside and fully developed. The question is, what do you want people to see? Better yet, what do you long to see?

Whatever it is, you must program that image in your mind by whatever means necessary. Persistence and determination alone are the chief reasons people are successful, and it's imperative you do whatever you must in order to bring these attributes to the forefront of your life.

> *Lord, grant that I may always desire more*
> *than I can accomplish.*
>
> —Michelangelo

PATIENCE

ANTICIPATION

One can't help noticing that the vast majority of our world seems to have grown completely impatient. Firmly entrenched in the age of instant gratification, most people have lost the art of exercising patience. Take a look around and you'll see what I mean. People get angry and frustrated if they have to wait more than five minutes for anything—at the bank, the grocery store, stop lights—you see it everywhere. Sometimes it feels as though people have gone absolutely nuts.

The problem is that most people want immediate results. Everyone wants to work out for a month and look like martial arts legend

Bruce Lee in his prime. If they don't make that benchmark, they are disappointed and either try steroids or drop the whole idea altogether.

Many of life's failures are people who did not realize
how close they were to success when they gave up.
—Thomas Edison

Worthy goals take time to achieve, so you must learn to exercise patience. Patience doesn't come easily or naturally to any of us. But just like discipline and self-motivation, it is a skill learned by choice and acquired over time.

Success is a journey; the real joy itself is more in the process of discovery than in the knowing or arriving at the actual destination. There are different levels of achievement throughout the continuum of one's career. If you don't learn the art of patience, you'll end up quitting when things don't go your way or happen quickly enough. It is far easier to quit something than to pursue it to completion.

Anything that's worthwhile takes time to accomplish. The important thing is that you continue to climb uphill, step by step. I like to visualize my life as a lengthy bicycle ride. As long as I know I'm pedaling and moving forward, I'm still in the race, and that's all that really matters. There are going to be times when you are just coasting and everything is going along smoothly, and then there will be times when you really have to struggle to stay upright. Pedaling uphill is hard for everyone, but if you keep going you will eventually come upon level ground and catch your breath for the climb that lay ahead. Climbing to the top of any sizeable mountain is going to take patience—and lots of it.

There is no road too long to the man who advances
deliberately and without undue haste; no honor
is too distant to the man who prepares himself
for it with patience.
—Jean de La Bruyère

Being patient really paid off for a friend of mine named Jon Clark. To Jon, it seemed like everyone he'd grown up playing with had scored a big gig while that level of success eluded him. Obviously, he wished he had been able to land some of those same gigs. But for one reason or another he never got the nod after he auditioned.

His disappointment continued for a number of years. Most people would have become disillusioned and quit, but Jon was persistent and it paid off big time. The first big gig he landed was the biggest pop gig of all time for a sideman. In 1987, he was hired by the King of Pop, Michael Jackson, to play on his Bad world tour, which lasted for over two years. Michael was larger than life and at the height of his popularity as a solo artist. Just think what would have happened if Jon had not been patient; he would have lost out on the opportunity of a lifetime.

Becoming really good at something takes a long time. Anything that becomes great and mighty does so over time—just look at the huge trees in California's Sequoia National Forest. They didn't get that way overnight; it took some of them more than 2,000 years to look that magnificent and reach such an incredible size.

> *When God wants to grow a squash He grows it in one summer; but when He wants to grow an oak He takes a century.*
> —James A. Garfield

We may be able to get an Internet connection at light speed and fast food in mere minutes, but maturing emotionally, creatively, spiritually, and personally still happens slowly over long periods of time—and that's not bound to change anytime soon. It's essential to remember this, or you will always be too anxious and expect things to progress faster than possible, thereby setting the stage for frustration and disappointment. Carving out a successful career as a sideman and developing into a seasoned musician are enormous undertakings. This can only be achieved through years of hard work coupled with ample amounts of patience.

Nothing in the world can take the place of persistence. Talent will not; nothing is more common than unsuccessful individuals with talent. Genius will not; unrewarded genius is almost a proverb. Education will not; the world is full of educated derelicts. Persistence and determination alone are omnipotent.

—Calvin Coolidge

THE ART OF LEARNING
KEYS TO DEVELOPING
YOUR TALENT

Music training is a more potent instrument than any
other, because rhythm and harmony find their way into
the secret places of the soul.

—Plato

Several years ago, I met a young man at Nashville International Airport. He recognized me as I deplaned and began to share his passion for music. Happy to speak with him, I further inquired about his interests.

After he shared some of his dreams, which included playing the guitar and writing hit songs, I asked him a question: "Are you studying privately or attending workshops or classes to help you develop your talent?"

"Well, no, not really," he replied. "I don't want anything to influence my style."

"Have you ever studied your instrument or the craft of songwriting through books, DVDs, or by any other means?"

"No," he said, rather sheepishly.

I thought to myself, "This is the stupidest thing I have ever heard!" I didn't tell him that, of course. I wanted to guide him, not slay him on the spot. But I did encourage him to take some classes and stressed the importance of learning the fundamentals.

It's absolutely ludicrous to think that, by avoiding essential basic foundations in music, you will magically have your own charismatic, original style. Actually, my misguided young friend was correct in one sense: with his ignorant approach to learning, he will surely have his own style. Except it's not an original style at all. Millions of other lazy and delusional wannabe musicians have already beat him to that sound, a sound no one will pay to hear because it's plagued with mediocrity.

I suppose it sounds harsh, but this guy's line of thinking has become far too common. It is disheartening on a number of levels. It's sad to see so many people today duped into thinking an education is somehow going to stifle their artistry. The truth is, education will only enhance it. In my opinion, this mindset is nothing more than a license to be lazy. A lack of education will only stunt your growth and waste whatever talent you may have. Nobody is too cool to learn.

> *The doorstep to the temple of wisdom is a knowledge of our own ignorance.*
>
> —Charles Spurgeon

STUDYING YOUR INSTRUMENT

HOPELESSLY DEVOTED TO YOU

Okay, so maybe you've watched the most recent concert DVDs of your favorite players and bands and checked them out on YouTube. Perhaps you've heard the hottest club bands in the area and listened to the latest Top 10 releases, and then said to yourself, "I can play that well." Maybe you can, but how do you go from practicing in your basement to landing a gig with a major recording artist?

The answer is multi-faceted, but one of the keys is to develop your playing to such a high level that your skill becomes undeniable and people take notice of you every single time you make music on your instrument. That kind of ability only comes about as a result of intense

In order to reign over the music and play it convincingly, you must understand how it originated and evolved into what it is today.

study and serious practice. In order to reach that level of proficiency on your instrument, you must have mastery over the language of music, and that comes about by listening and studying the works of great musicians who have preceded you.

Here's an illustration that should help validate the importance of knowing the history of your instrument. In order for a newly appointed government leader to reign effectively, he or she must understand the nation's history. It would be impossible to do a good job without a deep comprehension of the key events, political figures, and policies that have shaped the country.

Playing a style of music with authenticity is no different. In order to reign over the music and play it convincingly, you must understand how it originated and evolved into what it is today. History provides perspective.

Whether you are aware of it or not, all modern music is rooted in the past. Delving into history will help you understand the connection and relevancy to what we do today. As you study your musical forefathers, you will have a deeper appreciation and knowledge of the music you wish to master.

Michael Jackson, the King of Pop considered by many to be one of the greatest entertainers of all time, was known for his deep commitment to studying the legendary entertainers who preceded him. He immersed himself in James Brown, Gene Kelly, Sammy Davis Jr., Frank Sinatra, Chuck Berry, Jackie Wilson, and Fred Astaire, to name just a few. Jackson was not only influenced by their music and dancing, but also by their sense of style, charisma, and dedication to excellence. Through countless hours of hard work, Michael became a unique amalgamation of everything he had learned from the greats. As a result, he made an indelible mark on history.

> The direct relation of music is not to ideas, but
> emotions. Music, in the works of its greatest masters, is
> more marvelous, more mysterious, than poetry.
> —Henry Giles

I agree with what legendary UCLA basketball coach John Wooden once said: "Everything we know we learned from someone else." In light of that, make an effort to know the key players who contributed to the evolution of your instrument—from its beginnings right up to the present. Knowing what preceded you is vital to gaining complete understanding. When you clearly grasp the foundations of music, you can confidently move toward the future.

Skipping over this formative part of your education is like expecting to be a great classical pianist without studying the works of Mozart, Beethoven, Bach, Tchaikovsky, Brahms, Handel, Verdi, Liszt, Schubert, and Chopin. It's arrogant to think you can master a style of music without going back to its roots and doing some serious homework.

> *If I have seen further, it is by standing upon*
> *the shoulders of giants.*
>
> —Sir Isaac Newton

When it comes to playing music, learning the fundamentals is essential. Now, you might be saying to yourself, "As a creative individual, I thought that the rules in music were meant to be broken?" It's true that musicians have, at times, abandoned traditional approaches of playing their instruments and opted for more unorthodox techniques, but they *knew* the rules before they decided to discard some of them. A good producer or musical director can tell when you are breaking a rule intentionally and when you are breaking it out of ignorance and inexperience. Learn the rules first, and then break the ones you feel compelled to break, but only if doing so strongly contributes to the music in some way.

PRIVATE INSTRUCTION

TEACH ME TONIGHT

When I first began to pursue my dream of being a professional musician, I often fantasized about meeting my favorite bands. One of the groups I wanted to meet most was Earth, Wind & Fire.

In 1980, after I graduated high school in Eugene, Oregon, I moved back down to Los Angeles where I had originally lived. Shortly after I arrived in town, a special one-time concert called *Jesus at the Roxy* was being held at the famous Roxy Theater in Hollywood. It was a gospel concert that featured a variety of R&B celebrities, including a few members of Earth, Wind & Fire. I lived just down the street from the Roxy at the time, so I bought my ticket the minute I heard about the event. I was stoked!

> *Get your facts first; then you can distort 'em*
> *as you please.*
> —Mark Twain

After the show was over, I walked boldly onto the stage and introduced myself to the drummer for the evening's concert. It just happened to be Ralph Johnson, the drummer for Earth, Wind & Fire.

Ralph and I spoke for quite a while. And as fate would have it, that night turned out to be the beginning of a great relationship that would forever change my destiny. Ralph became my instructor, mentor, role model, friend, and a music figure in whose footsteps I wished to follow. I listened intently to every word he said.

After studying with Ralph for a short time, a friend of mine suggested I study at the prestigious Berklee College of Music in Boston, Massachusetts. I asked Ralph for his opinion, and he said that if I was really serious about playing music for a living I should definitely attend the school. Trusting Ralph completely, I applied for admission and was accepted.

> *Those who bring sunshine to the lives of others cannot*
> *keep it from themselves.*
> —James Matthew Barrie

Although I did gain a great deal of knowledge from my college professors, I learned the most about what it takes to become a professional working musician through private lessons, an opportunity commonly overlooked by musicians. I was fortunate to have three great teachers who mentored me in the early stages of my development: Eric Christianson, Kent Clinkingbeard, and Ralph Johnson. Each made vast deposits into my life that boosted my confidence and helped make all my achievements possible. After all these years have passed, I remain friends with all of them, and each one still holds a special place in my heart.

No matter how great a player you are, always make it a priority to study with the best teacher you can find in your area. If you live in a large city, study with as many great instructors as you can afford. If you have the opportunity to travel a bit, try to take private lessons from renowned teachers everywhere you go. As I toured throughout the country, I always tried to book a lesson with the most reputable teacher I could find in each city. Since each instructor had something new to impart to me, those lessons played a pivotal role in my development and caused me to experience tremendous growth on my instrument.

> *Music is God's best gift to man, the only art of heaven given to earth, the only art of earth that we take to heaven. But music, like all our gifts, is given us in the germ. It is for us to unfold and develop it by instruction and cultivation.*
>
> —Charles W. Landon

Being exposed to a variety of teaching regimens and philosophies will teach you many perspectives. Learning from a player who is already doing what you want to do, like I did with Eric Christianson, Kent Clinkingbeard, and Ralph Johnson, is the most direct avenue to learning what it takes to make it.

In many cases, a well-connected teacher can be your direct link to the industry. Being an industry insider, he or she can recommend you for opportunities you'd never be able to get on your own. That's exactly what happened to me while I was studying with Ralph. Besides really helping me hone my skills and preparing me for the professional world of music, Ralph recommended me to Philip Bailey, the lead singer of Earth, Wind & Fire. Philip had just released a solo album and was planning a concert tour to support it. I started off subbing for Ralph, who was Philip's regular drummer. When Ralph was unable to commit to the rest of the tour dates, Philip offered the gig to me!

Up until that point, that was my biggest break, and it was a great learning experience and an absolute thrill for me in every way! It gave me credibility and helped to spread my name and reputation around Los Angeles. Playing the gig also boosted my self-confidence, because for the first time I had a big-name artist to put on my resume. Many respected teachers who are active players on the scene will actually groom talented young students to take over gigs they no longer can or want to do, and that's what opened the door for me.

THE ESSENTIAL COACH

I BELIEVE IN YOU

Have you ever stopped and wondered why the greatest athletes in the world all have coaches? It's obvious they have the natural talent and necessary drive to rise to the top, so what purpose could a coach possibly serve?

The sports world has long recognized the need for the mental, physical, and emotional support of a coach. Since you're not always the best judge of yourself in the crucial moments of competition, a coach offers a second set of eyes and ears. As an outside observer, a coach can see you more clearly than you can see yourself and can help point out your weaknesses in an effort to strengthen your game. The coach with the right heart can become your confidant, personal motivator, and friend.

A seasoned coach will challenge you to give your personal best and encourage you to stay in the game until you reach your goals. Synergy comes when two individuals work together toward a common goal, and that synergy is prevalent in the relationship between coach and athlete.

A good music instructor serves the same purpose as any top-flight sports coach. Though the parameters are somewhat different, their function is identical. A wise student will take advantage of what a great teacher has to offer and will experience unbelievable growth in the process.

The glory of friendship is not in the outstretched hand,
nor the kindly smile, nor the joy of companionship;
it is in the spiritual inspiration that comes to one
when he discovers that someone else believes in him
and is willing to trust him.

—Ralph Waldo Emerson

Experienced teachers empathize with the struggles and insecurities of their students and are there to lift them up in times of doubt. The great ones will see your potential and coax it to the surface for all to see. Without the aid of a gifted teacher, the results of your growth will probably be disappointing. If you work hard and actually take heed of their instruction, it will be one of the best business investments you will ever make.

There are many places you can look for a quality instructor, but I would first try getting referrals from students, local professional players, music stores, and other teachers. If you happen to live in a city that has a musician's union, college, rehearsal studio, or music school, those are always great places to inquire about a solid teacher. If you live in a very small town with none of these opportunities, you can at least check with your local high school or junior high school. If you don't have any luck there, you can always try the Internet.

What Can a Good Teacher Do for You?

SHOW ME THE WAY

- Design a personally tailored curriculum that will eliminate wasted practice time

- Help you set realistic goals

- Honestly evaluate and critique your playing on a continual basis to help you reach your full potential

- Provide you with quality mentorship by offering wisdom, guidance, direction, incentive, and motivation

- Expand your musical horizons by exposing you to new music, techniques, concepts, and philosophies

- Become a good friend and a constant source of encouragement

- Recommend you for various gigs

INSTRUCTIONAL MEDIA

YEARNIN' LEARNIN'

In some cases, finding quality music instruction can be a challenge. If you live in the middle of nowhere, you may simply have no access to a quality teacher, workshop, or school within a reasonable distance. For others, job and personal responsibilities can make it nearly impossible to take lessons on a consistent basis.

In situations such as these, DVDs, CDs, music downloads, and instructional books with companion CDs are worth considering as viable alternative means of learning. One Google search will yield a huge variety of quality products that will suit your needs. Before you buy, though, read reviews and customer comments to ensure you don't waste your money.

> *Never let a day pass without looking at some perfect*
> *work of art, hearing some great piece of music and*
> *reading in part, some great book.*
>
> —Johann Wolfgang von Goethe

Musicians today are fortunate to have many great educational tools on the market that were not available when I was starting out. Grants Pass was by no means a thriving music capital, so the best thing I could do to make sure I was informed was to read everything I could get my hands on. Reading about the music business and the careers of celebrated musicians helped me feel connected to an industry that was hundreds of miles away.

In addition to vital information you can access on the Internet, you will find that larger cities have industry trade papers and other periodicals. Whether they are online or in print, these publications will give you the inside scoop on a variety of related topics. You'll see who's looking for musicians, musicians who are looking for work, where courses are being offered, announcements for upcoming clinics and trade shows, where local bands are playing, and other pertinent information.

Clinics and master classes are also great opportunities for learning. You can learn much from the players you meet at these venues and you will be enlightened and exposed to a variety of music concepts. All of this new insight will eventually work its way into your playing.

I will study and get ready, and perhaps
my chance will come.

—Abraham Lincoln

PREPARING FOR MUSIC SCHOOL

GET READY

If it's at all possible, I highly recommend that you attend a music school of some kind to further develop your craft. From major universities to renowned private music schools and trade schools, there are many fine institutions throughout the country from which to choose. It's up to you to do the necessary research to make an informed decision.

There are obviously many factors to consider when choosing a school, such as your overall music goals, your financial situation, and geographical location. Whatever the case may be, investigating all possibilities is certainly worth the effort if you are planning to make a profession out of music. Even if you cannot afford to attend long enough to earn a degree, studying for as little as a year like I did will still prove to be incredibly worthwhile and will help catapult your understanding to another level.

When I first began attending Berklee College of Music in 1981, I grew more rapidly as a musician than I had anticipated. By bathing in an environment of perpetual learning, I was exposed to more information than I realized at the time. My growth came not only from the instruction offered at the school, but from all the inspiration and motivation that lurked in the hallways, classrooms, and ensemble and practice rooms.

With all those creative musicians running around like busy bees there was a constant buzz in the air and an excitement about playing, learning, sharing, and growing! Although you can study many music concepts on your own, there is an energy released when a group of like-minded individuals celebrate and explore their mutual passions together. You simply cannot manufacture that kind of incredible synergy on your own.

You will be afforded the opportunity to grow by playing with other musicians, but there is another fringe benefit; befriending talented musicians who possess the vision and determination necessary to succeed is how many young musicians get their tickets into the industry. When a fellow student catches a big break in the business, they'll hopefully remember you and get you connected!

> *Make your friends your teachers and mingle the*
> *pleasures of conversation with the advantages*
> *of instruction.*
> —Baltasar Gracian

Aside from having access to great teachers, you'll meet determined students who come from all over the world to study at prestigious music schools. What you learn from them can be just as valuable as what you learn from the instructors. Everyone has his or her own way of approaching music and expressing creativity—a different perspective, edge, or twist on things—and you can learn something from everyone. My roommate, Dan Donifrio, and some other fellow students turned me on to some great new music, and I was inspired by all the new sounds.

Since piano, harmony, theory, arranging, and sight-singing are usually part of the curriculum for performance majors at most music schools, I strongly suggest you study those subjects with a private teacher. If you are not able to do so in person, there are plenty of DVDs and CDs that cover the material.

I went to school with several musicians who quit after the first semester because they were so overwhelmed with how much they had to learn about music. Most of them were decent players, but they never gave much thought to studying the other aspects of music necessary for becoming a great musician.

> *Taking first things first often reduces the most complex*
> *human problem to a manageable proportion.*
> —Dwight D. Eisenhower

The motto here is, "Where there is a will, there's a way." There are simply no legitimate excuses for neglecting to prepare. Don't let the fear of learning keep you from reaching your potential. And don't wait until you get to music school to get these skills together, at least on some basic level. The more prepared you are for school, the more you'll get out of it and the less overwhelmed you'll be.

BECOMING STREETWISE

THAT'S WHAT FRIENDS ARE FOR

In 1982, I left Berklee College of Music and moved back to Los Angeles. From that point on, hanging out in the local music scene became the biggest part of my informal education. Music schools are great for teaching you about playing music—and even a little bit about contracts, publishing, and copyrights—but the only way you'll really learn the business of being a musician is through the school of hard knocks.

Once you get to a city that offers a variety of employment opportunities for musicians, the next step in your education is to get acquainted with the local scene. You do this primarily through socializing, which is a fancy word for hanging out. There are bars, clubs, showcases, rehearsal and recording studios, restaurants, and a wide variety of other places where budding musicians with similar goals tend to hang out. Not only will you find others with a similar passion for music, but as you mingle in this environment, you will also inevitably find out about auditions, gigs, clinics, private teachers, master classes, and other useful information.

We cannot become what we need to be
by remaining what we are.
—Max De Pree

Seminars, conventions, and trade shows are also great venues for learning and networking. You'll make contacts and gain valuable information from players, producers, instrument manufacturers, and other industry people. There are a plethora of conventions around the world offering various forms of music or technical education and information, and you can mingle to your heart's content with your breed of people. One of my favorite conventions is the NAMM show (NAMM is the National Association of Music Merchants). It is held twice a year: in January, it's in Los Angeles; in June, it's usually in Nashville. NAMM is a great place to meet a broad range of music experts and enthusiasts.

Because this is such an unorthodox business, one learns the politics and ins and outs primarily through this social network. The key is to divide your time equally among practicing, performing, and socializing. Career-wise, it won't do you the least bit of good to become

> *It won't do you the least bit of good to become the greatest musician in the world if you don't have the first clue about how to earn your next meal as a working musician.*

the greatest musician in the world if you don't have the first clue about how to earn your next meal as a working musician.

The downside to all this fraternizing is that it can become addictive and time-consuming. I knew several musicians who overindulged in schmoozing to the point they never developed their playing skills enough to experience success.

Time spent networking will take you away from practicing and performing, so you have to learn to keep several balls in the air simultaneously. Becoming a master juggler is another important skill required to prosper as a musician. Remember, everything has its time and place. Balance is the real key.

THE QUEST FOR ANSWERS

I GOTTA KNOW

For as long as I can remember, I've been inquisitive. In many ways, my curiosity has helped me tremendously; I've probably learned more by asking questions than by any other means.

I was always the kid in school who asked the questions everyone else wanted the answers to but were too afraid to ask. My classmates knew that if they waited long enough I would ask the questions and they could continue looking brilliant. I knew they didn't understand what was going on either, because as soon as I asked the first eye-opening question everyone else joined in and asked the teacher to explain further.

I took on this icebreaker role because I valued the knowledge more than what others thought of me. I knew if I didn't ask I'd be totally lost as the class progressed. I was inspired to display such courage from this saying: "He who asks a question may be a fool for five minutes; he who never asks a question remains a fool forever."

The fear of looking stupid in front of our peers keeps most of us legitimately ignorant. The real stupidity is not being humble enough to ask others to share their knowledge. If knowledge is power, then ignorance is its counterpart, and to be ignorant is to be powerless. Sometimes it's downright shameful to admit we don't know something we think we should.

> *The beautiful thing about learning is nobody can*
> *take it away from you.*
>
> —B.B. King

Shamelessly asking questions is the most direct way to gain understanding and find out what is really necessary to accomplish a goal. If there is something in particular about music or the music industry that you don't know, be bold enough to ask, because that's really the only way to learn. To me, there is nothing as noble as a willingness to learn and a hunger for knowledge and understanding. It is precisely with that sense of urgency that humans have advanced our world in every way. Our glorious creative achievements have come into existence because of mankind's curiosity and hunger for answers. Seek out those who possess experience and knowledge and are willing to share their wisdom so you might be able to accomplish your goals.

ON-THE-JOB TRAINING

DO IT BABY

It's not enough to just practice out of a book, take lessons, and play along with music. You eventually have to get into the trenches and do it. While continuing to diligently study and practice, the next step is to apply the skills you are learning to real-life playing situations. The more you perform, the more your confidence will be boosted and the more comfortable you will be on your instrument.

> *Sometimes you have to play a long time to be able to play like yourself.*
>
> —Miles Davis

It is only by putting yourself in the driver's seat and launching out that you will find out what works and what doesn't. Playing in your practice room doesn't compare to playing in a live situation where you're under pressure. You'll learn the most when mistakes are made on the bandstand and you have the task of covering them up as smoothly as possible in order to move on unhindered.

One way to gain valuable experience is to audition for as many gigs as possible. You won't always get the gig, but the more you audition, the more comfortable you'll feel under pressure. You'll also meet other musicians and forge relationships that may prove beneficial down the road. Auditioning as often as you can is also a good way of getting your name around. The more musicians you circulate with, the more will eventually know who you are.

If you are still in high school or junior high, playing in the marching band, concert band, or stage bands will help you gain invaluable experience. College ensemble performances, theater productions, churches, and contests such as a battle of the bands or solo instrument competitions are also great outlets for performing. The pressure you will experience during these contests will groom you for the tension of real-life performances.

With experience comes maturity. It's not uncommon for recent music school graduates to overplay. They get so excited to show their friends back home what they've learned that they unleash their new-found knowledge like nuclear missiles. In a single bound, they perform all their newly acquired licks, reharmonizations, and polyrhythms. When you become secure with your playing and who you are as a person, you won't find it necessary to show people everything you know in the first 12 bars of a song.

There are no shortcuts to any place worth going.
—Beverly Sills

Mature players don't sound tentative like inexperienced beginners do; they play with authority, certainty, and confidence because they know their instrument intimately. Becoming a mature player begins in your mind. It revolves around knowing what's right for the music and being humble enough to carry it out. In music, what you leave out is just as important as what you play. It takes maturity to know the difference.

LIFELONG LEARNING

HIGHER GROUND

In January of 1997, I ran into my friend Steve Gadd at the NAMM show in California. Considering that Steve is one of the world's greatest drummers, I was really excited to show him a rough draft of my first book, *The Commandments of R&B Drumming: A Comprehensive Guide to Soul, Funk & Hip Hop.* Since I highly valued his opinion, I was eager to get his feedback on the material.

Much to my surprise, Steve seemed enthralled as he thoroughly worked his way through each page. The first thing he wanted to know was where he could get the CDs I recommended in the listening guide. Having been one of the busiest session players in the '70s and '80s, Steve had been so occupied with creating and innovating music that it would have been impossible for him to be hip to all the other music that was out there.

Steve was especially interested in the R&B material, primarily because it was not the music he grew up with in his formative years. I quickly learned why he's a master of so many feels; he maintains a burning desire to constantly evolve and grow—always a student of his instrument.

He had such a refreshing outlook. It wasn't enough that Steve Gadd had become an icon, a legend, a sideman of epic proportions who had redefined contemporary drumming in his lifetime; he still wanted to learn more. We should all strive to have the same unquenchable thirst for knowledge. I finally understood why some people achieve greatness, while others only dream of it; a humble attitude can make a huge difference in your life and your ability to learn.

> *A winner knows how much he still has to learn, even*
> *when he is considered an expert by others. A loser*
> *wants to be considered an expert by others, before he*
> *has learned enough to know how little he knows.*
> —Sydney J. Harris

My philosophy of education is to be like a sponge and soak up everything you can. If you are willing to live your life in such a way, you will undoubtedly experience consistent growth and continue to reach new heights. In contrast, if you're close-minded and think you've already got it all together, you'll never learn as much as you can.

Formal or informal, education in any capacity is by far the most important ingredient for becoming a great player. Mastering your instrument is a lifelong process; there will always be more to learn. Remember: it is one thing to know how to play an instrument, but quite another to make music with it.

> *The first law of success....is concentration—to bend all*
> *of the energies to one point, and to go directly to that*
> *point, looking neither to the right or left.*
> —William Matthews

THE ART OF PRACTICING
LEARNING METHODS FOR MAXIMUM GROWTH

*Success, real success, in any endeavor demands more
from an individual than most people are willing to
offer—not more than they are capable of offering.*

—James Roche

In 1983, an interesting performance opportunity came my way while I was on vacation in the Bahamas with my mother and little sister, Lisa. Eager to check out the local music talent, my first quest was to find the best live music I could on Paradise Island in Nassau. The concierge at our hotel informed me that the club downstairs was the most happening live music spot in the city.

I took his advice and eagerly went to check it out. I quickly discovered this really happening funk band that I was dying to sit in with. On their first break, I went up and introduced myself to the keyboard player and asked if I could sit in and play with them. He willingly obliged my request and I jammed with them for a good half hour, grooving on some of my favorite hit songs of the day.

A couple of days later when I was in my hotel room chilling out, I received a phone call from Harold Barney, the band's keyboard player. He also worked with a famous Bahamian singer named Marvin Henfield, who was in desperate need of a good drummer to do a quick cruise ship gig. Harold asked if I was interested.

"What the heck," I thought. "Let's live life on the edge a little!" How often would I have an opportunity to play with a famous recording artist from that part of the world? Excited about my new adventure, I boarded the ship the next day.

It turned out to be a great experience. I not only learned how to play calypso music from the masters, I also got

http://4wrd.it/A.BG6

to see a little bit of paradise—and get paid at the same time. I did the gig for a little over a week and then returned to Nassau to resume vacation with my family. The money I earned on the cruise was just enough to buy some new drum equipment I needed.

You just never know what casually sitting in with a band might lead to. I never expected to play on a cruise ship, and it sure was a memorable trip. All of my early playing opportunities gave me the experience I desperately needed to refine my playing skills. Your job will be to hunt down every playing opportunity and allow each one to shape and mold you into a better performer—even if some of them take you by surprise!

> *I recommend you take care of the minutes: for the hours will take care of themselves.*
>
> —Lord Chesterfield

THE DISCIPLINE OF PRACTICE

DON'T STOP TILL YOU GET ENOUGH

I practice every time I get the chance—on flights, in cars, even at the gym. Just about any playing surface will do. At the gym, I put a few towels on the handlebars of a LifeCycle and practice finger control and technique with a pair of sticks for 30 minutes. Concentrating on my practice and listening to music distracts me from the burning pain of the bicycling and helps to pass the time. No one has ever asked me to stop my tapping, because the towels absorb any audible noise. I have done this same thing playing on airline pillows stacked on my lap. Some people might think I look like a freak, but hey, at least it's just drumsticks and not a tuba!

Honestly people, who really cares? Most of us spend way too much time seeking the approval of others when we should be chasing hard after the dream God has placed in our hearts.

I've heard the saying "practice makes perfect" as far back as I can remember. Most of the time I love to practice, but sometimes it can be a laborious process. At times I procrastinate too long and suddenly find myself on a deadline to learn a bunch of new songs for an upcoming gig or audition. Under those circumstances, even cleaning out my garage is a temptation that is hard to resist.

The practice room is a place many of us dread, and we find every excuse under the sun to avoid its confines. After all, who wants to spend all day in a musty old practice room with no air-conditioning when you could be enjoying a nice breeze at the beach?

> *Some people regard discipline as a chore. For me, it is a*
> *kind of order that sets me free to fly.*
>
> —Julie Andrews

What is it about practicing that's such a drag? Quite frankly, practice is hard work that inevitably involves the "D word," *discipline*. To most musicians, discipline is like what a sunny day at the beach is to Dracula—deadly! More to the point, practicing is a solitary business that, in a way, represents the death of your freedom.

When you finally do buckle down and get into a serious practice routine, there always seem to be interruptions. People in your personal life won't always see practice as something serious enough to warrant leaving you alone. Those who work out of home offices frequently experience this same lack of consideration and respect.

Throughout my career, those closest to me haven't hesitated to interrupt me or ask me to do an errand if they knew I was practicing. To them, it was perfectly fine to break my concentration no matter how mundane and stupid the reason. To most folks, it seems like we're just goofing off and having a lot of fun. Sure, we can stop what we're doing to go to the grocery store and pick up some eggs. What's the big deal? It's just practice.

But for musicians, practice is a huge part of the job and one of our ongoing responsibilities. We are not alone in our solitary confinement. Athletes, actors, and many other professions share the same disciplines, especially if they hope to reach world-class status.

The fact is, if you are a serious musician who wishes to progress, you must treat your practice exactly as if it were a job and demand that others treat it the same. Practicing isn't always fun, but it has to be done at all costs.

> *What we do on some great occasion will probably*
> *depend on what we already are; and what we are will be*
> *the result of previous years of self-discipline.*
> —Henry Parry Liddon

Practicing isn't always convenient either, particularly for the players of certain instruments. If you are a drummer, for instance, you can't carry your drum set everywhere you go. Sticks, on the other hand are very portable. In my early days, I wore out three car dashboards from practicing at stoplights and during bumper-to-bumper traffic. Mind you, this is not a procedure endorsed by the Department of Motor Vehicles; I'm lucky I never got in an accident.

Unlike drums, which are rarely set up in public places for people to play, pianos are everywhere, like hotel lobbies, bars, schools, churches, and many other places. A guitar is too big, heavy and cumbersome to carry with you like a pair of sticks, but it has many options that you don't have with a drum set. You can practice the guitar acoustically in your house or a hotel room and make very little noise. If it is electric, you can use headphones or no amplification at all. No matter where you play it, a trumpet can drive people crazy because of its natural volume, unless, of course, you use a mute.

Unfortunately, practicing your instrument is always going to be a nuisance to someone, at some point. But to excel at all, you may have to be somewhat selfish at times. If I stopped playing every time I annoyed someone, I would never have become very good. When I was younger, I had my fair share of run-ins with the local police department because I was playing too loudly in my garage. Believe it or not, after all these years of playing, I only recently built a soundproof room in which to practice and teach. My wife is ecstatic!

We are what we repeatedly do. Excellence then is
not an act, but a habit.

—Aristotle

Unfortunately, repetition is the key to mastering your instrument and there is just no way to get around that. The more time you put in, the better you'll be. Practice takes a LOT of time. You will spend more hours practicing your instrument than you ever will actually performing with it, at least in the early developmental stages. That investment of time will be worth it if you want to reach excellence and make a living as a player.

The time you are able commit to your instrument will largely depend on your age and station in life. Finances, as well as job and relationship responsibilities, are huge considerations, and will ultimately dictate how much time you actually have to invest in your practice. If time is limited, as it often is when you're older, you may have to sacrifice other activities you enjoy. Still, there are plenty of opportunities to practice if you are willing and a little creative.

If possible, reserve substantial blocks of time for practicing each day, or at least a few times a week at intervals that are practical for your time constraints. The key to great results with any kind of practice is consistency. Highly focused small blocks of practice time on a regular basis can go a long way.

Every calling is great when greatly pursued.

—Oliver Wendell Holmes

COMMITMENT

TAKE IT TO THE LIMIT

During my junior year at Hidden Valley High School in Grants Pass, Oregon, I had an after-school job with the custodial staff of the school. Well, actually, the truth is that I was a janitor, a humbling job for a young man who desperately wanted to be cool. There was a popular cleaning product at the time called Janitor in a Drum, so students jokingly called me the "Janitor with a Drum." It was embarrassing, but I was nonetheless grateful for the job opportunity.

My junior year was also the first time I was in stage band. Since I was one of the school janitors, I had keys to all of the classrooms. The night before the state band competition, I let myself in the band room to get some much-needed practice. I stayed up almost all night long practicing my big drum solo that was going to be featured in a Maynard Ferguson arrangement of the opera classic *Pagliacci*. So as not to worry my mother, I told her I was spending the night at a friend's house. I practiced for nearly 12 hours straight, only sleeping for a couple of hours.

The following morning, when the students walked in and saw me crashed next to the drums in my sleeping bag, they asked why I was lying there. When I told them I'd been practicing all night, they couldn't believe it. My stage band buddies Bill Newman and Cory Graper helped spread the word of my sheer determination throughout the band and the school, garnering me a new level of respect. Bill played the guitar and Cory played the bass, and both of them encouraged me from the moment I started playing the drums. Through their obvious display of faith in my abilities, my confidence was catapulted and I was inspired to dig in even harder.

The all-night practice session paid off. When it came time for my drum solo, I was well prepared and came out blazing.

> *No one ever attains very eminent success by simply doing what is required of him; it is the amount of excellence of what is over and above the required that determines greatness.*
> —Charles Kendall Adams

After our performance, one of the judges came over to Mr. Kantola, our stage band director, and asked if he was a drummer himself because he thought the student drummer was so good. Mr. Kantola was kind enough to pass on the compliment to me, further fueling my efforts and boosting my self-esteem.

More affirmation came when Bill, Cory, and schoolmate Dave Day invited me to join them for a performance at a school cabaret. The three of them were in a band of their own called White Lightening, which was hugely popular on campus and in the local area.

We rehearsed long and hard every day after school in the choir room to prepare for our first show together. I had the time of my life playing extended versions of Led Zeppelin's "Stairway to Heaven" and Aerosmith's arrangement of The Beatles classic "Come Together," which they had just performed in the movie Sgt. Pepper's Lonely Hearts Club Band.

We were a huge hit, and after rocking out on the drums I was treated differently by my classmates. Suddenly, I was cool! That cabaret show in the spring of 1979 was my first official gig outside of the school band program.

Later in the year, we played at the school's *Gong Show*, a talent show modeled after the popular television variety show of the same name. We played a Cheech and Chong song called "Earache My Eye." And from that point on, I was consumed by my dream of becoming a professional drummer. I believed with all my heart it was possible.

> *The only limit to our realization of tomorrow will be*
> *our doubts of today.*
> —Franklin Roosevelt

A lot of great things transpired from being in the school music program and by staying committed to my instrument and vision. I was so inspired by those early performance opportunities at the high school that I read everything I could get my hands on about how to become a master musician.

One thing I remember reading in particular was how iconic jazz saxophonist John Coltrane would sit and practice just the C scale for eight hours straight, and then follow the same routine with another scale on the following day. "Man," I thought, "now that's discipline and determination!" Stories like his had a powerful effect on me, and I soon learned that they were not at all uncommon with great musicians. I became inspired to make that same kind of effort.

Hopefully the stories I've shared will give you the incentive to work hard, too, so one day you might have your own story to tell.

THE ROLE OF A NON-RHYTHM SECTION INSTRUMENT

ALL BY MYSELF

Since all instruments differ slightly in function, it's important to understand the general distinctions between the two major ruling classes of the commercial music empire: the non-rhythm section instruments and the rhythm section instruments.

Even though there may sometimes be some overlap between them in terms of their specific functions, for the sake of simplicity I will refer to drums, bass, guitar, keyboards, and percussion as rhythm section instruments and those from the woodwind, vocal, brass, and string families as non-rhythm section instruments.

Most frequently, background vocalists and musicians in the horn, vocal, and string sections are required to read music. If you are unable to do so, you will significantly limit your opportunities. These groups must play their parts exactly or the arrangement won't make musical sense. Just imagine what would happen if everybody improvised at the same time. It would be musical chaos!

> *The wise musicians are those who play*
> *what they can master.*
> —Duke Ellington

Besides being able to sight-read well, learning to solo comfortably over a variety of chord changes is essential for any non-rhythm section instrument. A major part of your practice time should be spent developing your skills in this area. The arrangement of the music will ultimately determine which instrument is best suited to engage in the solo. But in any case, you must always be ready to deliver.

Since most non-rhythm section instruments are melodic in nature, having a large repertoire of songs would be another requirement. To begin with, become intimately familiar with the standards for your chosen genre of music, whether it's rock, blues, jazz, or any other style. If you want to be an A-list player, this is a must.

ESSENTIAL SKILLS FOR NON-RHYTHM SECTION INSTRUMENTS

STAND BY ME

- Sight-reading
- Soloing over chord changes
- Phrasing
- Solid time
- Proficiency in all keys
- Melodic interpretation

- Intonation
- Playing by ear
- Improvisation
- Song repertoire
- Memorization

THE ROLE OF A RHYTHM SECTION INSTRUMENT

GOT TO BE THERE

The role of a rhythm section player is very different from that of a non-rhythm section musician. While every instrument's ultimate purpose is to support the musical arrangement and accompany the artist in some fashion, the primary function of a rhythm section instrument on most commercially oriented gigs is to provide solid time and a strong feel, whereas soloing is secondary. Of course, this requirement can vary depending on the style of music and which instrument of the rhythm section you play. Drummers, percussionists, and bass players tend to take far fewer solos in most pop styles of music than keyboardists and guitar players. The need to solo on a more frequent basis, and with extreme proficiency, would certainly be more common in progressive styles of music such as progressive rock, jazz-fusion, and jazz.

By design, rhythm section instruments are given more improvisational liberties when interpreting charts than non-rhythm section instruments. If you're a rhythm section player, the most essential skill needed is being able to groove. Your job is to lay down a strong foundation upon which the rest of the ensemble will be able to confidently build.

> *Your job is to hold the band together. Your job is*
> *to support everybody in that band. It's your job to*
> *give the band what they want, when they need it.*
> *Always, that's your role.*
>
> —Bernard Purdie

Although it's essential for all musicians to have good technique, feel should always take precedence for rhythm section players. Stevie Wonder is one of the best feel players I've ever heard. Stevie sings, plays keyboards, drums, harmonica, and just about everything else. Whichever instrument he's playing, he makes you move no matter how simple or complicated the part. Groove is the mission, and it will always be the most important function of a rhythm section member.

Remember: we don't get paid by the sheer amount of notes we play. If that were the case, there would be a lot more wealthy young musicians in this business since so many of them tend to overplay.

ESSENTIAL SKILLS FOR RHYTHM SECTION PLAYERS

DON'T DISTURB THIS GROOVE

- Timekeeping
- Grooves
- Styles
- Song repertoire
- Playing by ear
- Sight-reading
- Chart interpretation
- Intuition
- Phrasing
- Memorization
- Improvisation

PRACTICING METHODICALLY

GROOVE IS IN THE HEART

As time goes by, it's easy to lose sight of what we need to practice most. When our focus dissipates, we can end up spending a lot of time dinking around with little to show for our efforts. This loss of direction happens to most musicians after a certain point in their development. When I came to this point early in my career, I realized I needed to devise some kind of system that would help me concentrate on what was really needed most—to be able to play lots of grooves.

What I've learned along the way is that playing exercises out of method books alone won't ensure you get the groove. Exercises for technique, scales, patterns, chords, grooves, and rhythms will certainly help you develop the necessary coordination, but not necessarily the feel. You have to play along with songs in the style of a particular groove to make that happen.

In an effort to maximize my own practice time, I came up with a method for cataloging songs and directly targeting a variety of specific time feels. This system originally started on cassette tapes, but eventually progressed to CDs when that technology was introduced. I only wish there had been an iPod when I first started playing music; that would have saved me hours of time and allowed me to carry an incredible amount of music with me wherever I went.

In order to take advantage of this cataloging system, you'll need three things: an MP3 device, a wide variety of music, and the iTunes software installed on your computer. Once you download music to your iTunes library, you can begin to create multiple playlists broken down by categories and classifications.

It is only well with me when I have a chisel in my hand.
—Michelangelo

I have playlists based on eighth rock grooves, slow eighth ballads, sixteenth note grooves from slow to fast, quarter note grooves, etc. Then I have odd time signature playlists like 5/4, 3/4, 7/4. I also have a variety of triplet related feels like shuffles, slow swing, medium swing, fast swing, 6/8 Afro Cuban, 6/8 gospel, and 12/8.

I can break each one of these feels down even further and create subgenre playlists. For example, I have several playlists for the 12/8 time signature: 12/8 with a rock feel, 12/8 with an R&B feel, 12/8 grooves that are extremely slow, and then 12/8 grooves that are really fast. This allows me to target what I need to work on most in my practice time by going straight to the 12/8 feel that needs the most work. Like any other time signature or feel, 12/8 grooves are not all the same and have a number of ways to approach them stylistically. You may be able to play a slow 12/8 blues with no problem, but playing a fast 12/8 modern R&B groove may take you completely out of your comfort zone.

I also create playlists based on styles of music, particular eras, and tempos. I have playlists for individual players or groups that I want to transcribe and study more in depth. One of the absolute best things you can do as a musician is to create playlists of classic songs from various genres. In the music business, we call those classic songs "standards." I have playlists for classic rock standards, jazz standards, jazz-fusion standards, and funk standards. Some are then broken down into the decade such as 1960s soul classics, 1970s funk classics, or classic 1990s alternative rock songs. I even have old-school gospel standards and contemporary Christian standards.

There are an infinite number of ways you can categorize the music, so do what best serves your needs and ultimate purposes. This method of cataloging will evolve every day as you hear more music and download new songs into your music library.

> *Continuous effort—not strength or intelligence—*
> *is the key to unlocking our potential.*
> —Sir Winston Churchill

By practicing this way, you'll learn how to play different time feels and solo over them as they apply to a variety of real songs. Each tune will naturally feature different musicians and bands playing ensemble figures, kicks, rhythms, and accents that will help you understand how to authentically interpret those phrases in the music. Doing this eliminates wasted practice time by getting right down to the areas that need the most work. It doesn't really matter whether it's playing in a specific key, time signature, style, or groove, practicing like this will give you an opportunity to get a laser-sharp focus.

This technique of practicing has been great for my playing because it helped me identify my weaknesses and achieve my goals much more quickly. When I was required to play a gig that stressed a certain time feel I hadn't played in a long time, I was able to go to the appropriate playlist and hit it for hours. Eventually I had it nailed.

> *The true delight is in the finding out*
> *rather than in the knowing.*
>
> —Isaac Asimov

Here is another method of developing control over various tempos of a specific groove. Let's take a blues shuffle, for example. You can organize your playlist for this specific feel and put the songs in order of slowest to fastest. Before creating your playlist, grab a pen and piece of paper and give every shuffle song a BPM tempo marking using a metronome, and then write it down. Now, with that sheet of paper telling you the exact tempo for each tune, you can put together a serious playlist of shuffles from slowest to fastest.

> *Just like a body builder starts out with light weights and progresses to heavier ones, you should never blaze at the highest tempo right off the bat.*

It will take a little time to put together, but it's well worth the effort. By the end of your practice session for that playlist, you would have methodically worked your way up from the slowest shuffle you could find to the fastest. Just like a body builder starts out with light weights and progresses to heavier ones, you should never blaze at the highest tempo right off the bat. Warm up to those faster tempos or you'll get tendonitis. Once you do the homework, you'll stop wasting time in the practice room doing what comes easily and concentrate on your weak points.

For melodic instruments such as brass, woodwinds, strings, or vocals, consider creating playlists according to the keys you want to get comfortable with, and practice soloing over those chord progressions. If you play the saxophone, for instance, you could create separate playlists for each of your favorite sax players and your favorite solos by each one of them. If you are a piano player and want to do an intense study on ragtime music, you could simply create a playlist exclusively for that genre and then completely immerse yourself in it.

No matter what kind of music you want to play, it's wise to listen to a wide variety of it from various cultures to broaden your palette. Part of your practice time should be spent working on musical concepts that are out of your comfort zone. Another great tactic to improve your overall musicianship is to learn to sing no matter which instrument you play. This will inevitably make you a better musician and help you with articulation and phrasing. If you're strictly a vocalist, it would be good to learn a rhythm section instrument just to have a different perspective and be able to better communicate with the musicians in their own language.

> *Do you see a man skilled in his work? He will serve*
> *before kings; he will not serve before obscure men.*
> —Proverbs 22:29, NASB

Studying music in such an in-depth manner has many layers. In fact, getting to the core of a song is much more difficult than it might seem. On the surface it may seem easy to play, but you are really only playing it at an elementary level. The deeper you go, the more amazing the music will sound as you discover greater riches that you were unable to discern upon your first levels of listening.

Digging deeper into musical concepts reminds me of a big Maui onion. The first layer of the onion is the crispy peel on the outside, which is simple to peel off. However, if you were to take a knife and cut through the entire onion, you would find that there are many, many layers and veneers of substance to it. If you were to analyze the onion through a microscope, you would find even more layers than you could view with the naked eye—thousands of them, in fact.

Music is much like this onion: the deeper you get to the core, the more in-depth the layers are. Cutting through them will bring about tears just as slicing the onion did.

DEVELOPING YOUR OWN SOUND

THANK YOU FALETTIN ME BE MICE ELF AGAIN

One of the primary goals of undergoing the various aspects of musical training is to eventually create your own musical identity and signature. Most of what makes a player sound original is the unique way he or she blends the various elements of music together.

It's like being a master chef. All trained chefs have access to the same knowledge, tools, and ingredients. I mean, a carrot is a carrot, a chicken breast is a chicken breast, and salt and pepper are the same for everyone. The originality comes from how they use those raw ingredients to come up with their own signature recipes. What makes a chef excellent is a combination of knowledge and experience, fused together with daring imagination. When they're hitting on all cylinders, people will line up from miles around to partake of their culinary genius.

This same combination of attributes gives birth to innovative music people love to hear. My own groove was developed through intense study and total immersion in the craft: copping great grooves off records, playing to drum machines and loops, and learning a wide variety of songs. Eventually, your sound will be an amalgamation of every experience you've absorbed, and that unique blend of components will come out in the way you approach the playing of every note.

Most of developing an original sound comes from your conceptual approach to music, which involves studying the music and players who have preceded you, then taking those concepts, expanding upon them, and turning them into something of your own. It is important, though, to avoid purposely becoming a clone of any one particular musician. Be yourself and you'll always be number one because there is only one you. If you strive to be someone else, you will always be number two because that other person already exists.

Eventually you'll take the phrases and rhythm patterns
you've copped and begin to put your own mark on them.

—Eddie Van Halen

I went to music school with some musicians who devoted their practice time to transcribing just one or two players. Subsequently, they sounded exactly like them, adding nothing original to the mix. It would have been wiser to transcribe a wide variety of players to keep them from sounding like a clone of any one in particular.

Although you can get a certain amount of work as a musician by copping someone's sound, which is also a great way to first learn various musical dialects, it's really only those with a sense of originality who leave a lasting imprint or musical legacy. Learn to express yourself in truly unique ways that will celebrate your individuality. Making whatever music you play feel good with your own voice is what being a creative artist is all about.

> *Magic is that God-given, mysterious little something extra no one can quite put their finger on. Magic, or "mojo" as musicians like to refer to it, is what gives a musician seductive powers and charisma.*

Skill, attitude and emotion are key factors for making music feel good, but they are not the only characteristics that distinguish one musician from another. Passion, dynamics, touch, sensitivity, and a sense of timing also play roles. But there is one final ingredient that is the clincher: magic. Magic is that God-given, mysterious little something extra no one can quite put their finger on. Magic, or "mojo" as musicians like to refer to it, is what gives a musician seductive powers and charisma. Everyone is playing from the same technical bag of tricks, so when your mojo is working, you're absolutely inspired and on point.

Another attribute that sets players apart is the *way* they play what they play. I mean, the value of an eighth note is the same note value for everyone; the way you play them is what sets you apart. The way you hit that drum, pluck that bass, strum that guitar, or pounce out that chord on the piano will set you apart from other players.

Many inexperienced players will listen to a great classic recording and hastily say, "I can do that, what's the big deal?" But they mindlessly overlook all the subtle ingredients that make the music feel the way it does—and miss the whole point in the process. Various components working in tandem, and a unique chemistry amongst the musicians, cause something to feel great.

What makes musicians great is their creative intuition, the magic that allows them to hear the parts they're going to play in their heads before they come out in real time on the actual instrument. It's easy to cop something after the fact—all you have to do is listen to what's already been created and emulate it note for note. A true master always makes it look easy and effortless, because music flows out of them so beautifully. Their movements are fluid and graceful, their attitude confident, and their demeanor is relaxed. The ability to hear a great musical part in your head and then quickly and flawlessly execute it, is what separates the novice from the master.

It is possible to be a technically proficient and highly educated player who reads music well and keeps excellent time, but still be unable to come up with a great musical part because of a lack of imagination.

> *Imagination is more important than knowledge.*
> *Knowledge is limited, imagination enriches the world.*
> —Albert Einstein

The beauty of music is that a multitude of players can be playing the same exact part and each will interpret it in his or her own way. Each will have a unique take on the feel, accenting and emphasizing it according to how the music is personally felt. There is always room for evolution and originality within any genre of music.

Once you learn the basic rules and technical aspects of playing music through experimentation and risk taking, you will develop something of your own that will become truly unique, original, and ultimately you!

By using your imagination and adding your own personality to the music, you make it an extension of who you are as a creative being.

Once you learn the basic rules and technical aspects of playing music through experimentation and risk taking, you will develop something of your own that will become truly unique, original, and ultimately you! Styles and sounds are invented by those creative musicians who elaborate upon basic concepts and take them a step farther, or who approach something in a completely innovative way.

It's not always the specific notes that make musical passages infectious; it's the actual *placement* of the notes. There are exercises for all instruments that will help you develop the necessary control and coordination to play a variety of grooves, parts, chord progressions, and solos. It's essential to get the technique facilitated so that when you play you have the fluidity and phrasing to make the music flow. Once you have the fundamentals, you can leave the technical aspects behind and play the music from your heart.

When you get in that zone, nothing else matters. In the words of writer Henry David Thoreau, "It is only when we forget all our learning that we begin to know." One of the absolute best techniques for developing your sound is to regularly record yourself and listen intently to what you sound like. You will often be shocked by what you hear. It's kind of like the first time you heard your voice back on a tape, video, or answering machine. Yikes! Is that what I sound like? Of course it is. A recording doesn't lie.

Recording yourself is like standing in front of the mirror naked. The looking glass tells the truth, and what you see is what you really look like—good or bad. Likewise, what you hear on a recording is what you really sound like. It will reveal every inconsistency that you may not be able to discern when you are actually playing. So often we are so overcome with the emotion of the moment that we don't realize where and when we're going astray. The more you know what you actually sound like, the more you can actually improve that sound.

STRIVING FOR EXCELLENCE
YOU'RE THE TOP

Going from being a total beginner to becoming a good player is a relatively simple task if you are serious about it. The wide gap between being a good musician and a great one is paved with numerous subtle complexities. Making that final leap requires a mastery of concepts that are more difficult to grasp. It involves elements like articulation, pitch, tone, dynamic control, mastery of timekeeping, stylistic approach, and creative interpretation, as well as how quickly you can learn and flawlessly execute the music. Like Olympic athletes who are trying to shave a half second off their best time, your final increments of improvement can be painstaking. The farther along you get, the harder you have to work for minimal returns.

For the most part, the rapid improvement you saw when you first started playing will begin to slow down. To experience a noticeable change in your playing at higher levels requires a much more targeted strategy, along with far more diligence and dedication to your instrument. You will have to let go of your ego and scrutinize your playing on a consistent basis in order to reach that higher ground.

> *I saw the angel in the marble and carved*
> *until I set him free.*
> —Michelangelo

Unfortunately, there are many musicians who are notorious for their lack of discipline and trying to get something for nothing. They want to be great without paying the price, but true greatness is not achieved through laziness, apathy, complacency, delusional thinking, or by choosing the path of least resistance. If you want to be successful in this business, you must strive to be a specialist, an expert on styles, feels, melodies, harmonies, chord changes, and songs. You've got to do the necessary homework if you want to earn the title of a professional. If being great were easy, then everyone would be on top.

As important as practicing is, it's equally important to take time off after long periods of grinding it out in the land of solitary confinement. All serious musicians need time away from their axes to clear their minds and refuel, or they get burned out.

Time spent with loved ones, enjoying God's creation, and some of life's other magnificent expressions will revitalize your spirit. When you do go back to your instrument, you will feel refreshed and genuinely excited to play again. New ideas will emerge out of that period of rest that could not have come otherwise. In your quest for greatness, you must maintain a healthy balance between serious practice and divinely essential rest.

SURVEYING THE MASTERS
DEVOTION

In our individual journeys toward striving for greatness, it's helpful to examine some of the common musical attributes amongst the greatest musicians of previous generations as well as our time. Those great masters who have gone before us left us with their incredible artistry to enjoy, examine, and expand upon, and their influence has far surpassed their own lifetime. Future master musicians who are in the making today will have the same opportunity to make their mark in their own time and influence future generations to come.

The blueprint below will point you toward your own success. Even though every master musician is a unique creature, all truly great musicians have a number of common character traits:

Passionate: They intensely love expressing themselves on their instruments.

Musical: They consistently demonstrate tasteful playing with every performance.

Purposeful: They always play what's right for the music.

Proficient: They execute musical phrases in a seemingly effortless manner.

Sensitive: They intuitively possess restraint to let others shine.

Dynamic: They employ incredibly wide ranges of dynamic control.

Humble: They remain teachable despite their world-class status.

Professional: They do what they are called upon to do without an attitude.

Integrity: They can be counted on to deliver on their promises.

Consistent: They still sound great to others even on their worst days.

Supportive: They are cognizant of the musical needs of those who employ them.

Diligent: They have amazing work ethics and give 100 percent to every gig.

Studious: They are always students of their instruments and continue to grow.

Original: They have unique approaches to music that set them apart from others.

Expressive: They utilize the intellectual and emotional aspects of music with a depth of spirit and connect us to their hearts.

The greatest use of life is to spend it for something that outlasts it.

—William James

THE ART OF INTERPRETATION
MASTERING THE LANGUAGE OF MUSIC

Music is the universal language of mankind.
—Henry Wadsworth Longfellow

Several years ago, I played a New Year's Eve gig in New York City with American pop legends Frankie Valli and the Four Seasons. On this particular engagement, Paul Shaffer, David Letterman's musical director and sidekick since 1982, sat in with us. Now, I've had the pleasure of jamming with a number of celebrity musicians, including Steven Tyler of Aerosmith, Mick Jagger of The Rolling Stones, Slash of Guns 'N Roses, Stevie Wonder, and legendary saxophonist Grover Washington Jr., but Paul Shaffer was especially impressive.

What made him stand out from other players was that he not only knew the chord changes of the songs, which is a must because he's a keyboard player, but he also knew the parts of all the other musicians—the bass, horn, and guitar parts. I mean, he knew it all! Most cats just try to get up there and fake it, but he knew the music inside and out. That kind of respect for the music clearly demonstrates why Shaffer is a great performer and the musical director for one of the longest running shows in nighttime television history. You don't get to the top by accident; you get there by sheer mastery of your instrument, an act that is always intentional.

THE LANGUAGES OF MUSIC
TALK TO ME

I look at the language of music the same way I look at the English language. People speak English all over the United States, but they have different accents in different regions. In New England, you can drive a very short distance and hear a staggeringly different drawl. People speak differently in New Orleans than they do in Texas even though they

http://4wrd.it/A.BG7

are geographically close. Native North Dakotans sound significantly different than people in Alabama, even though they use the same basic language.

It's the same all over the world. English is the primary language in England, Scotland, Wales, Ireland, Australia, and South Africa, but in each part of the world there is a unique accent and spin on the same basic language.

If you want someone to think you are from their region of the world, you need to mimic their dialect. Otherwise, the minute you open your mouth and speak, it will be very obvious you are a foreigner. It's the same with music. In order to blend in with the locals, you have to sound like one of them. To sound like a jazz musician, you need to speak with the same inflection or accent that a jazz musician would have. The same thing goes for country, blues, bluegrass, pop, funk, rock 'n' roll, jazz-fusion, and any other genre of music.

All Western music is made up of the same 12 notes, but each style has a unique take on the core musical language and employs the use of rhythmic, melodic, and harmonic structure somewhat differently. Just like an actor studies the regional dialect of the character he's going to play before he begins filming a movie, mastering a musical style takes the same level of advanced study, research, and intense listening.

> *Half an hour's listening is essential except when you are very busy. Then a full hour is needed.*
> —St. Francis de Sales

Here is another analogy to bring it home. If you want to avoid getting a traffic citation in the U.S., you would be wise to obey the posted traffic signs, but on the German autobahn, there is typically no posted speed limit. As a musician, you need to learn how to drive in every kind of musical setting and always abide by the laws that are in place. Developing a deeper dialect of musical languages allows you to have more under the hood, ensuring you can handle any road ordinances and conditions.

Your goal is to be a musical Lamborghini, but when you're in that 30-mile-per-hour zone, you must respectfully abide by the laws that are written. When the opportunity arises for you to show what's under your hood, you should have the horsepower to pull it off effortlessly. A beat-up Volkswagen clunker from the 1960s that taps out at 50 mph represents the musician whose vocabulary is elementary and whose control over a particular musical dialect is very limited.

The Lamborghini, however, has crazy horsepower and an engine that can handle even the slowest of speeds with ease, finesse, control, and confidence. It understands what it's made of and knows it can blaze upon the word "go," and therefore has nothing to prove. This sports car is like a trained black belt karate expert who only exerts the release of energy when it's called for. Maturity like this accompanies the seasoned veteran musician who operates his instrument with musical wisdom.

> *You can have brilliant ideas, but if you can't get them across, your ideas won't get you anywhere.*
> —Lee Iacocca

Every style of music has a body of songs that best represents its language. Listening to music that embodies the style you intend to master is the most crucial step toward internalizing it. Even if you have ample technique, you simply can't play something you can't first perceive in your mind. Remember, you can't make music without *knowing* music!

Just like a painter needs more than one type of brush, roller, or sprayer to paint an entire house, a musician needs more than one pattern, chord, scale, lick, riff, or groove in order to play an entire song with any sense of mastery.

Everyone enjoys the great job the painter did giving the room ambience, but no one really appreciates all the tools it took to get the job done, nor the intricacy involved in bringing it to life. They don't need to know the details to appreciate the end result.

It's no different with musicians; the most subtle ghost note on a snare drum or grace note on the flute can take years to develop into something that ever-so-gently pushes the music along. Even though the average listener can't properly identify the magic ingredients, those little subtleties are what make the song a musical masterpiece.

With any groove, pattern, rhythm, or chord, there are literally endless combinations one could employ. Whether you're playing blues, hip-hop, country, or jazz, having a vast mastery over the authentic elements that originate from within those musical styles will only enhance your ability to execute them at a higher level.

THE FOUR T'S OF A MASTER MUSICIAN

I'LL TAKE YOU THERE

There are many aspects of musicianship you must develop in order to master your instrument and become a great performer. Much of the challenge lies in knowing what exactly you should be working on. The following are what I refer to as the four T's of a master musician: time, technique, touch, and taste. For a musician, these sensory perceptions are the equivalent of the universal five senses (sight, sound, touch, taste, and smell) that we use to receive and transmit information about our world.

You could look at the four T's as the operating system for your musical computer. By design, every musician uses this same operating system to create, but the beauty is that each responds intuitively in a unique way based on the software installed on his or her own hard drive. This software represents musical data that was input at some point in its development. In an effort to improve our software, we should be consistently backing up the information we have learned in an effort to retain it, as well as periodically making updates in order to acquire more knowledge.

I view all of this musical input like the colors assembled on an artist's palette. It's liberating to know that you have a potpourri of vibrant colors to choose from when you paint your masterpiece. Oftentimes, underdeveloped musicians use only primary colors like a child with a small box of crayons. However, it's reassuring to have exotic colors like chartreuse, indigo, and crimson, which only come in the big box of 64 crayons, for times when no other color would tell the story better. As musicians, we need every color of the rainbow to help us express our musicality.

> *Make preparations in advance. You never have trouble*
> *if you are prepared for it.*
> —Theodore Roosevelt

If you are a vocalist, your voice must be developed like any instrument. Most of the following musical principles, such as developing a strong sense of time, will relate to you, but in addition to those, you have some essentials that apply specifically to singers. Those key components to master are your pitch, tone, breathing, diction, and phrasing. When coupled with a sense of soul and style, total mastery over these elements is the recipe for a great vocalist.

TIME

ROCK STEADY BABY

No matter which instrument you play, you will need to define time in various forms. Whether you're grooving or soloing, all the chops in the world are useless if you can't keep them within the framework of solid time. Think of time as the process of creating and keeping a consistent pulse. It is comprised of three elements: meter, subdivision, and time bending.

Meter is the reliably predictable pulse of a quarter note flow at any BPM (beats per minute). The second component of time is the subdivision. Subdivisions are the various partials of beats evenly divided into smaller segments of time, such as eighth notes and sixteenth notes.

The third element is time within the time, which I think of as "time bending." It refers to the manipulation of time in any direction within any specified subdivided grouping. This involves bending the time ever so slightly to achieve a certain feel within the music. There are three terms most commonly used to describe this time bending concept. The first is known as playing "slightly laid back" or "behind the beat." As you play a pattern in time, you are always just a hair behind the quarter note pulse of a metronome, yet not so far behind that you actually get off beat and turn the metronome's quarter note click into the upbeat or the "and" of the beat. Turning the metronome's downbeat into an upbeat is a mistake known as "turning the beat around."

"Dead center on the beat" refers to playing a pattern so perfectly with the metronome that you bury the sound of the quarter note click and are totally synchronized with the pulse. In this second time bending option, you are neither ahead nor behind the metronome's perfect pulse, but right with it.

> It is only by mastering the combination of meter, subdivisions, and time bending that the full gamut of masterful timekeeping can be achieved.

Lastly, "ahead of the beat" refers to playing a pattern just a millisecond in front of the metronome's perfect quarter note pulse. You continuously push the pattern ever so slightly ahead of the metronome, but again, not enough to get out of sync with the metronome and turn the beat around. These time bending effects can be used throughout an entire song, for a short phrase or passage, or for a singular particular pattern, scale, fill, or riff.

Some players naturally have steady overall meter, but they are challenged when it comes to controlling subdivisions with precision or being able to bend time to achieve the desired feel of the music. It is only by mastering the combination of meter, subdivisions, and time bending that the full gamut of masterful timekeeping can be achieved. If there is solid meter but the subdivisions are inconsistent, the musical passages will waver and therefore be unstable. If a player is unable to delicately bend the time in multiple directions, then the music can tend to sound one-dimensional.

A good way of looking at these three elements of timekeeping is to relate them to the experience of watching a movie in 3-D. Movies in 3-D give a film a sense of realism that cannot be attained with a flat two-dimensional picture.

One of the best ways to develop a strong sense of time is to practice regularly with a subdivided "click track," a fancy name for an electronic metronome. There are many models available on the market and even a wide variety of phone apps that feature subdivision technology. At first, playing to the metronome might feel a little like having your hands tied behind your back and then being asked to karate chop bricks in half, but you'll get used to it in no time.

Start by playing any kind of repetitive groove, pattern, scale, chord progression, or whatever pertains to your instrument until you are comfortable with it. Practice with both a straight and swing feel, and play phrases that are slightly behind the beat, dead on the center of the beat, and pushed just ahead of the beat. Then you can practice short fills or riffs and longer solo ideas applying a variety of subdivisions.

You should also learn to feel short phrases, starting with two to four bars, then eight to sixteen bars, and then finally, thirty-two bars. When you get lost, go back to where you departed and start over. Your ear will get better as you go. This will help you hear and feel all of the subdivisions while simultaneously developing your internal clock.

Throughout your career as a musician, you will inevitably play every conceivable tempo, so it's imperative that you practice playing everything to a wide variety of tempos so you're comfortable with all of them.

> Usually I'm concentrating on the quarter notes. That's where my focus has to be to keep the tempo locked. Whatever subdivisions I play in those spaces, I make sure they're locked in with the quarter note so that I don't rush them... I just try to be part of the foundation.
> —Steve Gadd

One of the most difficult things about playing to a click track is making smooth transitions from one time feel to another. Playing any singular time feel, such as a straight eighth note groove, through an entire song is not nearly as difficult as going from one section of the tune to another with multiple time feels throughout.

An example would be playing a song that had an eighth note triplet shuffle groove in the A section, then a double time shuffle feel in the B section, then going to a double time gospel groove in the C section, and finally transitioning to an Afro Cuban 6/8 feel on the vamp.

This scenario would be similar to playing a medley that transitions through a number of feels in an arrangement. To do this with the utmost confidence requires you to make each musical transition with total precision with regards to the time shifting.

To improve the skill of transitioning from one time feel to another, let's try an exercise I call the "Time Machine." Start off by playing a slow eighth note swing groove at 40 beats per minute. Now without changing the tempo, smoothly and quickly transition to a sixteenth note triplet-based swing groove. If done correctly, you are now playing a double time, or duple meter, swing groove at 40 beats per minute with exactly the same pattern that you started off with, only it's played twice as fast—thus the name "double time."

With the metronome still remaining at the original 40 beats per minute, you may even be able to churn out one more upward time shift by transitioning to a thirty-second note triplet-based swing groove. Only this time, it's exactly twice as fast as the sixteenth note groove you just left. From the original swing eighth note subdivision you started with, this version of the same exact groove or pattern is exactly three times faster. Thusly, it is called "triple time."

By successfully playing that exercise, you have just learned to play three different subdivision variations of the same groove or pattern while the quarter note remained unchanged at the original 40 beats per minute. The point of this exercise is to develop your internal clock while making random shifts to all the various subdivisions for a particular groove or pattern. I call it "Gear Shifting," and depending on the BPM setting on the metronome, you can do this exercise with an endless variety of grooves or patterns, giving you limitless time shifting possibilities. Get creative and play every other time shift that you can think of until it all becomes second nature.

As a timekeeper, think of yourself as a chauffeur who wants to give his customers a smooth ride. Rather than driving them over a speed bump in a beat-up car with bad shocks, you would opt to drive them in a high-end SUV with new high-powered shocks. Going over the speed bump is the same exact science for either car, but the passengers of the thrashed car with terrible shocks would feel every little bump, making for an uncomfortable ride. Not so in the luxury SUV—those passengers would hardly notice that there was a shift in the pavement, because their ride had such good suspension and adjusted to the change in pavement instantaneously.

> At first, playing to the metronome might feel a little like having your hands tied behind your back and then being asked to karate chop bricks in half.

The top-of-the-line SUV with a skilled chauffeur is like a musician who makes transitions feel velvety smooth from one section of a song to the next.

The practice of playing space is often neglected, and that's where many musicians have trouble. In conjunction with practicing various rhythmic phrases and subdivisions, you should also practice playing very sparse rhythmic patterns with lots of wide-open time in between each lick or riff. This musical silence, or space, is known as a "rest." You can rest for the exact duration of whatever note value that you choose. Try playing a groove, pattern, scale, or melody along to the metronome, and then randomly make up a rhythmic figure and imagine that the entire band is playing that rhythmic figure with you. Now imagine that the ensemble figure you chose is followed by a break in the music. The break could be any length of time, from as little as one beat or less, to a three-bar break or longer, and any other infinite number of subdivision possibilities.

By doing this, you are training your ear to account for the silent space in which you playing nothing. Believe it or not, it's actually more difficult to account for the silent rests than it is to fill up that same space with actual rhythmic patterns.

> *Don't play what's there, play what's not there.*
> —Miles Davis

When trying to nail these rhythmic figures, there is often a tendency to rush the time. This is especially apparent when cutting loose and deviating from the original pattern or groove—players can get a little too excited and the time goes right out the window. The key is to stay relaxed and consciously make an effort to keep the time laid back when your adrenaline starts to flow. Learning to accurately play the note value of rests and controlling your enthusiasm is a mental skill that must be developed in order to reach a high level of musicianship.

When using a click track, bear in mind your headphone mix. The relationship between the click track and the rest of the mix is very important. In the early days of my career, I was afraid of getting off beat, so I had the click especially loud compared to everything else. Because of that, I found myself always "chasing the click," which is a term I use for trying to get in sync with the metronome by either slowing down or speeding up to the correct tempo of the metronome. Discipline yourself to keep the volume lower so it's not intrusive. That way you won't sound too mechanical.

> Think of the click as just another member of the band who keeps really good time.

Think of the click as just another member of the band who keeps really good time, and focus on locking in with it. This is, of course, easier said than done, but be of good cheer; the more you practice cutting loose and stretching out musically with the metronome, the better you will become at it.

There is one final point I would like to make on this subject of time. Even though your goal is to keep excellent time, you must also be flexible enough to adjust the time to the inherent demands of the particular style of music you are playing. You must also adhere to the natural time flow of the musicians with whom you are playing. In other words, don't be so dead set on keeping perfect time that you don't allow for the manipulation of time in the direction that may best suit the music. Remember, music is not a brick; it's more like an elastic rubber band that is meant to stretch and flow in multiple directions. You just have to know when to bend and when not to.

TECHNIQUE

DIDN'T I BLOW YOUR MIND THIS TIME?

We have just learned the importance of mastering the art of timekeeping. However, a big part of controlling time and subdivisions is purely technical. Technique is how you execute what you are playing. Regardless of the style, technique is required in order to make the music flow, and there is a definite technical art to singing as well as playing each separate component of your instrument.

Good technique involves a variety of approaches to your instrument and every instrument has its own unique set of variables. Depending on your instrument, this can range from finger and wrist control to intonation, tone, and proper breathing techniques.

Independence is also an essential element of every musician's technique. For a piano player, this would mean being able to play chords with your right hand while simultaneously playing a bass line on the lower keys with your left hand. For a drummer, it means being able to play something in one limb that is rhythmically independent from the remaining three limbs. Independence is merely the ability to play finger and limb configurations independently of one another to create some kind of rhythmic and melodic counterpoint. Playing one rhythm compounded against another one without losing the first rhythm is the basis of all independence and creates a polyrhythm which brings tension and excitement to the music. Great musicianship is achieved by employing a combination of techniques to serve the music with the greatest possible depth of expression.

You arrive at your sound and touch through the techniques you employ. I use a variety of methods; it's not an either/or, but rather an amalgamation of numerous unique approaches to my instrument. Some people are under the erroneous assumption that playing something simple doesn't involve good technique, but I am here to tell you that nothing could be further from the truth! It takes an incredible amount of facility—or "chops," as we musicians refer to it—to play any musical phrase or pattern in a smooth and confident manner.

If ya ain't got it in ya, ya can't blow it out.
—Louis Armstrong

Every instrument has its own set of technical challenges, and having highly developed chops is how you meet those challenges. I am not merely referring to being able to play a particular pattern at a blazing speed. You must also possess adequate chops in order to play specific parts, grooves, patterns, feels, and fills in a seemingly effortless manner. I call that "Groove Chops," and every musician, regardless of instrument, needs them. Chops are never the enemy of musicality. The enemy is the misuse of chops by using them in an unmusical fashion.

Overplaying is one of the best examples of being unmusical, and it's an offense practiced by many immature musicians. An example would be a singer who is asked to perform the national anthem at a ball game. Instead of just singing the beautiful melody the way it was written, they sing complicated vocal riffs throughout the entire song to demonstrate their technical prowess. They do this to bring attention to themselves rather than selflessly serving the song. Due to a lack of discipline and maturity, they butcher a perfectly beautiful song by over-singing it. Instead of leaving the proper rests in the song, they take it upon themselves to fill in every bit of space with more annoying and uninvited dramatic notes.

> *As a man grows older and wiser, he talks less*
> *and says more.*
>
> —Victor Hugo

Seasoned musicians refer to this overplaying as "musical diarrhea." The equivalent would be writers who constantly use fancy words to flex their literary muscles. In an effort to impress you with their vocabulary, they miss the whole point, which is to serve the story and communicate the message as clearly as possible in a way that serves the reader's needs, not their own.

Only a sensitive musician has the discretion to play just what's necessary for each song—nothing more and nothing less. If you have incredible technique, chops, rhythmic control, and independence, and know how to use it all, then you would be considered a great musician.

TOUCH

SMOOTH OPERATOR

At the end of the day, we're all playing from the same foundational music concepts. Touch is what makes each musician an individual, and the only thing that sets us apart from one another. Part of your touch is the unique way you produce a sound through your instrument and the actual tone you get out of it. Do you get a flat, squeaky, squashy dead sound, or a fat, plush, round, beautifully full tone that's based on a superior touch to the instrument? Touch also involves what I call your "Inner Dynamic Mix," or the tonal balance with which you play your instrument.

As a drummer, my Inner Dynamic Mix is determined by the natural balance with which I play my bass drum, hi-hat, ride cymbal, and snare drum. The volume relationship of these components is what constitutes the total sound of my instrument. In essence, musicians are really sound engineers who determine their mix long before there is a microphone or direct box anywhere in sight. Amplification devices will only reproduce the sounds emanating from within the tonal spectrum of your instrument, which inevitably comes from the way you play it.

A part of your touch also encompasses control of your instrument through a wide variety of dynamic markings. It's a great challenge to maintain steady timekeeping while engaging in drastic volume changes and dispersing random accents throughout an arrangement. It takes incredible control to play with fire and passion at ultra low dynamic markings, but playing quiet is not a license to be wimpy or indifferent. Playing quieter doesn't mean playing more slowly, but slowing down is often what happens when an unseasoned musician is asked to lower their volume. You can certainly roar like a lion at a soft dynamic marking, but that takes incredible touch. Intensity is often mistaken for volume when control is really the name of the game.

Conversely, playing louder doesn't mean playing faster, but speeding up is what frequently happens when an inexperienced musician is asked to play with more volume. All truly great players are able to play in time while expressing themselves within a huge dynamic range. Devoting serious time to practicing dynamics while maintaining the pulse of time will greatly enhance your ability to adapt to any musical situation and give the greatest range of emotional expression on your instrument.

> *When music fails to agree to the ear,*
> *to soothe the ear and the heart and the senses,*
> *then it has missed the point.*
>
> —Maria Callas

A masterful touch is one of the biggest indicators of great musicianship. I find myself naturally attracted to the sound of players who demonstrate a beautiful balance on their instruments and exemplify the essence of touch.

Touch is just as much about emotion as anything else. The amount of your soul you invest into the music will partly determine your touch. Are you all the way vested in the music or are you emotionally indifferent? What specific emotions are at play while you are performing on your instrument? Are you playing with a sense of joy or angst? There is no right or wrong emotion, per se; the question is whether or not the full state of your heart is engaged as you play.

There is no possible way to separate the emotional and spiritual aspects of your humanity from how you approach playing your instrument. This is what ultimately allows your musicianship to distinguish itself from others in a supernatural way.

> *Music is the electrical soil in which the spirit lives,*
> *thinks, and invents.*
>
> —Ludwig van Beethoven

TASTE

MY FAVORITE THINGS

Taste is your intuitive ability to play what's right for the music. This skill comes from listening and by developing a vast musical vocabulary. Knowing what to play at any given moment is an instinctive reaction derived from having studied the classic music that best represents the genre of music you are trying to play.

Long before the modern musical notation system came into being, music was perceived and conceived by the human ear. Though you may have incredible chops and independence, you will only be able to play what you can conceive in your mind. You can never play what you can't hear, so it is critical to broaden your musical horizons and take in as much music as you can.

Every genre of music has a standard set of songs, seminal recordings, and influential artists that define it. This vital information must be ingrained in your spirit if you are to perform it convincingly. If you wish to play anything authentically and tastefully, you must have intimate knowledge of the original sources of what you are attempting to emulate.

To me, the hardest thing about being a musician is knowing which musical choice to make at any given moment. The fact is that no one can be with you at the moment of musical conception when an idea is birthed. We're all alone at that time, and what we choose to play will be based on all of our past experiences, both as a listener and as a student of the music. What makes a musician great is what's in between the ears—musical intuition.

Sometimes it takes hearing a more experienced musician approach the music you're attempting to play before you can begin to hear other possibilities. By intensely observing the habits and performances of great musicians and then emulating them, you will eventually be able to discern what is required for each job.

Most recording artists and producers will reference music they are familiar with when trying to describe what it is they want you to play. In actuality, it would help you to think more like an actor than a musician. To the best of your ability, determine ahead of time what is needed and then show up ready to play that role. Don't be the actor who has no idea what the director's motivation is. You'll never land a gig as a freelance musician if you don't understand what the role entails. Your goal should always be to perform as a great accompanist and accommodate the needs of the other musicians by rolling out the red carpet for them.

I write the music, produce it and the band plays within the parameters that I set.

—Sting

When my children, Jarod and Jordan, were just three years old, I taught them the meaning of the word "wisdom." I broke it down into an age-appropriate definition a toddler could grasp: "Wisdom means making the right choice."

As musicians, we need the wisdom to make the right musical choices. In order to make those choices, however, you will need a paradigm shift in your thinking. It's not about you; it's always about the music. Serve the song, the artist, and other musicians, and facilitate their musical dreams. If you can do that, other musicians will naturally love to play with you.

QUICK PROFILE OF A MASTER MUSICIAN
YOU'VE GOT THE MAGIC TOUCH

- Emotional capacity to play with passion
- Touch, technique, and dynamic control
- Improvisational and interpretive skills
- Finely tuned listening skills
- Sight-reading skills
- Rhythm and timekeeping skills
- Cooperative spirit that best serves the music
- Humble spirit to take criticism and instruction well
- Intuition to come up with the right musical parts
- Ability to inspire and motivate others
- Repertoire of songs from a wide variety of genres

DEVELOPING A REPERTOIRE

WITH A SONG IN MY HEART

As I have stated before, every style of music has core songs that are most frequently played on gigs and requested by listeners. If you perform long enough, you're bound to play these standards somewhere along the way, and you'll be glad you learned them. To really own these songs, you must intimately know the song form, melody, chord progressions, groove, ensemble figures, lyrics, breaks, key, and your instrument's specific part.

When adding a new song to your repertoire, force yourself to attentively listen to it before attempting to play it. Let the music soak deep into your soul. Don't be misled by what may seem very simple; playing it can be quite another story. Before you can play it, you must first internalize it and learn it on a subconscious level. Listen to it over and over again in your car. Listen to it while you are waiting in line at the grocery store, on the school bus, getting your oil changed, working out, or sitting on the tarmac waiting for your flight to take off. Suddenly, places that would otherwise be time wasters will help you become more productive. For me, it's like programming my mind as if I were a human jukebox, storing up tunes to be retrieved at a later time.

Start a crusade in your life to dare to be your best.
—William Danforth

In many musical performances, the weakest section of the song is the passage that only occurs once, such as the bridge. If you practice a song with one bridge in the form 20 times from beginning to end, you'll have played the chorus or verse at least two or three times more than the bridge.

Whether it was a band I was in or one I was simply listening to, it always bothered me to hear a band fall apart or emit a tentative sound when they got to the bridge. Over the course of my career, I've made sure that breakdown wasn't caused by me.

Like most musicians, you've probably come to a section in a song that you could not comfortably execute. At that point, you need to stop before going any further and pinpoint what it is that's preventing you from mastering that passage. It may be the coordination or execution of a particular pattern, or it could be soloing over the chord changes. It might be playing the melody proficiently or reading and interpreting the rhythmic figures correctly. It could be that you don't understand what is going on rhythmically or harmonically.

Whatever it is, the song will always clue you in on what's needed on your part. Once you identify the problem, you can implement a very specific practice routine to remedy that deficiency. This technique of analyzing problematic areas of your playing will naturally lead you into uncharted territory that will demand more out of you, such as studying harmony on a much deeper level in order to play the chord progression from that song correctly. Whatever the case may be, just be sure to follow where the path may be leading you and be willing to undergo the process that's necessary to master the skills that are needed to play that song correctly. Inevitably you will run into those same technical challenges on future songs. It may take you several hours, days, or weeks to experience a breakthrough and master a musical concept that stretches you on the first go around. However, the next time you run into a similar demand, you will be able to nail it in minutes—not hours or weeks.

There is a huge difference between transcribing a song and jamming whatever you want over it—which takes no discipline at all. You have to really break it down and figure out what makes it work and why. I don't necessarily mean to transcribe it literally on paper, although that's fine if you know how. What I am talking about is mental transcription, which is learning a song note for note and then memorizing it until you can play it perfectly, just as if you were memorizing a great speech or monologue.

> *We all have idols. Play like anyone you care about but*
> *try to be yourself while you're doing so.*
>
> —B.B. King

The great players throughout history have spent countless hours learning songs and then mentally transcribing and picking them apart. It's tedious work that takes serious mental focus, but it's the best way to master the art of playing songs. Whatever style of music you play, and no matter what the setting is, you will be operating within the framework of a song. Whether you play in clubs, at recording studios, concerts, theaters, or churches, musicians play structured music as opposed to endless jamming without structure, or overplaying with a barrage of chops in an uncontrolled and pointless manner.

The end result of all your practice and musical knowledge should be the ability to play songs in a skillful manner. It doesn't matter if you have all the chops or hip licks in the world, or if you can solo your brains out in every key—if you don't know songs, it won't mean a whole lot. Everything revolves around the songs that will eventually be heard by the audience, and it's the fans of the music that keep us working.

Regardless of the style, there are universal truths in music. Playing an instrument requires an *ear* for the language of music, which is developed through the laborious study of melody, harmony, and rhythm. These elements are fused with emotion, creativity, and spirituality, which give the music the power to touch the soul. A musician is a linguist of sorts- -the more you listen, study, and practice, the more you develop an ear for the language and understand how your instrument should sound on a finished product.

> *There is never any end. There are always new sounds to imagine; new feelings to get at. And always, there is the need to keep purifying these feelings and sounds so that we can really see what we've discovered in its pure state. So that we can see more and more clearly what we are. In that way, we can give to those who listen the essence, the best of what we are. But to do that at each stage, we have to keep on cleaning the mirror.*
> —John Coltrane

8

THE ART OF PREPARATION
GETTING READY FOR THE AUDITION

*Concentration is everything. On the day I am
performing, I don't hear anything anyone says to me.*
—Luciano Pavarotti

One day, while I was waiting in an airport, I saw a woman wearing
a T-shirt that read, "Life is one audition after another." What a
profound statement. No matter what line of work you're in, you
have to continually audition if you want to advance. First, you will
interview for the position. In the modeling world, it's called a "go
see." If you are an actor, you will go on a "reading." If you're an
athlete, you will have a "tryout."

I used to think entertainers were the only ones who had to constantly
prove themselves in such scrutinizing, and sometimes humiliating,
ways to get a job. But when I read that T-shirt, I was reminded that
everyone in the world has to audition. Even when you do land a job,
you often begin on a trial or probationary basis, even if it is kept on
the down low. The pressure just never lets up.

FINDING AUDITIONS

SEARCHIN'

If you hope to get the opportunity to audition for big-name recording
artists, it's imperative that you live in one of the major music markets.
For the most part, auditions for these "A-level" gigs occur in Los
Angeles, New York, Nashville, Atlanta, Chicago, and Miami. There
are exceptions, of course, but your chances decrease tremendously if
you're not in one of the regions where all the action is.
If you don't live in or near one of those cities, or at least
have strong contacts there, it will be nearly impossible
to get a shot at one of those big gigs.

In light of this, relocating to one of those markets is your first, and most important, step toward landing a big gig. Since auditioning will always be part of a musician's life, it's important you learn all you can about the process and improve your skill in that area.

Most auditions for professional gigs spread through word of mouth; they're not advertised in the traditional sense. If a recording artist is on the lookout for a musician to round out his or her band, word is put out on the street. Band members, management, and musical directors then make calls and invite prospective candidates to audition.

If an artist is having trouble finding someone to fill the bill and they want to attract a lot of new players, they may set up a "cattle call," which is the industry term for an open call audition, and then place an ad in a trade publication or post it on the Web. This is how someone with no contacts gets a foot in the door. To keep abreast of what's going on, you must make routine phone calls to other musicians in the know, read the music papers, and stay on top of your local scene.

> *How you spend your time is more important than how*
> *you spend your money.*
> —David Norris

PERSONAL REFERRALS

DEPENDING ON YOU

The best way to find out about upcoming auditions is through word of mouth. You're most likely going to hear about what's happening through players who are already in the loop, circle, or scene—whatever you want to call it—so hang out with the players who do a lot of gigs in your area.

The musicians I became friends with taught me a tremendous amount about how the industry works. They shared personal experiences and intimate insights on what was going on politically in a certain scene, things about which I was completely unaware. They also helped me get gigs; if established professional drummer friends had an overflow of work, they recommended me for the opportunities I could handle without the possibility of embarrassing them. Time spent waiting in the wings for the right opportunity to present itself can be greatly reduced by building friendships and relationships with players who are already plugged into the scene.

> *Wherever there is danger, there lurks opportunity;*
> *wherever there is opportunity, there lurks danger.*
> *The two are inseparable. They go together.*
>
> —Earl Nightingale

Even if you don't get the gig you're going after, there's still a lot to be gained from auditioning. I at least ended up knowing what I needed to work on most in terms of my musical skills and how to perform under pressure.

During an audition, you'll have the opportunity to meet and exchange numbers with other players. I always made it a point to meet as many people as I could. It's particularly beneficial for people to see your face so you will come to mind when another opportunity presents itself. Any friendship made at an audition could eventually lead to a great opportunity. I met some of my best friends at auditions at which neither of us walked away with the gig, yet those relationships opened new doors down the road.

UNDERSTAND YOUR LIMITATIONS

THE FOOL ON THE HILL

Although I don't want to contradict what I said earlier about auditioning for everything possible, you must exercise some common sense with all of this. Know your strengths and your weaknesses, and for God's sake, please know your limitations! If you know the artist is looking for a vocalist with a special talent for harmonizing and who also plays percussion, don't bother going to the audition if you can't carry a tune. You'll look like an idiot when they ask you to sing and play the congas. Would a veterinarian go to an interview at a hospital that is looking for a board certified plastic surgeon?

I am well aware of my own personal limitations on my instrument. If there is an audition for a singing drummer I won't waste my time or theirs, because I can't sing my way out of a paper bag. I'm not afraid to pass on something if I'm certain I don't have what they need because I know what I do well and what I don't. Why give myself any unnecessary headaches, heartaches, or grief, and purposely look like a fool?

> *We are always more anxious to be distinguished for a talent which we do not possess, than to be praised for the fifteen which we do possess.*
>
> —Mark Twain

You'd be amazed at how many people I have seen in auditions who were ill-suited for the position. They were told in advance what the criteria for the position were, yet they somehow jived their way over the phone to get a spot and deluded themselves into thinking they could cover the job.

Showing up for an audition where you are clearly out of your league is totally idiotic and reminds me of the majority of the people who try out for *American Idol*. Situations like these are embarrassing for all concerned and can be avoided by simply exercising basic wisdom. As soon as you leave the audition, the band will mercilessly rag on you, and you'll get a terrible reputation that will be difficult to overcome.

THE AUDITION STRATEGY

GOT MY MOJO WORKING

Over the years, I have had discussions with some of the greatest musicians of our generation about auditioning. There has been unanimous agreement on one thing—they could all tell whether someone was happening or not in the first minute of an audition. If the player doesn't have what it takes, the remaining minutes of an audition are really just a courtesy. It's what's known as the "milk of human kindness." After all, nobody wants to be responsible for making someone commit suicide. Can you imagine how you'd feel if you heard someone yell out, "Thanks a lot...Next!!!!" after you'd only played three bars of a tune?

To avoid being the star of that scene, you need a strategy to help you give the best possible audition performance and increase your chances of walking away with the big gig. A number of factors come into play, but we'll focus on eight key tactics:

- Come Prepared
- Be Punctual
- Maintain a Winning Attitude
- Don't be Presumptuous
- Play the Part
- Stay Focused
- Choose a Prime Time Slot
- Market Yourself

COME PREPARED

YES, I'M READY

Every audition is structured differently, so there's no single formula for all of them. Some auditions are run by the artist, many are conducted by the musical director, and still others by the back-up band or possibly even the management. In certain instances, you may be told in advance the two or three songs you'll need to play, which will give you a chance to perfect your skills beforehand.

Unfortunately, in many cases, the artist chooses not to disclose this information, leaving you to go in blind or deaf. With a few phone calls to other players on the scene, however, you may be able to find out in advance which songs you'll have to perform. (Obviously, you may not get a lot of cooperation from musicians who are also auditioning for the gig on your same instrument; focus instead on players who aren't competing for the spot. They won't feel as threatened and are more likely to help out.) If you are able to obtain this information, learn the music like the back of your hand prior to the audition, and you will feel more confident and at ease when you are under the gun.

If you are auditioning for an established artist with several hits and albums, pinpointing the material that will be focused on will be much more difficult because they have so much to choose from. In that case, and if time permits, learn all of their previous hits. When an artist goes on tour, they usually like to promote their latest release, so you'll want to be sure to learn that material as well, or at least the song that's getting the most airplay or downloads. Learning all of this music is clearly quite a task, but if you do your homework, you'll definitely be prepared for anything they throw at you. In many cases, it will be impossible to get the inside scoop, so you will have to go in cold and be prepared for anything.

> *If I had eight hours to chop down a tree, I'd spend*
> *six hours sharpening my ax.*
>
> —Abraham Lincoln

From the perspective of the artists, the whole point of the audition is to see how quickly you learn and how well you can play their music. Depending on the type of music and the artists' preferences, this process can be conducted in many ways. Most of the time they will either require you to learn the music on the spot by playing a track a couple of times, or they will ask you to sight-read a chart. They may also want you to perform a solo to see what your chops are like.

The extent to which you are required to improvise depends on the style of music you're playing. For example, a jazz-fusion artist would require you to have much more technical prowess in the area of soloing than a pop artist would, because pop music is more song-oriented than player-oriented.

For some auditions, the entire focus is to see how accurately you can sight-read. This is especially the case if it's an audition for an orchestra or a Broadway show. For many jazz auditions, reading is also critical, but the artist may also want to get a feel for your ability to interpret the chart and improvise over it, and to hear how well you interact with the band.

On the flip side, there are big-name headliners who couldn't read a chart if their lives depended on it. In those cases, they may want to see how well you groove, if you accurately play your part, if you gel with the band, and if you're able to play with a click track or sequenced parts. If you're a vocalist, they will want to hear if you can sing in tune, nail your parts, and blend with them and the other background singers.

You never really know what the audition situation will be, so be prepared for anything. Of course, you'll definitely have an edge if you can find out what the audition agenda looks like. If you can't, you'll have to rely on your skills and training. Whatever the format of the audition, every bit of your experience will come into play when you are under pressure.

> *If you plan on being anything less than you are*
> *capable of being, you will probably be unhappy all*
> *the days of your life.*
> —Abraham Maslow

One thing that gives me an edge over other people auditioning is that I do some serious research on the artist and the players currently in the band. For instance, if it's an established name band you can go online and find out who influences them musically. Find out their favorite players, artists, songs, and anything else you can about them. The more you know about each player, the more you can relate to them. When you talk with them you'll know the music that has a special place in their hearts and be able to speak their language. It always makes me feel great when I talk to another player who has an affinity for the same kinds of music I love, and anyone else will naturally feel the same way. It's a bonding experience; it's just like when you're shooting the breeze with a new acquaintance and find out that your favorite restaurant is also theirs. All of a sudden, you're bros and feel more connected to one another! It's the same with our musical tastes and influences. Once you understand where a player is coming from, you can come at the music with that in mind, giving them one more reason to choose you over another candidate.

BE PUNCTUAL

GIVE ME FIVE MINUTES MORE

It never fails; when you really need to be at an audition on time, the exit you need is closed or you can't find a parking spot. Not only will you be flustered if you're late, you may not end up getting a fair shake. First of all, you'll look like a flake—definitely not a great first impression. Second, if there are other players scheduled for certain time slots and you mess up that schedule you may not be able to audition at all.

Whatever time you are told to arrive at the audition, make sure you give yourself plenty of wiggle room to account for traffic jams, delays, detours, and the horrendous parking problems that are commonly associated with overcrowded rehearsal studios. Plan to leave extra early to allow for all contingencies—there's nothing worse than working yourself into a panic or cold sweat before you have even played one note.

> *He who sows hurry reaps indigestion.*
> —Robert Louis Stevenson

Here are some sure-fire ways to ensure you won't be late for your big audition. If the studio is in an area with which you're not familiar, get directions in advance. You can easily print out turn-by-turn directions from an online mapping site like mapquest.com or googlemaps.com, or you can invest in an inexpensive GPS system. Many mobile phones also have a GPS application.

Still anxious? Why not drive to the studio the day before the audition and scope out the location and parking situation ahead of time? That way you'll know exactly where you're going before it's time to show your stuff.

Not only will you be more relaxed if you get there early on the day of the audition, but you may also get a chance to find out what your competition is doing. Players are usually lined up outside the door of the rehearsal studio just like patients in the waiting area of a county hospital emergency room. That's where you can get the scoop before it's your turn to play; not only will you be able to hear the other candidates through the door, and thus hear the songs you are going to perform in advance, but you might also converse with the ones who have already finished their audition and get some valuable insight. Knowing what is expected of you before you have to play can give you just the edge you need and help you to discern a last-minute audition strategy.

MAINTAIN A WINNING ATTITUDE

WE ARE THE CHAMPIONS

If you are like me, you do your best playing when you are in complete control and show no signs of anxiety or nervousness. I'll never forget walking into one of my first big auditions and freaking out when I spotted other candidates more experienced than myself. Competing with me were big-name players with stellar resumes—some were even the top dogs of the business.

An overwhelming feeling of fear came over me, and for a minute I let myself feel intimidated and nervous. I convinced myself

> *Self-doubt will surely set in if you give it an open doorway.*

there was no way I would get the gig with that kind of competition. In a moment of desperation, I dug deep and pulled myself together emotionally and was able to do my very best. Even though I was the underdog in my mind, I still landed the gig, and I learned that, for a variety of reasons, artists don't always want the top cat.

Self-doubt will surely set in if you give it an open doorway. Never count yourself out. Despite how many others are in line for a job, don't let yourself be intimidated or overawed by someone else's credentials. You might very well be the perfect person for a gig just like I was.

You often hear about people who seemingly came out of nowhere and suddenly score a big gig. How did they do it? Well, they auditioned just like everyone else, and the artist or their band clearly liked something about their playing and/or personality. This could just as easily happen to you if you are fully prepared and the right situation presents itself. Don't feel threatened by your competition. Just do your best and stay positive.

There is little difference in people...
The little difference is attitude. The big difference is
whether it is positive or negative.
—Clement Stone

Every artist wants to hire a confident musician, someone who knows how to take control of their instrument. But remember: there is a fine line between what is perceived as confidence and arrogance. No one wants someone with a bad attitude or a player they sense may be difficult to deal with. People can easily pick up on arrogance through your vibe and will choose to stay away from you if they sense it. What they are really looking for is assurance. Demonstrate your confidence by the way you play your instrument and by having a winning attitude. True confidence is a natural result of experience. The more music you play, the more confident you'll become.

Let's face it—you aren't going to be perfect for every gig. Sometimes you'll be the right person, but sometimes you won't. So when you audition, you should always be yourself. If you try to put on an act or pretend you're someone that you're not, you are asking for trouble. Eventually, the real you will come shining through, and if you were hired because you gave them a false impression, somebody will be very disappointed.

If you remain true to who you are, you won't have to carry on in a pretentious manner. Promote your own individuality, and stay away from the cookie-cutter mentality practiced by so many others. Your uniqueness will set you apart. It's freeing just to be yourself, knowing that in certain cases you will be the perfect fit.

> *All I would tell people is to hold on to what was*
> *individual about themselves, not allow their ambition*
> *for success to cause them to try and imitate the success*
> *of others. You've got to find it on your own terms.*
>
> —Harrison Ford

DON'T BE PRESUMPTUOUS

LISTEN TO WHAT THE MAN SAID

In my capacity as a drummer for big-name acts, I have been involved in the auditioning process of countless musicians. As one of the band members, I was able to cast my own vote and use my influence when it came to selecting the musician to hire. Believe me—how you present yourself can make or break your audition. Players are often passed up because they presume they are going to get the gig, and that arrogance comes shining through. I've seen it happen many times.

Never assume anything. Some players will come into an audition talking like they've already got the gig, simply because they were asked to audition. Just because you are asked to audition doesn't mean you are the only one being considered. Being good friends with someone in the band doesn't mean you are an automatic shoe-in, either. Even if your chances are better than most, don't act like the gig is yours; there may still be other band members who are going to screen you. It rubs other players (and artists) the wrong way when you come in with a cocky attitude.

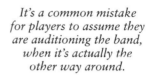

It's a common mistake for players to assume they are auditioning the band, when it's actually the other way around.

When people audition you, they like to feel a sense of control; it's all part of the ego trip that goes along with their position of power. Go ahead and let them feel that way—at least until you have the job. Just because everyone digs your playing and starts asking about your availability doesn't mean you are the chosen one quite yet. Sometimes they are just being inquisitive but non-committal!

In the final analysis, the one who gets the gig will either be chosen by the recording artist, the musical director, the band, or a combination thereof, so you need to find a way to appeal to all of them.

Another thing to keep in mind is that you can irritate people by asking too many detailed questions about the gig before they have even expressed a serious interest in having you fill the position. As curious as you might be, the answers to most of your questions won't mean squat unless you land the gig. Even if your chances seem pretty good or they are talking like you have the gig, remain as understated as possible until they actually make you an offer—then fire away with your questions. It's a common mistake for players to assume they are auditioning the band, when it's actually the other way around.

While you don't want to appear presumptuous, you don't want to seem indifferent either. Don't act like you don't really need the gig or couldn't care less if you get it. On the other hand, you don't want to appear desperate; no one wants to be around someone who is needy.

Think about it from a romantic perspective; nobody is attracted to a potential partner who appears to need them too much. It reminds me of the 2003 hit movie *How to Lose a Guy in 10 Days*, which is about a magazine reporter who intentionally hooks a guy and then does everything she can to get him to dump her. She does all of the dating faux pas, from being desperately needy and controlling, to moving her things into his apartment right from the start of their relationship. She was a huge turnoff.

Even if you are desperate, which is not uncommon for someone choosing to play music for a living, nobody needs to know it. Carry yourself with dignity.

PLAY THE PART

LISTEN TO THE MUSIC

One of the keys to being a successful musician is to think more like an actor than a musician. If an American actor wants to be convincing in his role as an Englishman, he needs to study the accent. It's about authenticity. Look at the incredible job actor Forest Whitaker did in his portrayal of Ugandan dictator Idi Amin in the 2006 film *The Last King of Scotland*. He was so convincing that he received an Academy Award for his work. Whitaker took the time to study his subject and perfect the accent, and because of his diligence, he was believable.

Music is the same way; every style of music has its own authentic language. Blues, for instance, has a distinct language that is different from any other genre of music. Within a musical

> *An audition is not the technical program of the musical Olympics!*

language, there are also different dialects. Jazz has several different sects including big band, be-bop, jazz-fusion, and swing with vocalists like Frank Sinatra. All these styles of music are like vastly different languages.

I worked with Lenny Kravitz for a long time. He draws from many different styles of music, so one minute he wanted me to play like the drummer from Led Zeppelin or Jimi Hendrix, and the next minute he wanted me to sound like I was playing behind Curtis Mayfield or Frank Sinatra. Then he'd turn around and want it like James Brown or Earth, Wind & Fire. Because I know all of these musical languages, I was able to meet his needs.

Highly skilled musicians with incredible chops and technical ability sometimes fail to get certain gigs because they consistently overplay. It's like a recent college graduate trying to sound intelligent by using ten-dollar words when one-dollar words better communicate the message.

Players of all experience levels make the mistake of going into an audition and trying to show everything they know how to do within the first five bars of a tune. An audition is not the technical program of the musical Olympics! If you are in the rhythm section, major recording artists will be most concerned about your groove factor; they want to see if you can play good, solid time that feels great. If you're a background vocalist, string, or horn player, the primary concern of the artist will be to see if you can hit all the notes, play all the right parts, and blend with the other musicians in your section.

> *Each man is capable of doing one thing well.*
> *If he attempts several, he will fail to achieve*
> *distinction in any.*
>
> —Plato

Truly great musicians play from the heart first and the intellect second. They play what is right for the music, not what they want to play for themselves. It would be like a supporting actor trying to steal the thunder of the lead. Each has a distinct part to play.

A song is a hit because the music is arranged with specific parts. You need to play the exact part on the record, not what you think it should sound like. This isn't the time to do your own thing; it is the time to serve the song. Musically speaking, you might think of it in terms of being a giver and not a taker. Musicians who are givers walk away with the majority of the gigs and are in the biggest demand—year, after year, after year. Every situation is unique, and each band has different criteria for choosing musicians, but how the players blend musically with each other is always a big part of it and creates the overall chemistry.

As you are preparing for an audition, ask yourself the following questions:

- What part are you going to play?
- Who are they looking for?
- Are they looking for an experienced pro or some new blood?
- Are they looking for a player who has little training, but plenty of heart and soul?
- Are they looking for a musician with a hard attitude or a more laid-back demeanor?

Think in terms of the band's sound, and then put all of the clues in your mental computer and figure out how you can show up sounding like the player they are scouting.

STAY FOCUSED

NICE 'N' EASY

In the Olympics, it's not necessarily the most talented athlete who wins the gold medal; it's whomever delivers the best performance under intense pressure on that special day. Being auditioned also tends to get the old adrenaline flowing. Not only are you nervous about the performance, but the prospect of playing with a particular recording artist can be so exciting that it becomes hard to concentrate.

You'll probably have a thousand thoughts running through your head: "What do they think of me? How am I sounding? Do I fit in with these cats? Did they hear how I fumbled that lick? Are they all staring at me or am I tripping out? Why am I rushing so much? How do I sound compared to the other players? Should I have worn that other outfit? That last person sounded great, I should just pack it up!" Distracting thoughts like these will take your mind off the main event and reduce the likelihood of playing your best.

*I don't care how much power, brilliance or energy
you have, if you don't harness it and focus it on a
specific target, and hold it there you're never going to
accomplish as much as your ability warrants.*

—Zig Ziglar

Instead of letting your mind wander, do your utmost to focus on doing whatever it is they're asking. You accomplish this by continually pushing competing thoughts out of your head and refocusing your lens on what's going on in front of you. When your mind is drifting, take a deep breath, and as you let it out, picture all of your anxiety going with it. This is a learned skill, and if you can successfully master it, you'll be surprised at how quickly you can regroup.

One thing musicians have in common is that we all play our best when no one is watching and there are no demands placed on us. The real trick to landing big gigs is learning to play to the full measure of your ability while you are under pressure—that's what being a performer is about.

You're not auditioning so you can play in your practice room; you're auditioning so you can play at concert venues in front of thousands of people. In an audition situation, the musician who usually walks away with the gig is the one who can stay focused and perform well while under tremendous scrutiny. Grace under pressure is the key.

CHOOSE A PRIME TIMESLOT

JUST ONE OF THOSE THINGS

Auditions vary greatly; there could be anywhere from three to fifty candidates vying for one spot. So whether the auditions go on for a day or two weeks, the time slot you get can make a huge difference in the outcome. It's certainly possible to be the first guy who walks in the door, totally nail the music, and immediately get an offer—for some artists, time is of the essence and they don't want to pussyfoot around. But more often than not, artists like having choices. It's like shopping for a car; when it comes to spending our hard-earned money, most of us like to have as many options as possible.

*Bravery is the capacity to perform properly even when
you are scared half to death.*

—Omar Bradley

Some artists have all the time in the world and enjoy going through the whole screening process. However, the artist usually isn't present at preliminary auditions; the musical director and band usually conduct the first round. At times, cameras may even be used to record prospective players. The artist or musical director then reviews the recorded performances later to determine who to invite to callbacks.

For some artists, it's an ego trip to see how many people come out to audition for a chance to play with them. An extremely popular rock band recently held a cattle-call audition looking for a new guitar player. They held a nationwide search and auditioned nearly four thousand players for the job. That's not a cattle call—that sounds more like mad cow disease to me! Did they remember what each player sounded like? Did number 3,000 even get a fair shot? Yeah, right! The whole charade was really just a publicity stunt that propagated false hope with aspiring musicians around the country. In the end, they hired somebody they already knew.

You may not always have control over the day or time of your audition appointment, but if you do, opt for a timeslot toward the end. I honestly feel I have a better chance of getting the gig if I'm one of the last musicians heard. This is especially true if it's a cattle call that has dragged on for days. By the time the decision makers get to the end of the schedule, they have already heard so many players that their minds are overwhelmed with all the possibilities. In most cases, they are more inclined to remember the good prospects that played near the end.

It's kind of like the old saying, "Out of sight, out of mind." Even though excellent players auditioned at the very beginning, things get a little hazy the further back you go in time.

MARKET YOURSELF

UNFORGETTABLE

After you have played, you may be asked to leave behind a business card, resume, bio, photo, demo, or DVD. Sometimes they'll even ask you for a list of the equipment you own so they'll know what they might need to supply you with for the gig. Having the foresight to bring promotional materials with you will set you apart and give you the appearance of having your act together.

On the other hand, there are plenty of musicians who land gigs without any promotional materials at all; they get jobs based on sheer ability. If you haven't played with anyone notable or do not have any promotional materials, don't worry about it; your playing ability will have to speak for itself. Besides, what you sound like on paper means nothing if you're not happening in person. The truth lies in what you are able to execute at that precise moment, not in how well you can pad a resume or how good you look in a photo.

Even if you don't get the gig, providing prospective employers with your promotional materials can only help them become familiar with you for future opportunities.

A wise man will make more opportunities than he finds.
—Francis Bacon

Networking is always the most effective form of marketing. Self-promotion in the truest sense isn't just obnoxious hype, it's simply being personable. Introduce yourself to everyone you possibly can, and gather contact info when appropriate.

Sometimes the person who lands the gig can't do it for some reason, so the artist has to go back to the drawing board and select someone else. It's like having a second runner-up in the Miss America Pageant. It helps tremendously if the artist can reach into a pile and pluck out your photo and resume. No matter what, you have nothing to lose by leaving a good impression—and possibly everything to gain. It's just one more thing to stack the deck in your favor.

LAST-MINUTE AUDITION REMINDERS

PEOPLE GET READY

- Double check to be certain you have brought all the equipment and personal supplies you will need to play your best.

- Listen to the music you will be playing just prior to the audition so it is fresh in your mind.

- Take the appropriate measures to make certain you arrive on time: bring directions or a map, or scout out the location and parking situation ahead of time.

- Try to remain calm, cool, collected, at peace, relaxed, and in control during the audition.

- Like an actor, go to the audition in character to land the part.

- Focus diligently when you play, and repel competing thoughts that could be distractions.

- Play the music authentically—don't play any less or any more than the part calls for.

- Before you leave the audition, make sure you have provided all of your contact information and promotional materials.

- Try to meet as many people as possible and leave a lasting impression...without brown-nosing!

*Before everything else, getting ready is
the secret of success.*

—Henry Ford

9

THE ART OF UNDERSTANDING
MAJOR FACTORS FOR LANDING THE BIG GIG

*I have been up against tough competition all of my life.
I wouldn't know how to get along without it.*

—Walt Disney

When I first started auditioning for major acts, I was completely unaware of how many factors went into the decision-making process regarding who would walk away with a gig. Naive, I assumed all I needed was to be good enough and I would land the gig. But I was wrong; plenty of musicians are good enough.

Of course, the music is essential, but after that need is met, several other factors clinch the deal. Unfortunately, you won't have control over many of them. The following considerations are taken into account when artists and their bands make the final decisions on which musicians to hire:

- Politics
- Reputation
- Experience
- Vibe
- Image
- Age
- Musicality
- Compensation
- Transportation
- Geography
- Showmanship

POLITICS

YOU'VE GOT A FRIEND IN ME

What happens when the auditions are over and three equally qualified players are still in the running? Who will be selected? At this point, it's no longer about talent. The question may be one of political positioning. Are you buddies with the musical director? Do you know the recording artist personally? Are you friends with any of the band members? If you have an established relationship with anyone in the organization it will definitely give you a leg up on your competition.

The position could even go to someone as a returned favor. Perhaps you hooked up the current bass player on the gig with some other really cool gig in the not-so-distant past. Now it's payback time and his or her turn to lobby for you to try and get you onboard. It's the old adage, "You scratch my back and I'll scratch yours."

The "good ol' boy" mentality runs rampant throughout the music business, and it can be very cliquish. Politics are involved in every situation, and who you're in with can either work for you or against you. It's not easy to discern what's happening politically at an audition, and in the end, you just have to accept that politics are always a hidden factor and learn to take the good with the bad. That's why it's so important to circulate in as many performance situations as possible and have friends scattered throughout the industry.

REPUTATION

TELL ME SOMETHING GOOD

After the silent political battle takes place between all the decision makers and everyone is finished shamelessly lobbying for their best friend, the next deciding factor is your reputation.

> We always look at dependability and reliability being
> the two main criteria we require for our team.
> —Mark Shapiro

Your reputation consists of your attitude (how you act) and your behavior (what you do). Although your reputation is based on how you are perceived, your character is established by real-life actions that reveal who you really are. Your character is usually communicated via word of mouth by those who have had prior experience with you. Whether it's based totally on factual information or not, what others share about you will impact how you are perceived throughout the industry.

Your character will be under heavy scrutiny during and after the audition process, and it will ultimately play a huge part in the artist's final decision. A great reputation is what's necessary to land a good job, but noble character is what allows you to keep it. For a working musician, a good reputation is like money in the bank!

EXPERIENCE

THE SONG REMAINS THE SAME

Audition decision makers will take a thorough look at your resume to determine your level of experience and see where you are coming from musically. They'll look to see what kind of gigs you have done in the past, what you are currently doing, and if you have played with any name acts in the past. In some cases, they want a seasoned professional who has extensive experience working with big-name acts. In the eyes of some, that makes you a proven commodity, which lessens their risk.

> *Experience is not what happens to you, it is what you do with what happens to you.*
>
> —Aldous Huxley

In other cases, artists look for less seasoned players, because they don't want to pay the wages experienced players demand, or deal with the possible egos that often go along with a successful sideman. Low-budget shows are great places for newcomers to break in; they are usually anxious to take gigs at any price to build their resumes.

VIBE

MORE THAN A FEELING

Vibe isn't something you can easily put your finger on, but people can certainly sense if there's a good vibe in the room and whether or not everyone is gelling with the new player.

Playing with other musicians is a lot like romance... some relationships click, while others don't. The right chemistry must be present from the onset for it to work; you can't manufacture that perfect union of people in marriage or in music.

The perfect vibe is difficult to achieve because it requires several intangible elements to line up in a cohesive manner. Personality, chemistry, attitude, and musical interpretation are all part of the eclectic mix. Since music is spiritual by nature, you also have deeper considerations that cannot be seen by the naked eye but are definitely discerned through our spirits. All of these factors contribute to the overall vibe.

> *Almost every man wastes part of his life in attempts*
> *to display qualities he does not possess.*
> —Samuel Johnson

In an audition situation, your personality and attitude will be on trial and closely observed. Are you playing confidently and with a spirit of teamwork? Are you personable and a good communicator? No one truly has control over the chemistry that will be created between groups of musicians, but we all have control over our own attitudes. Remaining positive and selfless will go a long way.

IMAGE

SOMETHING ABOUT YOU

The current music market is a lot more than just the sound of an artist who inspires someone to become a fan. An artist's image is a powerful force and a major contributing factor to his or her popularity and overall marketability. To the novice eye, the image portrayed by an artist may seem unassuming, but the truth is that just about every aspect of that image is carefully calculated. Many of today's recording artists are selling an image along with their music, so if you want to be part of the group, your image must fit into the total package.

The recording artist and band members conducting the auditions will size you up the minute you walk through the door. Before you even hit your first note, you may already sound bad to them because you don't look the part. Very often, people will audition you with their eyes before taking the time to actually listen to you with their ears.

Don't fool yourself for a minute; this is show business, and looks and appearance have everything to do with who gets a gig. If you're an actor trying out for a part in a movie, you'll have two specific needs to fill for the director: the first is that you can act, and the other is that you fit the look and profile of the character. In our industry, you have to be able to play the music convincingly, but you also have to look the part and blend with the overall image of the band.

Whether or not your image is a deal maker or a deal breaker depends a lot on the style of the music and the particular needs of the artist. Unfortunately, more than ever before we live in a plastic society that places more value on the way one looks than on what one can do. The entertainment industry perpetuates this kind of thinking to the highest degree. The minute you decided to become a part of it, you opened yourself up to tremendous scrutiny and prejudice.

With the exception of plastic surgery, most of us can't change what we look like too much. You do, however, have control over some elements of your image and overall physical appearance. Living a healthy lifestyle and looking as fit and trim as possible will enhance your position and increase your longevity.

Accept the challenges, so that you may feel
the exhilaration of victory.
—General George S. Patton

I have never seen someone get passed up for being in good shape, but I have seen plenty not get a second look because they looked beat and haggard and were overweight, especially with high-profile pop acts.

I am not saying that if you are overweight you will never get a good gig because it happens all the time. If you are an absolute ridiculous monster on your instrument or a legendary sideman, you may get all the great gigs despite aspects of your appearance. Musical virtuosos can get away with a lot of things those with mediocre talent cannot. It's the same with any celebrity in the limelight. If you're already famous, you can always bend the rules, and in many cases, never follow them in the first place. But if you are not a legend, you may as well do all you can to improve your chances of being chosen.

Race and gender are sometimes factors as well. An artist may be going for a particular multicultural look, and depending on whether they already have their desired quota of a specific ethnicity or gender, you may not get the gig. It's not about overt racism toward any one ethnic group or gender, but about going for a certain look that has a broader appeal to the general public. It's like they are making a big banana split and need strawberry ice cream because they already have vanilla.

AGE

THIS MASQUERADE

Because a good portion of the music industry is marketed and geared toward youth, there is a tendency for newer acts to discriminate against older musicians. But at what point is one considered "old?" What is the magic number?

Much of your marketability depends on your overall physical appearance, which really comes down to how well you take care of yourself. Your sense of style or fashion also plays a big part in your "hip factor." Older players can look younger than they are simply by dressing hip and being physically fit. Younger players who have not taken good care of themselves can certainly appear much older than they are, especially if they drink, do drugs, or smoke in excess. Partying will age you faster than a New York minute.

The age factor is a bigger concern for some styles of music than for others. The pop culture definitely leans toward the younger set, but an established jazz legend will have no problem hiring someone significantly younger if they play extraordinarily well. In that realm, musicianship supersedes age and image because it's more about the music than the image.

A man is not old until regret takes the place of dreams.
—John Barrymore

Your age can also directly impact how well you'll fit in with other band members. If the generation gap is too wide, it can be difficult for players to relate to one another and awkward to hang out. Even though you may gel just fine musically, you won't connect on a personal level. Good communication skills will certainly help, but eventually your age may not allow you to overcome the major differences between generations. Obviously, a retro punk band with an average age of 19 won't be overjoyed by the prospect of playing with a guitar player who uses Extra Strength Efferdent to clean his dentures and talks about how often he has to get up in the middle of the night to go to the bathroom.

No matter how talented you are, your age will always be on trial at an audition. You'll be too old for some gigs and too young for others. That's just a fact of life, so try not to take it personally.

MUSICALITY

THAT'S THE WAY I LIKE IT

You might be considered the greatest guitar player in town. You may be a virtuoso keyboard player with more speed than the space shuttle, but unfortunately, raw talent alone won't get you the big gig—it's how you play and interpret the music of the artist who is hiring.

I once witnessed a world-famous rock star work in a new musician for an upcoming tour. The new guy was a renowned musician in his own right and more than capable of cutting the gig. After about three weeks of rehearsals, the artist decided to cut the new guy loose and call back the musician who originally held the position. Though the original player displayed less technical prowess than the new one, he played the recording artist's music the way he wanted to hear it. In the end, it came down to who made the music feel right.

> *It takes time to succeed because success is merely the*
> *natural reward of taking time to do anything well.*
> —Joseph Ross

There could be a hundred bassists playing the same part, or a hundred background vocalists singing the same line, but everybody will perform a piece with a slightly different feel. Despite your best efforts to conceal your unique style and approach to your instrument, the real you will always surface. The one who finds the secret formula will be victorious. Sometimes your approach will have the magic pixie dust the artist is looking for, and sometimes it won't. The more you can do musically, the more your value will increase and the more desirable you will make yourself to a potential employer. If you sing well in conjunction with playing your primary instrument, you will be far more marketable in some genres of music than someone who only plays. Doubling on other instruments can also increase your value and potentially command a higher salary. The more musical skills you have and the more you bring to the table, the more likely you will be chosen over someone with less versatility.

Before your audition, make sure you have all the gear you need to achieve the sound the artist desires. FYI, on low-budget gigs you may be required to already own all the necessary gear. On major tours with huge budgets, however, that might not be an issue at all. If you're the right person for the gig, they'll buy you the gear you need. Some artists will give you the equipment at the end of the tour, while others will make you pay for it—most likely at a discounted price.

COMPENSATION

GAMES PEOPLE PLAY

Legendary opera singer Beverly Sills once said, "You don't always get what you ask for, but you never get what you don't ask for... unless it's contagious!" The truth is, everything is negotiable when it comes to the business side of music. There are no absolutes when it comes to financial compensation for musicians because the parameters are huge. I will go into more detail on this in "The Art of Touring" chapter, but for now there are a couple of approaches you could consider. First, if you know ahead of time that the gig isn't going to pay you what you need, don't bother auditioning. Second, don't concern yourself with the compensation piece until you are actually offered the job. Why worry about something that may never come to be?

On several occasions, I have landed a gig and been well into rehearsals before my salary was negotiated. I knew the longer they waited the better my position would be, so I didn't bother to bring it up. I also knew that the closer we got to the starting date of the gig, the more difficult it would be to make a last-minute change. Sometimes it's just easier for them to pay you what you want (within reason), than to bicker over a few bucks.

> *Our patience will achieve more than our force.*
> —Edmund Burke

No matter what the gig is, compensation will be a major consideration for both the artist and the player, and it will naturally weed out certain candidates. If you're a veteran player auditioning for a newer artist with a small budget, he or she most likely won't be able to pay you what you're used to getting. On the other hand, if you are auditioning for a well-established artist, money won't be an issue. He or she may want the best players available and is willing to pay for them. Surprisingly, some big-name artists opt to hire musicians who are barely good enough so they can save money.

Compensation depends on a wide variety of circumstances. Part of it is dependent on the genre of music; if it's a serious symphonic gig, the level of player is going to matter a lot more than if it is a Disney Channel pop star.

It is not uncommon for established artists who are less commercially successful to pay more than an artist who is huge. Sometimes it's because the star's management knows that great musicians will line up to do their gig just to have the artist's name on their resume. At other times the artist makes the call. It ultimately comes down to whether the individual is a cheapskate or generous. When it all comes down to it, the music business is first and foremost about money, and compensation will always be a major factor in choosing musicians.

The more knowledge you have of the situation and the motivations of those with whom you are negotiating, the better positioned you will be to get what you want. You need to understand the fair market compensation for your services and then be prepared to negotiate diplomatically.

He who has learned to disagree without being
disagreeable has discovered the most valuable secret
of a diplomat.

—Robert Estabrook

So, how do you know how much to charge? You need to understand what the market will bear so you can determine how much your services are worth. Your negotiations must be based on relevant information, not random figures plucked out of the clear-blue sky.

There are three things to consider in determining your worth. The first is your level of experience, the second is the going rate for that type of gig, and the last factor is to determine how much the artist wants you on the gig. You gather this kind of inside information by asking other musicians who are doing the type of gigs you are going after. There's a fraternity of sorts amongst backup musicians, a spirit of camaraderie because of our shared struggles. Consequently, most musicians are happy to help. Be sure to ask what the going rate is per gig and per week. If you try to negotiate way above those numbers, you're going to look ridiculous. If you are lucky enough to get the gig, don't be too hardnosed in your negotiations, but at the same time, don't get ripped off.

The most important trip you may take in life is meeting
people half way.

—Henry Boyle

TRANSPORTATION

CHITTY CHITTY BANG BANG

Although it seems ridiculous to even mention transportation as being a hiring issue, I have seen plenty of capable players get passed up because the band knew they didn't have reliable transportation. I've actually known musicians who expected other members of the band to pick them up and take them home after rehearsals!

Being needy is not how you make yourself attractive to a prospective employer. No major artists or the members of their bands will put up with that "can I bum a ride" mentality for long. If you want a good gig, it's imperative that you have dependable transportation. This is common sense, but for many musicians, basic logic is something of a scarcity. Remember, no show equals no dough.

GEOGRAPHY

JUST TO BE CLOSE TO YOU

Where you reside can be either an advantage or a disadvantage. For example, a notable British act may not want American musicians for logistical reasons. It is important that band mates live within a commutable distance so they can rehearse conveniently without incurring additional expense to the artist. With some acts, however, just the opposite is true. For a while, many French acts were willing to incur the extra expense to hire top-notch American musicians, fly them across the ocean, and put them up in hotels while they were rehearsing in France.

Some artists use different bands in different cities or countries. For example, the legendary singer Tom Jones, who is a native of Wales in the United Kingdom, has been known to use one band for his American tour dates and a British band for all his dates in Europe. Some oldies acts have two bands, a West Coast band for dates closer to that side of the country, and an East Coast band for dates in that region. Although it would be easier to always use the same musicians, it all comes down to economics and convenience.

The two most important requirements for major success
are: first, being in the right place at the right time,
and second, doing something about it.

—Ray Kroc

Geography doesn't always play a role in who gets the gig. Some established acts don't carry anyone; they always use pick-up bands; local concert promoters hire local musicians who prepare the music in advance of the artist's arrival. Other artists carry only a conductor or musical director and then hire local rhythm, horn, and string sections in each town, as needed. Since artists tend to hire musicians who live within close proximity to where rehearsals are held, you should wisely choose where you live. There's nothing worse than having the goods to deliver, but be stuck someplace where you are unable to make the delivery.

SHOWMANSHIP

THE WAY YOU LOOK TONIGHT

Showmanship is the essence of many live gigs. After all, this is show business. If you are auditioning for a symphony or an orchestra position, they couldn't care less if you can move like one of the classic ol' skool Soul Train dancers, or how far you can swing the microphone into the audience without killing someone. But showmanship has always been a huge part of the popular music culture.

> *Ability is what you're capable of doing.*
> *Motivation determines what you do.*
> *Attitude determines how well you do it.*
>
> —Lou Holtz

The need to have a player who can entertain as well as they play is growing. Sometimes you can be an asset to a band if you are comfortable talking on the microphone, or if you're able to get the crowd going, or give them something interesting to look at. Use whatever you've got—this is show time and million-dollar careers are built on such things. The better you look on stage, the more of an asset you'll be.

In most pop environments, background singers and horn players are almost always expected to do some kind of choreography to enhance the live show. If you're a background singer seeking to do live work, it would be a good investment to take some dance lessons so that you can get comfortable with the combination of choreography and singing. In many cases, women are expected to invest in their clothes, hair, and make-up to look as attractive as possible at show time.

THE ENVELOPE PLEASE

IT AIN'T OVER TILL IT'S OVER

In the final analysis, everything we have just covered is up for grabs. Fundamentally, the player who walks away with the job is the one who fulfills the most essential requirements of the gig and makes the decision makers the happiest.

Some factors are in your power and some are completely out of your hands. If the artist wants a fine-looking blonde female background singer and you're a greasy-looking wooly mammoth with warts on your eyelids, it might be hard for you to fill the bill.

After doing the best you can, the rest is left up to fate. After the audition, just let it go. If you don't get the gig, don't worry about it too much. It won't be the first—or the last—time you experience rejection if you stick with music long enough.

Always imitate the behavior of winners when you lose.
—George Meredith

Auditions can be nerve-wracking and most players (including me) hate them, but they are necessary evils if you hope to build a world-class career. You could be the greatest basement musician in the world, but if nobody knows about you, that is all you'll ever be. Auditions are direct paths to the big gig, so you must learn to not only endure them, but also to thrive in that environment.

I've missed more than 9,000 shots in my career.
I've lost almost 300 games. Twenty-six times I've been
trusted to take the game-winning shot and missed.
I have failed over and over and over again in my life.
And that is why I succeed.
—Michael Jordan

10

The Art of Reacting
Coping with the Audition Outcome

*You have to accept whatever comes and the
only important thing is that you meet it with
the best you have to give.*

—Eleanor Roosevelt

I first met Mick Jagger of The Rolling Stones when I was on a European tour with Lenny Kravitz. Mick sat in and played with us on a few occasions, and I had the time of my life. One night, Mick and I had a great conversation about music, and I felt like we connected on several levels.

Several months after the tour was over, I received a phone call from his manager. I was excited to learn that Mick liked my drumming and wanted me to audition for his next big solo tour. At the audition, I played with Mick and his band for nearly an hour. I thought it went really great, but for whatever reason, I didn't get the gig.

To this day, it's a mystery I still can't solve. I knew from experience that an audition doesn't last very long when someone isn't interested in you, but in this case, Mick seemed to like what he heard. He often turned back and gave me a big smile and nod of approval.

Only a half dozen drummers were asked to try out for the spot, so even though I didn't get the job, I was honored that the lead singer of The Rolling Stones remembered me and thought enough of my playing to invite me to audition.

I never minded losing out on a gig if I knew I'd played to my full ability and had given it my best shot, like I did in the case of the Mick Jagger audition. But I absolutely hated blowing an opportunity when I knew I hadn't sounded my best. That happened plenty of times earlier in my career.

After many of those failed auditions, I sang chorus after chorus of the "if only" blues: "If only they could hear the way I sound when I am at my best, when I'm really on top of it, when I'm playing relaxed, controlled, and confident." Or, "If only they could hear me when I'm wailing all alone in the privacy of my practice room with no pressure." For a musician, that's truly a sad song, and one many of us have learned to sing well.

> For the sake of your sanity, learn to let it all go after the audition is over.

For the sake of your sanity, learn to let it all go after the audition is over.

HANDLING REJECTION

DON'T DO ME LIKE THAT

Once you finish auditioning, you have to deal with a number of different issues, most of which are psychological. If you do end up getting the gig, there's a lot you must do correctly in order to keep it. If you don't get the gig, you have to work through your feelings in a healthy way so you don't stay in a place of discouragement.

In this business, rejection is inevitable. It is impossible to get every single gig you audition for...you'll be right for some of them, but for others you just won't be the perfect fit. The trick is to learn from experience so you are better at the next audition. It amazes me when musicians get rejected time and time again, yet refuse to address any of the possible reasons why.

Occasionally, the reason you're rejected may have more to do with politics than talent, but you must not discount the fact that you might be passed on because of something you lack. In order to increase your odds of success, make an effort to identify your weaknesses and then address those problems. As long as you choose to remain blind, you will not be able to see your flaws.

> Don't be afraid to fail. Don't waste energy
> trying to cover up failure. If you're not failing,
> you're not growing.
>
> —H. Stanely Judd

After each audition, I conduct a mental examination of how well I thought I did and write down what I can improve upon for future auditions. It's kind of like an audition journal. An area of improvement could be an element of my playing, or it might be that I need to learn how to relax more in order to play better under pressure. Whatever it is, I target what needs to be improved most and implement some practical steps toward mastering the problem. Use each audition as an opportunity to pinpoint the areas of your playing and personality that need the most work and then do what's necessary to improve!

If you invest the necessary time to develop your missing attributes, you will be far more likely to land a good gig. There are tons of musicians who are strong on passion, but short on work ethic and skill. Everyone wants a good gig, but only a few are willing to work hard enough to be worthy of one. You must balance your desire with hard work and honest evaluation in order to increase your chances next time around.

Sometimes you might have been the best choice an artist could have made, but out of sheer ignorance they decide to pass on you. Choosing a musician, much like choosing a spouse, is not an exact science and can prove to be quite a difficult process. There is no foolproof system, and in the end, hiring a new musician is a gamble.

There have been many times I have known an artist or band to regret the choice and heard them say something like, "Gee, we should have gone with that other cat. We blew it and passed up on a good thing; now we're stuck with this joker for a while."

The man who wins may have been counted out several times, but he didn't hear the referee.
—H. E. Jensen

In certain cases, you may have the goods to deliver but the timing isn't right, and you have to learn to accept that situation and move on in spite of the disappointment. Never take it personally or allow rejection to interfere with the pursuit of your dreams. Auditions may speak to where you currently sit regarding your abilities, personality, and relationships, but they certainly can't speak to your potential. In other words, the audition is not the end of the story, only what the present tense of the story happens to be. The future hasn't yet been written, so try not to let that rejection undermine your potential.

Countless stories exist of notable individuals who were rejected by those who could not see their potential, and then wound up doing something utterly amazing later. Thomas Edison, Abraham Lincoln, Albert Einstein, and the author of the Harry Potter series, J.K. Rowling, were all initially overlooked, and we know how they turned out!

No one who achieved anything great in life did so without enormous opposition, so how can you expect to experience anything different in the pursuit of your big dreams?

God created each of us with limitless potential, so don't give other people the power to determine your future. Learn to be resilient and positive, and always keep your eyes fixed on your untapped potential— that is worth more than all the treasure on earth. During times of great disappointment, I have found the serenity prayer to be a great source of peace and comfort. It would be a wise time investment for you to commit it to memory in preparation for the discouragement you will inevitably face as you push toward your dream.

> *God grant us the serenity to accept the things*
> *we cannot change, courage to change the things we can,*
> *and wisdom to know the difference.*
> —Reinhold Niebuhr

THE CALLBACK

WHAT'S GOING ON?

Waiting for a callback can be frustrating. Naturally, you will be eager to know if you are in the ball game or if you totally struck out. As you wait for the phone to ring, your mind will probably ponder all kinds of scenarios of what life could be like if you land the big gig. After years of doing this, I trained myself to push these kinds of thoughts away until I knew for sure I had the gig. It's just takes too much concentration and energy that could be better utilized elsewhere.

Although it is difficult to do, my mental strategy after an audition is to try and forget about it as soon as I leave the studio. I do that for a couple of reasons. First of all, I don't want to get anxious about something that may never happen. Second, I need to focus on whatever I was working on before I heard about the audition. If I dwell only on getting invited to the callback, my other work will suffer because of my lost concentration.

There is no standard response time before you can expect a callback. It can be very frustrating when a decision drags on and musicians are left hanging in the wind for days, weeks, or even months. After a couple of days go by, you feel like a leper from the island of Molokai.

I've been told after many auditions that I would get a call later the same evening to let me know where I stood, only to never hear from them again. By the time they settle on a player, decision makers often don't want to be bothered with the chore of calling all the players who didn't get the gig just to give them the bad news. In actuality, I considered it a huge relief just to know I didn't get the gig so I could completely close that door and move on with my life.

> *You may be disappointed if you fail, but you are*
> *doomed if you don't try.*
>
> —Beverly Sills

I have also encountered decent artists who at least had their road manager or musical director call and say, "Thanks for coming down. We appreciate your time and effort, but the artist decided to go with so and so. You sounded great, though, and we've got your number if anything changes." More than once I received a call to replace someone they originally hired, so you never know what might happen. Every recording artist reserves the right to change his or her mind.

After screening all of these players, those in charge of the audition process narrow down the field to a select group of candidates. The recording artist usually listens to the final "cream of the crop" players and is part of the final decision, but not always. Sometimes the final say is left to the musical director, the entire band, or a combination of the two, but every situation is different. In other cases there may be no audition at all, and the musical director or the band comes to an agreement and hires someone they know who is qualified for the job. This way they are able to avoid the hassle of the audition altogether.

No matter how famous you are, or how impressive your resume, you may still have to audition for major acts. I have worked with artists who made me re-audition at the beginning of each tour even though they were intimately acquainted with my musical skills.

> *Winning is not a sometime thing; it's an all-time thing. You don't win once in a while; you don't do things once in a while; you do them right all the time. Winning is a habit. Unfortunately, so is losing.*
>
> —Vince Lombardi

In 1935, every major Hollywood starlet read for the part of Scarlett O' Hara for David O' Selznick's production of the epic motion picture *Gone with the Wind*. Instead of casting any of the top box office stars of the day, the producers chose Vivien Leigh, a relatively unknown actress. The film catapulted Leigh to enormous fame, and she went on to become a Hollywood legend. None of the big-name actresses got the part, yet they all had to audition.

If you're fortunate enough to be called back, you have a good shot at getting the gig; usually less than five percent of the musicians get called back. At this phase of the audition, experience, preparedness, and confidence are the keys to giving your best performance, so by all means, go home, do your homework, and be ready to slam!

KEEPING THE GIG

FOOL IF YOU THINK IT'S OVER

So you pass all the preliminary auditions, get the final call back, and are offered the position. *Woo hoo you got the gig!* Not so fast! Unfortunately, that's not the end of the story. There is always an unannounced trial period that can be quite nerve wracking. Right now you're probably thinking, "You mean to tell me that after all that, I still may not have the gig totally locked down, even though they committed to hiring me?" That is correct. I have seen many players pass all the auditions, get the gig, rehearse for a week or two, and then all of a sudden the bottom falls out and they're out of there. It can be very disheartening to be let go after seemingly climbing to the top of the mountain.

Regardless of what you're told, trust me—you're still under a microscope for quite a while, and they can change their minds at any given moment. The powers that be want to see how well you adapt to playing their music, get along with their camp, and deal with the politics of their environment.

They generally won't tell you about this probationary period, because they want to make sure they have someone locked in place to cover the job. But they reserve the right to cut you loose at the slightest provocation. "Hey, that's not fair!" Well, get used to it, life in the music business is never about being fair.

Believe it or not, I know many artists who have hired big-name players and if they didn't click musically or personally, they got rid of them real fast. No one is fully immune to the harsh decisions of a temperamental artist or an unconvinced band. That's not to say, of course, that musicians don't bring about their own dismissal on occasion. Sometimes they do such stupid things that they don't have the right to feel like a victim.

Here's another scenario that is all too common. Let's say a band hires you to replace their original guitar player who blew it and fell from grace. Just to cover their bases, they never tell anyone auditioning that there is a possibility they will hire back the original guitarist. If they did, fewer musicians would turn out for the audition. Unless you are a complete fool, you wouldn't blow off your commitments, quit your day job, and make all the necessary arrangements to accommodate the artist's work schedule. How many players would go through all that if they were told, "Yeah you got the gig, but if our old guitar player gets out of rehab before the tour starts, we'll have to let you go?"

In this scenario, you would just be an insurance policy used by the artist to straighten out the original guitar player. Perhaps the threat of losing a job would be all the guitarist needs to get his or her act together. Many artists could care less if you've changed your whole world to accommodate them, because for many, the world revolves around them.

I never allow myself to become discouraged
under any circumstances.
The three great essentials to achieve anything are,
first, hard work; second, stick-to-itiveness;
third, common sense.

—Thomas Edison

REPLACING MUSICIANS

CHANGES

Recording artists are notorious for changing their minds. One minute they may know exactly what they want, and the next minute they abort the whole idea and contract amnesia. They may be holding auditions merely for the sake of seeing what's out there and may not have anything specific in mind. They may be in no big hurry to fill the position and just feel like playing the field, so to speak. It's a lot like when you're single and not in any big rush to settle down and get married. You date a variety of people before you find the ultimate mate and are ready to commit.

Unfortunately, for those of us looking to marry into a good musical situation and settle down, we don't enjoy being in limbo after an audition, not knowing for sure how we did. This icy silence can be enough to give you frostbite.

Sometimes during the course of auditioning, the artist and musical director hear someone that makes them totally change direction. For instance, they may have been looking for a background singer who plays a little percussion, when all of a sudden, a monster percussionist who plays guitar, sax, and keyboards but doesn't sing at all walks in, and they impulsively talk themselves into hiring this person. Then a month later, when they come back to their senses and remember what they were looking for originally, they decide to let the new musician go.

Personally, I have never felt comfortable with a gig until I was well into the tour, but even that's no guarantee. Artists make changes in the beginning or even in the middle of a tour, sometimes for legitimate reasons, sometimes not. I've seen people get sent home during final production rehearsals for an outbound tour, and I've even seen some get sent home during the middle of a very hot tour.

> *You can't build a reputation on*
> *what you are going to do.*
>
> —Henry Ford

I was once on tour with a world famous recording artist who hired a particular bass player to do the tour. Let's call him Spazmo. Amazingly, Spazmo had managed to stay employed for the first three months of the European portion of the tour even though he had a horrendous attitude and major difficulties getting along with most of the band. The arguments were wicked! Spazmo even succumbed to spitting in the face of one of the band members during a sound check. Of course, the other guy later retaliated by pushing the unsuspecting, and fully clothed, Spazmo into a swimming pool just before a show. Mind you, rock 'n' roll is a crazy world, but this was over the top even by musicians' twisted standards.

After this nonsense went on for a while, most of the musicians were fed up with the freak show and brought Spazmo's seemingly juvenile behavior to the attention of the artist. The artist was an extremely nice person who really believed in giving a person a chance to reform, and because of his patience and compassionate spirit he was reluctant to fire Spazmo. On top of that, management really didn't want to change horses in the middle of the stream.

Then the last straw broke the camel's back. When the time came for players to negotiate their own separate deals for the recording of a live album, Spazmo used a risky tactic to get what he wanted: hostility. Spazmo went off on the manager, cussed him out, called him every name in the book, and then asked for an unsubstantiated amount of money to do the recording. The kicker was that this was Spazmo's first tour, so his demands were totally unwarranted...he was lucky to be employed in the first place!

After going on a rampage with some rather colorful expletives, "!@#$&^%!," the last thing he uttered to the manager was, "I'm not playing if I don't get what I want," and basically held him up for ransom.

When the artist's manager walked out of the meeting he murmured, "No one has ever talked to me with that kind of gutter mouth and disrespected me like that—and no one ever will again." Although he'd been hearing the band whine about Spazmo for a while, now it was personal. He then confronted the artist to seek permission to fire Spazmo.

> *My father said: "You must never try to make all the money that's in a deal. Let the other fellow make some money too, because if you have a reputation for always making all the money, you won't have many deals.*
>
> —J. Paul Getty

Despite the fact that we were scheduled to record the live album in three days, the manager implemented secret plans to replace Spazmo. It was a heavy decision because we were tight as a band, having done extensive touring together. No artist really wants to bring someone in cold at the last second to do a live album recording. So much of what makes that type of recording good comes from the time the musicians spent getting tight prior to the taping. There is no guarantee the chemistry will be there with a sudden change in personnel.

Despite having all those obstacles staring him in the face, the manager flew in another musician the day after Spazmo's outburst to replace the musician for the recording of the live album and the remainder of the tour. It was a gutsy move. Spazmo didn't see it coming. Cocky, he assumed the demands he had placed would be met.

> *Conceit is the most incurable disease that is known to the human soul.*
>
> —Henry Ward Beecher

It was unimaginable that the manager could even contemplate getting another bass player that late in the game. When Spazmo was handed a plane ticket after the show that night, he was utterly baffled.

The new musician worked out great and did a sensational job on the live album and the remainder of the tour was smooth sailing. I haven't seen or heard from Spazmo since the night he was fired. That may have very well been a career-ending move.

Spaz's story should serve as a wake-up call. Once you land a big gig, it's crucial to stay on top of it professionally and personally. Being on the team doesn't necessarily mean you'll stay there unless you keep doing what it is you were hired to do and you are gelling with the rest of the ensemble. Always make sure you are doing everything you can to make yourself as easy to work with as possible.

> *Glass, china and reputation are easily crack'd and never well mended.*
>
> —Benjamin Franklin

GETTING FIRED

ONE MONKEY DON'T STOP NO SHOW

I have seen players get fined, fired, and blackballed for a variety of reasons. They range from constant tardiness, to unscrupulous behavior and other needless stupidity. One guy, we'll call him Scambone, was fined his week's pay because he was got caught selling his own backstage passes before the show. He was also busted scalping his personal guest tickets. The road manager became suspicious because Scambone always asked for four guest tickets for relatives or friends at each stop of the tour. Nobody has that many contacts in every city in the country! It finally caught up with Scambone one night; he was so busy selling his tickets in front of the venue that he was late for the show. Oops.

Being late to an arena gig has huge ramifications for everybody concerned. For a period of time, I worked with a notoriously unpunctual musician we'll call "Count Flakeula." The Count could never get it together.

On one particular occasion, the Count was late one too many times. After a show, we were all to meet at the tour bus at a designated time. He had been told the departure time like the rest of us, but he was so used to us waiting on him hand and foot that he didn't care. As usual, we waited and waited for the Count to show up so we could head to the next city. Finally, the musical director got so ticked off and tired of babysitting that he told the bus driver to leave without Flakeula.

Everybody, soon or late, sits down to
a banquet of consequences.
—Robert Louis Stevenson

This was very serious business; it was a very long distance to our next show, which was scheduled for the following night. When we arrived in town early the next morning, there was no sign of Flakeula, not even a phone call. When show time rolled around, he was still nowhere to be found. We waited as long as we could, but 25 thousand screaming fans were going to tear down the house if we didn't hit the stage. The sound would be a little empty without his keyboard parts being played, but we had no other choice but to go on without him.

Just as we were getting ready to start the last tune of the entire concert, out of the clear blue sky the Count jumps up on stage to join us. There we were in our hip stage clothing and he showed up wearing a Hawaiian shirt and shorts looking more like Toucan Sam from the cover of Fruit Loops cereal than part of the group. It took a lot of gall for him to chime in at the last minute looking the way he did. Not only was Flakeula socked with a hefty fine after the show was over, management decided not to use him on the next leg of the tour.

Spazmo, Scambone, and Count Flakeula are excellent examples of what can happen if you don't keep your house in order. Neither of these characters was ever called again to work for these artists. In fact, I don't think they've landed a big gig since they were terminated. Talent was never the issue; they were all extremely talented, but they had no self-respect or respect for others and took the gig for granted. It makes no sense to practice all your life just so you can blow it all when you finally have the opportunity to build a credible career.

The price of greatness is responsibility.

—Winston Churchill

DEALING WITH THE ARTIST

IT'S MY PREROGATIVE

Every job has a set of skills that are required to qualify for it, and being a freelance musician is no different. The difference between success in the music business and most other industries, however, is that music has a unique byproduct: fame. When some artists reach superstardom and become idols, big changes can take place in their hearts and minds. Working for someone with a monstrous ego can be an emotional challenge. Temper tantrums, freak-out sessions, conniption fits, irrational rage, unrealistic expectations, control, and manipulation are emotional shrapnel that can test even the most even-tempered sideman.

One of the most important skills you must acquire has nothing to do with music. It's called diplomacy and it will help you in every facet of your life. Understanding how to deal with people will make dealing with artists a far more pleasurable experience.

The most important single ingredient in the formula of success is knowing how to get along with people.

—Theodore Roosevelt

Working successfully with recording artists, songwriters, and producers can be just as much a testament to your personal skills as it is to your musical skills. It's about learning how to intuitively read others and give them what they want. If you work with artists who are great singers but don't know diddly squat about your instrument, it will be a test of your patience to take instruction from them. Musicians who learn how to interpret the gibberish of artists and comply with their requests will most likely become successful in the long term.

To accomplish this, it is necessary to walk in utter humility. This is not an easy prospect for any musician, least of all an accomplished one. Until you are a recording artist yourself, your job as a sideman is to give artists what they need. Since music is a people business, studying the fine art of psychology will better equip you for the job that lies ahead. Players with huge egos and short fuses who fly off the handle at the first sign of direction or criticism often seal their own fates. Learn to keep your cool, and be eager and willing to follow the artist's suggestions even when you think they are stupid.

Some artists are complete pleasures to work with and make your job rewarding. The difficulty comes when you have to deal with those who are complete tyrants. In those cases, you just have to bite the bullet and do your best. Look at each situation as an opportunity to get your people chops together, and realize that every new experience teaches you a little bit more about human interaction and the art of diplomacy. If you can keep from being riled up, you'll save yourself from getting ulcers and increase your longevity. Over time, I have learned to take everything with a grain of salt.

> *Always do right. This will gratify some people and*
> *astonish the rest.*
>
> —Mark Twain

MY BIG BREAK

BACK DOWN MEMORY LANE

At one time I played in a Top 40 band in Los Angeles called Nu Breeze. Early one evening, as I shut my front door on the way to a club gig with the band, I heard the phone ring. Not being one who likes to miss calls, I quickly jammed the key back in the door and ran to the phone.

It was my buddy, Lenny Kravitz, calling to let me know that he had scored an audition for me with New Edition, the most popular black teen group of the 1980s. Lenny suggested I stay overnight at his house and go to the audition together the following morning since he was also going to try out for the guitar spot. On the way to my gig I dropped by Tower Records and purchased the latest New Edition recording. I wanted to familiarize myself with their music before the audition.

I didn't get to Lenny's house until after 3:00 a.m., but thankfully he was still up. We hung out the rest of the night and talked about how great it would be if I landed the gig. When we got to the audition the next morning, we discovered it was a typical Los Angeles cattle call—everybody and his brother were there trying out for the gig. I was a little intimidated when I recognized a couple of big-name drummers who were also after the gig, and I knew I had to gather my composure or I would be too nervous to play my best. Lenny reassured me that I was a better fit for the gig than the other guys.

It was a "do or die" situation for me, so I gave it my all, I mean, like everything I had. The members of New Edition weren't there; it was up to their musical director, Carl Smith, and the back-up band to narrow down the field to the best possible candidates before the artists got involved. I played with the band for about 20 minutes, left a copy of my resume, and Lenny and I headed home.

Back at my house I tried to forget about the whole audition, but I couldn't keep from wondering what they had thought of me or how I compared to the others. Every time the phone rang over the next couple of days I ran to answer it, hoping it would be good news.

After a few disappointing days, though, I quit sprinting to the phone. Then, surprisingly, when I was done being overly anxious, Carl Smith called and asked me to come down and audition again for the final callbacks. This time rather than just playing for the back-up band like I had before, I would be playing for the guys from New Edition.

Carl asked me if I was playing anywhere locally so the band could see me in a live situation. I told him about my gig that night at the El Gato Club with Nu Breeze. I was shocked when New Edition's back-up band all showed up at the club. Fortunately, Nu Breeze was a really good band and the gig showcased what I could do well. I laid down the groove for hours, a great way for my prospective new employers to see my stamina and consistency.

Now, this is where it pays off to do your homework. I always learned all the songs for Nu Breeze exactly like the original records we were covering, which is how they really wanted them played. It was extra work to learn so many tunes authentically instead of faking it, which is apparently what all their previous drummers had done.

Great things are not done by impulse, but by a series of
small things brought together.

—Vincent Van Gogh

Coincidently, Bruce Soto, the lead singer of Nu Breeze, just happened to call out a New Edition song called "Cool It Now," during the set we were playing. He had no idea I'd been to the audition or that members of the group were in the audience scoping me out for further consideration.

Even though we hadn't played the New Edition tune in quite a while, I still knew exactly how the beat went. It was a fairly tricky groove because it was programmed on a drum machine and had a difficult kick drum pattern. I always prided myself on my kick drum work and I nailed it that night. Boy did that feel good!

You should have seen the look on the faces of the New Edition guys when they saw a Top 40 band playing one of their original songs. They gave each other that "Let's see how well these cats play our song" look. Luckily, nothing could have been better than for them to hear me play that particular song, and more importantly, slam it down just like the record.

Callbacks were scheduled for the following day and only five other players were in the running. I felt much better than I did on the first round, because they seemed to dig what I was doing at the club. I was even more anxious to get the gig because it had suddenly become a real possibility. The five singers that made up New Edition were like the 1980s version of the Jackson 5. They were red hot on the charts with sellout concerts everywhere, so I was thrilled at the prospect of being their drummer.

When you're that close to getting a big gig, the let down can be very disappointing, so it was nerve-wracking waiting to audition. The anticipation was killing me. I had a chance to listen to a few of the other drummers through the door before they called me in, which helped me prepare mentally for what was to come.

We conquer—not in any brilliant fashion—
we conquer by continuing.

—George Matheson

Finally, it was my turn to play. This time, the guys from New Edition were present, and their choreographer, Brooke Payne, directed the drummers who auditioned. He instructed me to accentuate their key dance moves on the drums by nailing every rhythmic figure with embellishments on my hi-hat cymbals and snare drum. The guys were all about their live show, and total synchronicity between the drummer and the choreography was their greatest concern for the drum chair.

Brooke wanted me to catch every little dance swoop they were doing, while at the same time playing the actual grooves exactly like the record. This combination was extremely difficult to execute and it stretched me more than I had ever been stretched, both musically and technically.

As the afternoon wore on, the group decided to take a break for dinner and have me come back after that. I was so scared that I just wanted to go home and call it quits. For a moment, I entertained the idea of retreat more than victory. But something inside me didn't want to give up no matter how many times I contemplated it. I guess you might call it hope.

A champion is one who gets up when he can't.

—Jack Dempsey

As nervous as I was, I couldn't possibly think about eating, so I got into my car to try and get my head together. I just wanted to go back into the rehearsal studio and play to the best of my ability, but unfortunately, my nerves were getting the best of me and preventing me from doing that. I needed some supernatural help to chill out, so I said a little prayer and asked the Lord to give me peace and courage.

As I was sitting in the driver's seat trying to get myself together, a guitar player named Louis Metoyer walked up to my car. I had met Louis earlier that year at a city park when we were playing at a battle of the bands contest for an L.A. radio station. Although we were in competing bands, we hit it off after the show. Louis and I hadn't spoken since, so it was a surprise to see him at the New Edition audition.

I asked Louis what he was doing at the rehearsal studio and he said that he had just landed the guitar spot for the New Edition gig. They had asked him to come to the studio and play so that they could audition the remaining drummers with the entire rhythm section. I instantly felt better because I knew he'd liked my playing that day at the park. At least I now kind of knew someone in the band.

Louis gave me a word of encouragement just before he headed in to get his sound together. "You would kill this gig, man, it's right up your alley. I'll be rooting for you in there."

> *Words are the most powerful drug used by mankind.*
> —Rudyard Kipling

Louis convinced me that I was the perfect guy for the gig. I sat in my car a little while longer, only now I was beaming with positive energy that he helped to bring out. I believe the Lord answered my prayer at that crucial moment by sending Louis to boost my confidence, which gave me the courage to go back in there and fight for what I wanted.

I did some serious mental warfare with positive words of affirmation, telling myself, "You are the cat. This gig is yours. You are prepared. This is your time. Your name is written all over it. This is your vehicle and your road to success. Go in there and take what's yours."

Talk about hyping yourself up—I was totally pumped! A miraculous change had taken place in my attitude and spirit, which ultimately had a profoundly positive effect on my drumming. My usual tenacious spirit, which had been temporarily shot down, was now back in full swing and I went in there like Arnold Schwarzenegger in *Terminator* ready to stomp all over the gig. Everyone saw a new Zoro after the dinner break—I felt great! I was attentive and in total control, and I nailed everything they asked of me.

As Brooke yelled out breaks and accents like one of those dictatorial choreographers straight off the set of dance movies like *Saturday*

Night Fever, Moulin Rouge, and *Chicago,* I was able to stare him down and catch everything he threw at me. I was on fire! When I left the audition, I felt like I had stepped up to the plate and done my absolute best.

When I woke up late the next morning, my mom informed me that New Edition had called and said rehearsals would start that night. I was in! Words cannot properly describe the overwhelming joy that came over me. This single victory had made up for all the times I hadn't walked away with the gig at previous auditions.

I wanted to impress everybody at the rehearsal by knowing their names, so I studied the inside sleeve of the album cover and matched faces with names. When I walked into the studio I surprised them all by saying hello to each one of them by name. I could tell they were a little shocked. "This dude's on it," I heard one of them mumble as he walked off. Well I certainly was trying to be.

After two weeks of the most intense rehearsals of my life, I did my first gig with New Edition at Disneyworld in Orlando, Florida. That night was not only magical because we were in the Magic Kingdom, but because it was the biggest show I had ever done. The New Edition set an attendance record that night when more than 80 thousand people showed up for the show.

I was with New Edition for three years, and I was eternally grateful to my friend Lenny Kravitz for setting up my audition with the group and for believing in me.

> *I am a success today because I had a friend*
> *who believed in me and I didn't have the heart*
> *to let him down...*
> —Abraham Lincoln

That incredible experience established me in the major leagues and made all the hardships I'd previously experienced worth it. I know I wouldn't have been as appreciative of this golden opportunity had I not previously gone through so many disappointments and setbacks.

That was by no means the end of my auditioning days, but it built my confidence and gave me a real future in a business in which getting your foot in the door is sometimes the hardest step of all.

> *All big men are dreamers. They see things in the soft*
> *haze of a spring day or in the red fire of a long winter's*
> *evening. Some of us let our dreams die, but others*
> *nourish and protect them, nurse them through*
> *bad days till they bring them to sunshine and light,*
> *which always come to those who sincerely believe*
> *that their dreams will come true.*
>
> —Woodrow Wilson

11

THE ART OF GIGGING
CARVING OUT A LIVING

*Destiny is not a matter of chance, it is a matter of
choice; it is not a thing to be waited for, it is
a thing to be achieved.*

—William Jennings Bryan

Over the course of my career, I've played in just about every situation imaginable—from the sublime to the ridiculous. I've endured the smallest, stupidest, dorkiest gigs known to man, and was eventually rewarded with the unimaginably cool gigs I dreamed of as a kid. I've experienced everything from playing in the back of pickup trucks, onboard cruise ships, and on busy street corners where no one cared, to playing for screaming fans at sold-out concerts in some of the biggest arenas and most unique venues in the world and before millions on prime time television shows. I even got to play a concert in an 11th-century fortified castle in Carassonne, France! It's been an incredibly wild ride, but like everyone else, I had to start at the beginning.

Shortly after my 1980 high school graduation in Eugene, Oregon, I landed a steady gig with a local family act called The Robell Brothers. They played at bars, lounges, resorts, restaurants, Elks and Moose lodges, and weddings.

Pat and Gordon Robell reminded me of the characters played by brothers Jeff and Beau Bridges in the movie *The Fabulous Baker Boys*. Kevin was the youngest, but all three brothers were older than me and had ten to fifteen years more experience.

The band played a variety of standard tunes ranging from jazz and country to rock and funk, so I learned how to play it all. Early on, I gained invaluable experience that helped me build a musical foundation.

PAYING YOUR DUES

MEMORIES ARE MADE OF THIS

One classic gig I played with The Robell Brothers was at a wonderful establishment called The Pump House, which was located in a podunk little community on the outskirts of town. The place was a smoke-filled dive, like a scene right out of the movie *The Blues Brothers*. There wasn't even a floor for the band to set up on, just dirt with pool tables all around us. The Pump House was just about as far away from upscale as you could get.

The name should give you some indication as to the type of crowd they drew; it was definitely not a place frequented by the Royal Family. For some reason, the fact that I got paid 13 dollars that night has always stuck with me, but not as much as the 550-pound drunk man who hung a moon directly in front of me while I was playing the classic Surfaris drum song "Wipe Out." His rear end looked like those pictures of the moon you see on TV, complete with peaks, valleys, and moon dust. The whole interplanetary experience. It was a humiliating moment for an 18-year-old kid who took drumming seriously, but I still gave it my all. That's what you call paying your dues.

Standing in the parking lot after the gig was finished, I vowed to The Robell Brothers that I was going to make it big someday as a drummer, and when I did, I would tell this story to everyone. Now, over 30 years later, I have, indeed, fulfilled that promise.

> *A musician must make music, an artist must paint,*
> *a poet must write, if he is to be ultimately*
> *at peace with himself.*
>
> —Abraham Maslow

BEING A TEAM PLAYER

HAPPY TOGETHER

Besides great musicianship, the most important attributes for a working musician are strong communication skills and a sense of team spirit. The combination of these two qualities will help you to stand out in the crowd and make you attractive to all perspective employers. Developing each on a high level is imperative to your success.

Teamwork is the foundation of any successful organization, especially the music business. Unless you are a solo instrumentalist, such as a solo violinist or pianist, you're always going to be working with other people and therefore part of a bigger picture. A team only succeeds if individual members work together to become a unit with one set of goals.

All your strength is in union.
All your danger is in discord.
—Henry Wadsworth Longfellow

Approach being a musician in the same manner an athlete would approach being on a team. Music is very much the same, because a successful performance depends on the cooperation of a variety of creative individuals working in sync toward a common purpose. Musicians with team spirit will sacrifice their own desires for the betterment of the team and acknowledge that the team is really the big star. If you think and act like a team player, your servant's heart will be evident in the way you approach the music.

Most artists, producers, contractors, and musical directors in this business tend to hire players who are good communicators, possess a sense of team spirit, and are pleasant to be around. Musicians who understand their role and play well for their team are the most attractive to those doing the hiring.

Because being an effective communicator is a big part of being a team player, good communication skills are essential. Communication is a two-way street; while most people are pretty good at expressing their feelings, the real challenge is listening, taking direction, and being corrected.

Far too many musicians have problems taking instruction or criticism and can't figure out why nobody wants to work with them. No one will ever want to work with you if they feel like they can't confront you about something. If you can make those you work with feel comfortable telling you anything on a professional level, and then earnestly and authentically deliver it, you will have a long line of people seeking your services.

*The most useful person in the world today is the man or
woman who knows how to get along with other people.
Human relations is the most important science in the
broad curriculum of living.*

—Stanley C. Allyn

The sign of a true team player is someone who willfully listens to suggestions and then eagerly applies what's been learned to perform better. If you can put your guard down and check your ego at the door, you'll be miles ahead of the rest. Being a valued member of the team means putting the needs of the group before your own. Never forget that you are just one of many spokes in the wheel. However small your contribution is, it is a privilege to be part of something that is bigger collectively than you are individually. Being part of a great team gives you an unbelievable sense of belonging that cannot come about any other way.

GIGGING FOR A LIVING

BREAD AND BUTTER

Since the title of this book is *The Big Gig*, it is my assumption that the desire of most of you reading this book is to land a big gig with a major artist. However, in order to do that, it will be necessary to pay some dues along the way. "Paying your dues" means working your way up the food chain by putting in some serious time on lower-level gigs. You pay those dues by doing your best on every gig, which, in turn, will groom you for the A-level gigs you have your heart set on.

Gigging serves two purposes: one, it is the place where you hone your skills as a musician and learn to serve; and two, it is a source of financial revenue that enables you to earn an income while you're in pursuit of the dream gig. All gig opportunities come out of personal relationships that you have built over time with other musicians and contacts in the business. For players, this has been, and always will be, a word-of-mouth industry; it's imperative to build positive relationships as bridges to every possible playing opportunity.

The way to rise is to obey and please.

—Ben Johnson

The most consistent sources of live work are general business (GB) gigs, referred to by some musicians as "corporate gigs." At the top of that list is what's called a "casual," a West Coast slang term for any private event that hires a band for purposes of entertainment or atmosphere. On the East Coast these are called "club dates," even though they are not actually played in clubs, and in the South they're known as "society gigs," but they all refer to the same exact type of working gig.

Casuals include various types of parties, weddings, bar mitzvahs, corporate functions, holiday gatherings, balls, street festivals, and any event where music is needed that is not a club, concert, television show, or recording studio. Countless musicians have spent time working in this market to develop their skills and pay the bills. In an effort to keep a little cash flow coming in, A-list players have been known to revisit this type of work in between major tours and sessions, or when they are out of the more prestigious work.

In most large cities, there are agencies that specialize in booking these kinds of engagements, and they maintain a roster of local bands from which clients can choose. The easiest way to find these agencies is through other musicians who are dialed into the local scene. You can also do a Google search in your area for wedding bands or corporate event entertainment, and you will inevitably run across some of these agencies.

If you want to pursue this kind of work, it's a good idea to become familiar with the agents who book the entertainment. Schedule in-person appointments to let them know you are eager to work with them, that you are available for work, and that you'd be happy to sub for their regular players if they are unable to make a gig. You'll also want to give them a promotional package highlighting your experience. (I'll go into more details in an upcoming chapter about what should be included in a promotional package.)

Throughout previous chapters, I've stressed the importance of knowing songs. This is especially true in the GB gig market because you'll be playing a variety of jazz, pop, rock, country, and R&B

standards. You need to have a well-rounded repertoire together in order to meet the job requirements and increase your chances of getting called back for more work. If you don't know the songs, you definitely won't be on anybody's "go-to" list.

Playing live in clubs is certainly the preference of most musicians, but because of the decline in live club work in recent years and the low pay scale, GB gigs have become a main staple for many musicians in regions of the country where club work is either scarce or non-existent.

I long to accomplish a great and noble task, but it is my chief duty to accomplish small tasks as if they were great and noble.

—Helen Keller

THE THRILL IS GONE

Most musicians prefer club and concert work over casuals because the audience is there to listen to the music. On GB gigs the band is only there for background music or dancing. Musicians are hired by wealthy individuals or corporations that have the money to create the musical atmosphere they desire, but for the most part, the audience is distracted and unengaged in the performance.

GB gigs can sometimes make you feel like a second-class citizen, especially weddings and corporate events. Sometimes just finding the ballroom in huge hotels is the hardest part of the gig; you might be told to schlep all your gear through the hotel kitchen, up and down service elevators, and through tiny corridors rather than entering through the front door. By the time you find your way through the maze and get to the ballroom where you're playing, your shoes are all greasy and you feel disgusting. Then you have to set up your gear and get dressed up in your tuxedo after sweating like a pig.

You may not be invited to eat, and you'll have to get used to drunks asking you to play "Proud Mary," "Smoke on the Water," "Freebird," "Brown-Eyed Girl," "My Girl," or "Mustang Sally" at every event. And you'll have to learn not to take it personally when people say you're playing too loud. Receptions like these are not what most serious musicians are hoping for after spending countless hours in the practice room.

While the fool is enjoying what little he has, I will hunt for more. The way to hunt for more is to utilize your odd moments...The man who is always killing time is really killing his own chances in life.

—Arthur Brisbane

Fortunately, this kind of treatment doesn't happen on the concert circuit, because the audience comes to hear you and gives you their undivided attention and respect. By the very nature of a GB gig, you are a hired servant, much like a court jester. Times haven't changed much since the days when musicians were used to entertain the royal courts or were brought on board a long sea journey to keep passengers and crew entertained.

Very few musicians have been able to skip past a tour of duty in the GB marketplace. Those who succeeded have created other avenues of revenue that allowed them to escape this type of work. It's a drag loading the gear into your vehicle from home, driving to the gig, parking, unloading, setting up, tearing down, loading up the gear again, driving back, and finally unloading at home, but playing the music will refine your skills.

One half of knowing what you want is knowing what you must give up before you get it.

—Sidney Howard

Most of the musicians I know don't really enjoy doing GB gigs all that much, but these jobs are often their bread and butter. That's why many of my friends in Los Angeles refer to them as "casualties" instead of "casuals." A bad casual can either make you feel like quitting music altogether or motivate you to work harder in order to escape the vicious cycle. Overall though, it sure beats most day jobs, because at least you're playing music and getting better on your instrument.

YOU'VE GOT A FRIEND

On the plus side, some really good gigs and connections can come out of playing in the GB gig circuit. It happens mostly in the major music centers like Los Angeles, New York, Nashville, Miami, Atlanta, Chicago, Austin, and a few other cities where you meet highly skilled, well-connected players. Some players get the chance to audition for really big gigs as a result of being recommended by a player who is a band member of an established artist's touring band. It just so happens they were on the GB gig when they heard that new player and then later recommended them.

That can be a big break for the person who never had an opportunity to get a foot in the door on A-list gigs. In the right region of the country, GB gigs can help establish relationships with A-list players who have the connections to lead you to bigger and better gigs, but in smaller cities, GB gigs are less likely to help you land the dream gig. Don't get me wrong, GB gigs do serve a purpose, but you must realize that they lead to nowhere fast as far as a real career as a sideman is concerned. They should be viewed as a starting place or a springboard, not a final destination or resting place.

Since the focus of this book is how to score the big gig, not how to stay in GB gig land for the rest of your life, utilize these gigs to gain the necessary experience and as a means of avoiding a regular day job. You're certainly not going to be able to set up any kind of retirement plan built on a life of playing GB gigs unless you are the agent or the leader who is pocketing the lion's share of the money. The players on these gigs frequently get reamed compared to what the leader is taking home. Somehow, leaders get away with paying ridiculously low wages to sidemen who are desperate for work of any kind.

Music is forever; music should grow and mature with you, following you right up until you die.
—Paul Simon

COME SAIL AWAY

Another form of casual work can be found on cruise ships. Think of them as floating casuals, only you can't go home after the gigs are over. Royal Caribbean and Carnival are a couple of the major cruise lines, but there are a variety of other vessels and opportunities—from evening cruises that only leave the harbor for a few hours to vacation cruises that travel to exotic destinations all over the world. Some are four or five days long, while others last up to a month. Cruises can depart from any port-of-call in the country where there is water. Miami and Los Angeles are big hubs for many major cruise lines, but there are ports throughout the country. There are even opportunities in land-locked locations; yachting expeditions that travel on lakes instead of the ocean also hire musical entertainment.

Musicians and crewmembers employed on cruise ships must abide by a number of rules and regulations. Unless you are a celebrity, you're not allowed to mingle with the guests, which can certainly make you feel like a caged animal from the circus that only comes out to amuse people upon command.

The casino lounge circuit is another area of possible work. Opportunities exist in Las Vegas, Reno, Lake Tahoe, Atlantic City, New Jersey, and on the many Indian reservations throughout the country that have legalized gambling. Some of these gigs actually take place on Mark Twain style river boats that travel very short distances, or not at all. Believe it or not, some of these boats remained parked on small bodies of water because of loopholes in the gambling laws. Bottom line—there are gigs for musicians wherever legalized gambling exists.

Music doesn't lie. If there is something to be changed in this world, then it can only happen through music.
—Jimi Hendrix

THAT'S LIFE

All in all, the most fulfilling work for a musician is not found in GB gigs, it's in doing major tours behind established artists, having your own solo project, being an equal member of a hugely successful band, or playing in the studio on creative recording projects where you are allowed to shine and assert your individuality. There is no heaven here on earth when it comes to gigs, but I certainly know that a bad corporate gig can be like hell. The movie *The Wedding Singer*, which stars Adam Sandler, does a good job of putting this corporate gigging lifestyle into perspective in somewhat of a hilarious manner.

Being treated as an artist and a serious professional is a wonderful feeling, and one every player hopes to experience. If you work hard, pay your dues, excel on your instrument, and maintain a humble attitude, you deserve a little respect. Most dedicated players want to play great music with master musicians for people who truly appreciate, understand, and respect their art, and there is nothing wrong with setting your sights on that goal.

> *Most of us serve our ideals by fits and starts. The person*
> *who makes a success of living is the one who sees his*
> *goal steadily and aims for it unswervingly.*
> —Cecil B. Demille

Until you hit the big time, you may have to endure a fair amount of drudgery; it just comes with the territory. Climbing your way to the top is crazy hard work, but it is definitely something worth fighting for.

Here are some of the ways you can pay the rent while on the way to your dream gig:

SOURCES OF LIVE WORK

FOR THE LOVE OF MONEY

- Nightclubs, coffee houses, hotels, malls, and stores
- Casuals, club dates, and society gigs (weddings, bar mitzvahs, holiday parties, and corporate functions)
- Casino lounges
- Street corner gigs
- Showcases (playing behind up-and-coming solo artists or bands)
- Broadway shows
- Cabaret
- Plays (colleges, high schools, and junior high schools)
- Musical theater (in-select-cities-only and traveling show companies)
- Amusement parks
- Trade and industrial shows
- Cruise ships, yachting expeditions, and river boats
- TV shows (house bands)
- Orchestras

The pay for these gigs varies greatly, so it's useless for me to try and give you numbers. The pay scale is completely different in different markets, and everything is negotiable to some degree. The best counsel I can give you is to speak with other musicians who are doing the type of work you are seeking and ask them about the general financial parameters.

The life of the arts far from being an interruption,
a distraction, in the life of a nation, is close to the center
of a nation's purpose—and is a test of the quality of a
nation's civilization.
—John F. Kennedy

THE ETIQUETTE OF SUBBING

IF I CAN'T HAVE YOU

Because working as much as possible is a means of survival for the freelance musician, it is often necessary to send in a substitute to cover for you when you are double-booked or unable to do a gig. Subbing is a big part of any working musician's life. One of the main reasons to send in a sub to cover for you is if something better comes along and you have an opportunity to play a higher-profile, more lucrative gig. Of course, the intent isn't to lose your steady gig or burn any bridges with your current relationships, but it's very common for freelance musicians to play in several bands at the same time, and that can cause scheduling conflicts.

Knowing how to handle these situations from a political standpoint is the key to maintaining positive working relationships with all of your employers. There are obviously some artists and bands that will not allow subs; subbing is a more common practice in the working club circuit or GB gig market than it is with mainstream recording artists. If you're a regular band member for a big-name recording artist who only works occasionally, they may allow you to send in a sub if they come to the realization that such itinerant work doesn't give them the right to exclusivity.

Let's say, for example, that you've been working for an artist for a couple of years, but there are only a few dates each month. What do you do if you get an offer from another artist to do a full-fledged six-week tour? In order to take that new tour offer, you will have to miss out on a few dates with your main employer, but the money from the new gig is just too good to turn down. At the same time, you need to keep the working relationship with your original employer intact, because in six weeks when the other tour is over, you'll be looking for work again. If you play your cards right and are fortunate enough to work with an understanding artist, you may be able to do both. This is where sending in the right sub is of great importance.

Only those who will risk going too far can possibly find out how far one can go.

—T.S. Eliot

Unless you are being paid a retainer by Employer Number One, it's hard for him or her to demand your loyalty. A retainer is a portion of your normal salary that an artist agrees to pay you when they are not working. The purpose is to keep you on the hook; if a concert date suddenly pops up, they know they can count on you. In essence, it guarantees your availability. By agreeing to accept a retainer, you promise to be available any time you are needed and blow off all other offers that conflict with those engagements.

A retainer is an insurance policy for the artist so they don't have to keep working in new musicians for every new concert date—a practice that is costly and time-consuming. However, a retainer isn't usually enough money to live on, and musicians are forced to seek out other sources of income. Even if on retainer, most musicians accept every gig offer that doesn't conflict with their primary employer's schedule. If the artist secures an unexpected new date that causes a conflict, you will need to get a sub for gig number two. Because the artist who has placed you on retainer takes top priority, you have no choice but to honor your agreement.

One of the first principles to follow when sending in a sub is to make sure you choose someone who is completely reliable and on the same playing level as you. It's not uncommon for a musician who struggles with insecurity to send in a sub with a lower level of skill to make sure the new player doesn't lessen their chances of getting the gig back.

Sending in a low-level sub is a no-no, and a sure way to anger the person who hired you in the first place. No matter what the circumstances are for sending in a sub, there is always a chance you might lose that gig; the artist might actually have better chemistry with the sub and like his or her vibe, feel, look, and personality better than yours. It's like asking your best friend to look out for your girlfriend when you're out of town. In some cases, your best friend is truly noble and can be trusted, but sometimes you'll find out your girl has moved in with your best friend when you get back to town! That's a chance you have to be willing to take when you opt to bring in a sub.

The outcome of your subbing experience depends on who you're working for and the character of the sub. Some artists are totally loyal and would never dream of replacing you, while others look for any chance to ditch you because of something you did in the past that they didn't dig—like sending in lame subs or putting their gigs lower on your list of priorities.

There are so many possible scenarios that it is impossible to predict what might happen when you choose to send in a sub. Only sub out a good gig if it's absolutely necessary or if you feel the opportunity for landing a better gig is worth the risk. In the end, it's a gamble, but so is life. You'll never get ahead if you don't take chances.

> *If you can't accept losing, you can't win.*
>
> —Vince Lombardi

If you are the one being sent in as the sub, always show up on time and be prepared to do the best job possible without trying to snake the gig from their regular player. Albert Einstein asserted, "Try not to become a man of success, but rather a man of value." Remember that demonstrating a lack of character eventually catches up with you. Doing a good—and honest—job as a sub may bring about the lucky break you've been waiting for.

THE BUSINESS OF SCHEDULING WORK

ALL OR NOTHING AT ALL

The "feast or famine" principle seems to be a universal hardship shared by all self-employed people. Personally, it has been one of life's most annoying challenges. It never fails; I always seem to get two or three great calls for work at the same time and no offers when I really need them. Why can't the excess calls come in when the work is dry or non-existent? Why can't I take rain checks on the great gigs I hate to pass up? Why can't things just work out smoothly in my calendar all year round?

There have been many times when I missed out on incredible playing opportunities with major artists due to conflicts in my schedule; after all, I can only be in one place at a time. I may have only had a week left to finish one major tour, but that was the week the new artist needed me to start and I couldn't very well jump ship on the last week of a tour! On other occasions, I had to pass up major gigs because I wasn't available on the exact day they needed me—but I was totally available a day or two later.

I've always hated deciding which gig to take when I was offered more than one at a time; my stomach will be in knots until I make up my mind. I can sit and debate the pros and cons in my mind for hours: Which gig pays the best? Which would open up the most prosperous future situations? Which has the best players? What is the best career move in the long run? What music do I prefer the most?

> *Progress always involves risks. You can't steal second*
> *and keep your foot on first.*
> —Frederick Wilcox

In the end, I have always been guided by pure, gut instinct. Unfortunately, without a crystal ball I'll never really know if I made the right decisions. I could be better off now or worse off, who knows? Sometimes, by waiting until the last possible moment to make my final decision, things had a way of working themselves out and the path I was supposed to take became more obvious.

Not knowing exactly where I would be in my immediate future has always been a challenge, but I knew it was something I had to contend with if I wanted a career in music. During times of uncertainty, it was easy to envy people with fairly predictable day jobs and more structured lifestyles. They always seemed to know where they were going to be far ahead of time, and they knew precisely what to expect when they got there. I assumed they couldn't possibly stress out as much as a musician who never knows anything for certain from one year to the next.

If you're the kind of person who has the need to plan every aspect of your life in advance, you won't enjoy the unpredictability that permeates the lifestyle of the freelance musician.

What can you do about all of this uncertainty? Absolutely nothing. Through the years, I have learned to live by faith and enjoy the great adventure. Worrying will never change one thing or give me any more clarity on a matter, but it may jeopardize my health, shorten my lifespan, and rob me of my joy. All you can do is prepare yourself as much as possible for times of famine, for at some point the drought will most definitely come.

> *There is one thing which gives radiance to everything.*
> *It is the idea of something around the corner.*
>
> —G.K. Chesterton

PREPARING FOR CANCELATIONS AND UNEMPLOYMENT

HANG ON IN THERE BABY

In the music business, things can, and often do, change at a moment's notice. Work can get canceled at the very last minute and make it nearly impossible for you to fill in your calendar and make up the lost money. It's difficult to rustle up new work without advanced notice, especially since most employers have already booked musicians well in advance. Some artists are decent enough to pay freelancers for cancelations, but others are completely unsympathetic. The philosophy of some artists is, "If I didn't get paid, why should I pay my musicians?"

Some artists couldn't care less that you passed up other opportunities and are unable to pay this month's bills as a result of the canceled booking. This has happened to me more times than I care to remember, but since it's part of the business, you must learn to prepare yourself in the best possible way to ride through the storms of uncertainty.

On one occasion, a concert I was scheduled to play in Chicago was canceled the very morning of the gig, but nobody informed me before I got on my flight. Consequently, I flew all the way from Los Angeles to Chicago and then had to turn around and fly back. That's certainly not my idea of fun. I've even had entire concert tours get canceled. Talk about inconvenient!

*Success is to be measured not so much by the position
that one has reached in life as by the obstacles
which he has overcome.*

—Booker T. Washington

Gigs are called off at the last minute for a variety of reasons. Sometimes it is due to illness on the part of the artist you're backing up. Some shows are canceled because of flaky club owners, unscrupulous promoters, weak ticket sales, deals that went bad, or conflicts with artists' schedules.

While there are a multitude of reasons why gigs get canceled, none of them change the fact that you're out the money. Unfortunately, in this industry there can be a lack of respect and consideration for musicians, which is typically expressed in the manner we are paid. Most conventional, non-musician jobs compensate employees on a consistent time schedule of some kind, such as getting paid every week, bi-weekly, or monthly, but when you do session work and GB gigs, you may have to wait a while for your money.

In some cases, I've had to stoop to hassling people to get paid for work I did months earlier. That can make you feel more like a collection agency than a musician. Personally, I'd much rather concentrate on lining up new work than chasing down account receivables. Trust me, this happens more often than you can imagine—even on high-profile gigs. I once did a live video shoot for a major pop star and waited nearly an entire year to get paid for my services. I have been stiffed by many supposedly legitimate organizations, even with a signed contract.

When it comes to live work, contracts with sidemen aren't worth the paper they're written on. If someone wants to break their promise to you, they can and they will. Once the gig is over, what are you going to do—take it back? Unless you are prepared to file a lawsuit, a process that is very time consuming, costly, and frustrating, there's not a whole lot you can do.

*I would advise you to keep your overhead down and
avoid a major drug habit.*

—James Taylor

This is an uncertain line of work, and it's difficult to know when your next gig will come, so you must think ahead. The best way to prepare for dry seasons is to keep your expenses low. When the workflow is good and the money is rolling in, put aside a substantial cushion to keep you afloat as you wait on past due monies to trickle in. That way you won't be in desperate need of each of those checks.

Even if they are phenomenal players, very few musicians work 52 weeks a year. Work fluctuates with the seasons and at the whim of the public. Most of our work is project-based and sometimes there can be problems: the project fails to get off the launching pad, the start date gets pushed back, or the project ends early. It's the same for anyone who runs their own business; they must also prepare for times of famine during times of feasting. Tax accountants, commissioned salespeople, and seasonal businesses also contend with the cyclical nature of income flow and prepare themselves the best way possible.

After a certain point in their careers, many freelance musicians diversify into other areas within the business to even out the ups and downs. Some pursue educational endeavors such as writing instructional books, teaching private lessons, conducting clinics, doing consulting work, or anything else that will utilize their talents and help keep cash coming in during slow periods or times of total unemployment. Only the strong survive; you'll have to learn to be a pretty good money manager to have even the slightest chance of sustaining yourself in this business.

> *The toughest thing about success is that you've got to keep on being a success. Talent is only a starting point in business. You've got to keep working that talent.*
> —Irving Berlin

There is no such thing as job security in the life of a freelance musician. I have known several notable A-list players who were locked into steady gigs with some of the biggest rock stars and groups of all time. After several years, it was easy for them to assume they were on the lifetime retirement plan, but stuff happened and suddenly some episode of drama took place or something political went down and bam—they were fired. After years of service and loyalty, they were back to the drawing board looking for another big cushy gig. In some instances, this terrible blow came without much of a severance package.

Loyalty and honor are not real big in this line of work, and the word "fair" is not often part of the vernacular. Even if you are the subject of an implosion such as the one I just described, things can turn around if you hang in there and ride out the storm. A positive attitude will get you to the next place during genuinely difficult times.

8 SUCCESS STRATEGIES FOR THE WORKING MUSICIAN

DON'T STOP BELIEVIN'

- Establish yourself geographically in one of the major music market cities

- Develop a high level of playing skill

- Network and build healthy working relationships with as many musicians as possible

- Keep your living expenses low

- Put money aside for lean times

- Cultivate a sense of humor as you face the challenges of a freelance musician's lifestyle

- Diversify your skills and plan for other sources of revenue within the industry

- Maintain a positive attitude throughout periods of unemployment and surround yourself with equally positive people

If a man is called to be a street sweeper, he should sweep even as Michelangelo painted or Beethoven composed music or Shakespeare wrote poetry. He should sweep streets so well that all the hosts of heaven and earth will pause to say, "Here lived a great street sweeper who did his job well."

—Martin Luther King Jr.

THE ART OF RECORDING
SUCCEEDING IN THE SESSION WORLD

*Anybody can make the simple complicated. Creativity is
making the complicated simple.*

—Charlie Mingus

My first big recording session was a memorable one, but unfortunately, it isn't one of my more pleasant memories. For some reason, my bass drum pedal made all kinds of squeaky noises, all of which were picked up by my microphones. No matter how well I played, the awful noise of that pedal could be heard on the master tape.

I was just 18 years old at the time, and I was caught completely off guard during that session. I thought it would be easier to play in the studio, and it was evident from my lack of skills that I was not ready to break into the big-time session world—nor was my equipment. I felt like a failure!

Sadly for me, my drum tracks were replaced, but that grave disappointment spurred me on to work harder so that when my next opportunity arose, my gear and I would both be ready. Thankfully, a couple of years later, my time of redemption came. It would be the beginning of countless hours spent recording in the studio on a vast array of musical projects.

By that time, I was living in the epicenter of the recording world, Los Angeles, California, and I was happy about all of the prospects that were waiting for me in the City of Angels. Hooray for Hollywood was my anthem!

Without a doubt, living in one of the major music markets such as Los Angeles, New York, Nashville, Chicago, Miami, or Atlanta is one of the most important prerequisites to flourish as an A-list session player. Even if you don't live in one of those cities, there

http://4wrd.it/A.BG12

is still a vast amount of secondary market recording activity in small production houses found around the world.

Musicians are needed for all kinds of projects, including music for computer and video games, church messages, announcements, video shorts, documentaries, cell phones, conventions and various industry trade shows, cable television, infomercials, local TV commercials and news shows, and a plethora of Internet sites. But before you can even contemplate the idea of breaking into the music industry as a studio musician, you have to make sure you have the musical goods to deliver.

Unlike backing up an established artist onstage, playing in the studio is not about image. All that matters in this arena is your skill on your instrument.

> *It's easy to play any musical instrument: all you have to do is touch the right key at the right time and the instrument will play itself.*
>
> —Johann Sebastian Bach

Versatility is another key ingredient necessary to making it in the music business. Being adept at a variety of music styles comes from being a well-versed listener. It is important that you are able to emulate a variety of players and the latest sounds. Great sight-reading skills and a quick ear are also essentials.

To become truly accomplished, you'll need to spend a lot of time copping your instrument's major contributors, past and present. Be very aware of current musical trends and players so when you're asked to give that "so-and-so" sound, you'll be able to nail it. At the same time, practice the original concepts that are unique to your own style—but only insert them in the music when it best serves the artist, producer, or arrangement.

SESSION WORK

ANYWAY YOU WANT ME

Securing a place in the studio scene differs slightly from getting roadwork. Staying in town on a consistent basis is one of the trade secrets and keys to making it as a session player.

The peak years for the studio musician as a breed were back in the '60s, '70s, and early '80s. Back in those golden years of the recording scene, working studio musicians rarely traveled out of town for fear of losing their close relationships with the producers and contractors who hired them on a regular basis.

Being a steadily employed studio musician wasn't always ideal. The primary complaint from musicians who played in the studio day after day was that it got a bit monotonous. Playing on record dates and recording jingles all day could be confining because it required very focused and controlled musicianship. That didn't always allow for the sideman to stretch out musically. To keep from being musically stagnant, most session musicians in New York, Los Angeles, and Nashville played live club gigs late at night.

At that same time, some musicians spent the majority of their time out on the road playing behind the famous recording artists of the day and became known as touring musicians. Doing too much roadwork has drawbacks, too. Constant travel can make it difficult to develop relationships with the producers, contractors, arrangers, and engineers who are the keys to getting session work. Those doing the hiring want to know you are available any time they call, and they prefer players they can count on without having to adjust their production schedules to accommodate them.

*It's all about finding the right note at the right place
and knowing when to leave well enough alone.
And that's a lifelong quest.*
—David Sanborn

Although a good road gig can definitely lead to some session work, there seems to be a strange stigma attached to being a touring musician. Inexplicably, some artists and producers just won't call touring musicians to play on their records. It's like there are invisible labels on players; you're a studio cat, a touring player, a Broadway musician, or whatever other classification they attach to you.

It's the same thing in the acting world. If you're known as a great comedic actor, not many directors will consider you for the lead role in a serious drama, even though you may be fully capable of playing the part convincingly. There are mindsets, perceptions, and preconceived notions in many of the creative arts fields that limit how one's potential is viewed, and there just doesn't seem to be any way to change that.

Playing effectively in the studio requires a different set of skills than playing live, and unless producers know you possess those recording skills, it's very unlikely you'll be called.

The majority of musicians who break into session work are discovered by other players in a live setting. Playing live has its own set of challenges and unique skills, and it is how most musicians develop their craft and establish beneficial relationships.

There are many skilled sidemen who manage to juggle session work and live dates, and that combination provides steadier cash flow and the chance for broader musical expression. Today there are many more self-reliant bands than at any other time in the history of the music industry. They play on their own recordings as opposed to hiring session musicians. Naturally, that cuts out a rather large amount of the work session players were accustomed to getting in days gone by, when popular bands hired top session pros to play on their records instead of attempting to play themselves.

> *Getting ahead in a difficult profession requires avid faith in yourself. That is why some people with mediocre talent, but with the inner drive, go much farther than people with vastly superior talent.*
>
> —Sophia Loren

In the not-so-distant past, the majority of recording studios were large professional facilities located in major cities. Today, however, advances in digital technology mean you no longer need a million-dollar studio to make a great recording. Small, privately owned home studios are scattered all over the world. These modern studios take up far less space and are more cost effective, making it possible for practically anyone with a reasonable budget to have their own home studio and cut a professional-sounding record.

That's both good and bad. On the down side, it opens the door to anyone with musical delusions of grandeur and floods the market with mediocrity, bringing down the overall level of musicianship. On the up side, the emergence of home studios has created new opportunities for session work. For many musicians, this is a great place to gain invaluable experience before trying to wedge themselves into the scene with the heavy hitters. It is an apprenticeship of sorts, and the pay scale is much lower than working with a major recording artist who has a real budget, but it is a great way to become an all-around session player.

> *A pessimist sees the difficulty in every opportunity;*
> *an optimist sees the opportunity in every difficulty.*
> —Winston Churchill

Even for super-pro session players, much of the work has moved from those big studios to small, private ones. Many session musicians now record in the comfort of their own home studios and send the fully finished digital files to the client over the Internet. With the World Wide Web, you can do sessions for literally anyone in the world who is willing to pay. That has been a real blessing for musicians who were willing to invest in home studios and immerse themselves in new technology. For every setback our industry has faced, there are an equal number of setups, especially for those who are willing to view opportunities in a new light and grab hold of them.

Producers, contractors, audio engineers, studio owners, and other players are the key contacts to help you get studio work. While most musicians know what producers, sound engineers, and studio owners are, many are unfamiliar with the function of a contractor. A contractor is a musician employed by the producer to hire the other freelancers for the session, similar to what a casting director does for a film. In both cases, they acquire a lineup of capable talent for the project.

Whether a contractor is used to hire musicians on a session is dependent on the type of music being made, the preference of the producer, and the recording budget. With some styles of music, there are separate contractors for each group of musicians. For instance, on larger projects there could be a contractor for horns, one for strings, one for the rhythm section, and one for background vocalists.

> *The quality of a person's life is in direct proportion*
> *to that person's commitment to excellence, regardless*
> *of chosen field of endeavor.*
>
> —Vince Lombardi

In most cases, contractors are proficient musicians with great ears for talent who have established relationships with the players they hire. But in some cases, contractors are not great musicians but have good ears for talent and know how to schmooze their way into positions of power with producers. Either way, the producer counts on the contractor to bring reliable musicians to the project who are team players and will get the job done in a timely manner.

Contractors are also hired by musical directors to facilitate the hiring of musicians for their live dates. Since most artists routinely carry their own rhythm sections with them, contractors will provide horns, strings, and sometimes even an entire orchestra. On a major tour, there is often a different contractor for each city, although some cover multiple regions or might be used to employ the same musicians for the entire tour.

Although many producers know which players they prefer to work with, they hire contractors to assemble the musicians and book them for the session. A great deal of work goes into lining up the musicians and filling out the necessary union paperwork, and by delegating this work to the contractor, the producer can concentrate on selecting the songs for the artist, choosing the studio, working with the arranger, and conferring with the sound engineer and record label on the project's vision.

Based on your strengths as a player, begin to make a list of key producers your playing style may fit. In order to do this, you must be aware of the music that's hitting the charts and the most popular song downloads—and who is producing them. You can determine who the producer is by reading CD liner notes, industry trades such as *Billboard* magazine, and Googling the information online. Once this information is documented, find out where the producers live, which players and studios they use, and which record labels they frequently work with. Then begin making inroads with them any way you can.

KEY CONTACTS FOR GETTING SESSION WORK

NEW KID IN TOWN

- Producers
- Contractors
- Musical directors
- Musicians
- Engineers

- Studio owners
- Managers
- A&R directors at record companies
- Agents

Since timing is everything, don't fix your sights on the big dogs until you are totally ready to hang on their level. Remember, you don't get a second chance to make a first impression.

> *One of life's most painful moments comes when we must admit that we didn't do our homework, that we are not prepared.*
> —Merlin Olson

Assuming you get the green light from musicians whose opinions you respect, find out if anyone you know has a relationship with the producers or players and engineers they use who might be willing to introduce you. This is why it helps to develop as many strong friendships in the industry as possible. Don't give up; popular producers are obviously very busy, and more than likely they won't notice you the first or second time around. Keep pounding on those doors. Be persistent and patient, but make sure you have your playing together so that when the door opens you can seize your moment and maximize your opportunity.

Major music industry cities like Los Angeles, New York, Nashville, Chicago, Miami, and Atlanta have clubs where session musicians play that are regularly attended by key music industry figures. Your job is to find out where these clubs are and start hanging out there on a regular basis. The best way to do this is by asking local musicians where the action is. Your goal is to meet these musicians, develop friendships, and eventually sit in and play with them so you can be heard by industry decision makers. Sometimes it's not what you know, but who you know that really matters.

> *Be persistent and patient, but make sure you have your playing together so when the door opens you can seize your moment and maximize your opportunity.*

Being heard is the ultimate goal for the independent musician, and it is how you will slowly break into the hard-to-crack session world. Very few freelance musicians are hired for major session work by handing out demos of their playing. This is still a word-of-mouth industry, and it is difficult to assess a player's level of skill by listening to a few tracks on a demo CD. You simply don't know how long it took to nail the part, what kind of temperament the musician possesses, or how versatile he or she is until you have actually worked together.

Once you've established yourself as a credible musician, contractors and producers may take a chance booking you for a session based on a recommendation from someone they trust. The ability to effectively build relationships with a variety of players is critically important for the aspiring studio player; you have to be a serious networker to get a shot in the session world. Get your playing together first and foremost, but when you feel you're ready to try and break in, you must also get your socializing chops together or no one will ever hear you.

> *Music is given to us with the sole purpose of establishing an order in things, including, and particularly, the coordination between man and time.*
>
> —Igor Stravinsky

TYPES OF RECORDING SESSIONS

A SONG FOR YOU

While they are in law school, aspiring attorneys usually choose a specialization upon which to focus, such as divorce, bankruptcy, or criminal law. Just because someone is an attorney does not mean he or she understands all types of law equally. The same is true with session musicians. There are a variety of recording sessions a musician can specialize in, and even though there are similarities, these types of sessions are different in many aspects.

There are four major types of recording sessions. Understanding what is required for each of them should help you decide what kind of session work interests you most and whether you possess the necessary skills and temperament.

RECORD DATES

GOOD TIMES

Record dates are sessions that will inevitably end up being released in CD format by either a record label or independently by an artist. They are still referred to as record dates even though the masters are burned onto CDs and formatted for digital downloads rather than being put on vinyl. Although most major record dates take place in Los Angeles, New York, and Nashville, nowadays they can happen literally anywhere on the planet.

> *Play always as if a master were listening.*
> —Robert Schumann

The most essential skill needed to be successful on record dates is a great set of ears. You must have an intuitive ability to interpret the music in a manner that is pleasing to the producer and the artist. Depending on the style of music being played, sight-reading may also be an absolute must.

When it comes to sight-reading, it's best to think about the entire road map of the chart first, and then look at the major sections, phrases, and key ensemble figures, rather than just focusing on the actual notes you're going to play. Good sight-readers always read ahead of where they are playing—sometimes by as much as a bar and a half. By doing so, more difficult passages and rhythmic figures won't take them by surprise.

Train your eye to look ahead, and then learn to memorize certain rhythms that are common in all music. This comes from repetitive practice and is really the identical process that you followed when you first learned how to read words as a child. In our case, it is rhythmic, harmonic and melodic recognition.

Genius is one percent inspiration
and ninety-nine percent perspiration.
—Thomas Edison

The genres of music that naturally lend themselves to more sight-reading are the more harmonically and rhythmically complex styles such as jazz, big band, jazz-fusion, and symphonic music. Due to their slightly more simplistic nature and structure, heavy metal, rock 'n' roll, blues, funk, and hip-hop require less sight-reading, and they are generally performed by smaller ensembles. These styles are no less significant or artistic than the previously mentioned ones; they are just entirely different animals as far as the level of sight-reading that is expected.

The larger an ensemble is, the more likely you are expected to sight-read. Twenty-five musicians can't realistically improvise over an arrangement with any hopes of sounding musical. The larger the group, the stronger the need for specific parts and structure.

For instance, if a session is in Los Angeles for a big band record, proficient reading skills are a must because everything is charted out in the arrangement and time is of the essence.

If you're doing a session in Nashville for a country artist, the scenario will be completely different. In this case, producers will use what is called the Nashville Number System, a unique charting system that was developed in the late 1950s by Nashville studio musicians. It is a shorthand method of writing musical arrangements based on the degrees of scales. By writing chords as numbers, the music can be transposed more easily. If you're doing a session in Miami for a hip-hop artist, you most likely won't be doing any sight-reading, because in that environment it's all about ad-libbing and improvisation and detailed charts are rarely written out.

No matter what kind of music you're playing, good sight-reading skills are never going to hurt you or keep you from doing certain sessions, but not being able to sight-read will definitely limit what kinds of session work for which you'll be qualified.

Music is the shorthand of emotion. Emotions which let themselves be described in words with such difficulty are directly conveyed to man in music, and in that is its power and significance.

—Leo Tolstoy

JINGLES

LIFE IN THE FAST LANE

Jingle dates are recording sessions of music to be used exclusively for commercials. These sessions can take place anywhere, but the main centers for national commercials have traditionally been New York, Los Angeles, and Chicago. Ad agencies subcontract the music production to various independent producers who can be located anywhere. Players for jingle sessions are usually hired by either the music producer in charge of the ad or by the composer of the jingle.

Time is money, so in order to be chosen for this kind of session work you must be able to nail your part very quickly. Expectations are high, and producers assume you'll have the music laid down perfectly in two or three takes. If you take too long, you will inevitably cost them too much money and they will never call you back.

Men are alike in their promises. It is only in their deeds that they differ.

—Moliére

Because of the nature of this type of work, you won't have a lot of time to be creative with your parts or experiment with your sound like you would on a record date where the environment is relaxed and more open to a creative spirit.

For jingles, it's essential that you're able to comfortably cover a wide range of styles and deliver a huge palette of sounds from your instrument. Sometimes there are written charts, but many times there are not, and you'll need to rely on your ears.

In the world of commercials, filming usually takes precedence and the music is often the last component to come together before the spot is released. That means there is almost always a sense of urgency to get it done yesterday! To survive in this intense environment, you must be able to play under extreme pressure and scrutiny; if you are thin-skinned or unable to adapt on the fly, this might not be the gig for you.

TELEVISION AND FILM SESSIONS

WORK TO DO

The majority of television and film session work occurs in Los Angeles, the undisputed home of the movie industry, with the bulk of the remaining work taking place in New York City. Of all the available types of session work, this is probably the most difficult to break into because it can be very lucrative and demands the absolute highest level of skill from the musicians. Only top-flight players get a chance do to this kind of work, and calls are routinely placed to a very small clique of players.

Contractors and independent film composers are usually the ones who hire session musicians for TV and film dates. This elite group of individuals holds all the keys to the kingdom, and if you're not in with one of them, it's extremely tough to get a shot.

> *There are two golden rules for an orchestra: start together and finish together. The public doesn't give a damn what goes on in between.*
>
> —Sir Thomas Beecham

Good sight-reading skills are a plus with jingle sessions and record dates, but when it comes to TV and movies, they are imperative. If you're not a monster sight-reader, you would be wise to forget about this kind of work entirely. Aside from being able to play almost anything stylistically, you must also be able to follow a conductor, since many of these sessions go down live with an orchestra. You must be able to execute your part with very few mistakes.

As with jingle sessions, this environment is not really about creativity, per se. In film work, it's all about playing exactly what's written on the music, nothing more and nothing less. With upwards of 70 musicians who could be present at the recording session, there is little room for experimentation or tolerance for error. The huge labor expense involved in pulling off TV and film sessions puts incredible pressure on the musicians to be near perfect.

> *People forget how fast you did a good job—*
> *but they remember how well you did it.*
> —Howard W. Newton

In addition to this already mounting pressure, you may be called upon to "play to picture." This is an industry term describing a musician who watches the picture on the screen for visual cues and then comes up with music that intuitively supports the action. This type of work is totally improvisational, and it requires a sixth sense to some degree. This call and response method requires a musician to see a picture and then capture the mood the director wants to set for the audience. To do this effectively, you will need a wellspring of musical knowledge.

> *Musical ideas pursue me to the point of torture.*
> *I cannot get rid of them, they stand before me like a*
> *wall. If it is an allegro that pursues me, my pulse beats*
> *faster, I cannot sleep; if an adagio, I find my pulse*
> *beating slowly. My imagination plays upon me*
> *as if I were a keyboard.*
> —Joseph Haydn

DEMOS

LET'S STAY TOGETHER

Playing on demo sessions is a great place to get your recording chops together. Over time, doing so could lead to getting dialed in with bigger producers. Demo producers occasionally become notable record or jingle producers, and they often hire musicians with whom they already have a rapport. In some cases, they are already successful producers who just happen to be cutting demos for future projects.

You will meet a number of musicians on demo session dates, and some of them may already be major session players. It's not uncommon for A-list session players or producers to do demo work when they are not booked on major record dates just to keep money coming in. Since relationships with these types of players and producers are what open doors for major sessions, it's to your advantage to work with them as often as possible.

> *Don't be afraid to give your best to what seemingly are small jobs. Every time you conquer one it makes you that much stronger.*
>
> —Dale Carnegie

THE DEAL ON CARTAGE

CARRY THE WEIGHT

If you play keyboards, bass, guitar, or drums, you will need a wide variety of equipment for each recording session. Since most of this gear is too large to throw in the trunk of your car, it is customary for the producers of most professional recording sessions to pay for cartage—the industry term for transporting, or carting, all of your gear to the recording studio. Most working session players store their recording gear at rehearsal facilities that often offer cartage as well. This service is very common in Los Angeles, New York, and Nashville. Cartage companies usually bill the producer of the session directly for transporting the equipment, but bill you for storing your own personal equipment at their facilities.

Many musicians do their own cartage and bill their producers under a separate company name. Since cartage has to be paid for by producers anyhow, some musicians would rather make the extra money. If players choose this option, they usually keep the fact that their own companies are providing the cartage on the down-low, since it can make them look a little money hungry. Sometimes players will hire students to do the cartage for really low fees and then charge the producer just enough to make a slight profit on the deal.

REAL WORLD TIPS FOR RECORDING SESSIONS
IT'S YOUR THING

Here are some tips that will help you when you finally do get on a session. First, make sure to be respectful of the other players, the producer, engineer, and contractor, and be eager to please everyone. Don't go in with a "this is the way I play and that's just all there is to it" attitude. Flexibility is the name of the game, and you will succeed only to the degree to which you serve a purpose higher than your own personal music interests.

Don't make any suggestions, comments, or critiques unless you are asked to give your opinion. This is yet another example where silence is golden. With many producers this can be a touchy area, and you best not forget that you are there to facilitate someone else's musical vision—not yours. Always comply with the engineer's requests and be flexible about how he or she wants to record your instrument.

When you are running down a rehearsal take of the song, play with the full volume and passion that you intend to play on the real take. It's very common to play with lower volume and less zeal when you are just running the tune down than when the adrenaline hits and you are really recording. This can give the engineer a headache managing instrument levels. Be consistent with how you play so that there are no surprises when the engineer hits the record button.

When it comes to doubling your parts or "punching in," as it is referred to in the business, remember exactly what you originally played because it has to be identical. Play with the same dynamics, tone, intensity, pitch, and emotion on each subsequent overdub or punch so that they match. Learning to memorize parts quickly should be one of your major goals and a huge part of your practice regimen at home prior to entering the recording world.

> *Unless you try to do something beyond what you have*
> *already mastered, you will never grow up.*
> —Ronald E. Osborn

When layering one part upon another as a vocalist, horn player, guitar player, and percussionist would do, you must play something that complements the original part you laid down. Each new part must fit the previous parts like a well-designed LEGO set. Knowing how to effectively play multiple parts on top of your original track comes from your intuitive sense of arranging, which will come from all the listening you have done in the past.

Be sure to bring business cards along that contain all of your contact info. Don't hand them out, though, unless you get the feeling someone actually liked your playing! To do otherwise would be presumptuous and ultimately futile. In the session world, being low key is actually to your advantage, because hype really isn't tolerated. Your playing should do the talking.

> *The superior man is modest in his speech,*
> *but excels in his actions.*
> —Confucius

To ensure you leave a good impression, only take sessions you can confidently handle. Doing a session you're not legitimately qualified for will be the early death of your career as a studio musician, and your name will spread like wildfire—and not in a good way!

It takes a long time to build a positive reputation through consistent and strong performances, but it takes practically no time at all to destroy your reputation when you blow it. Bad news always seems to spread faster than good news, so resist the temptation to jump in over your head. Be sure to get well acquainted with your strengths and weaknesses as a player, and guide your decisions by those truths.

Now that you've got the gig, there are some ways to ensure your success. First, make sure you arrive at the session at least 45 minutes before it begins. Doing so will help take off the nervous edge and enable you to give your best performance. You may even have the opportunity to check out the charts in advance. If you see a difficult passage in the music, try working your part out in your head before you actually play it.

> *If you're afraid of what's coming up technically,*
> *you just won't be free to do the even harder job of*
> *creative interpretation.*
>
> —Harvey Mason

Also, make sure your equipment is in tip-top shape, ready to go, and ultra quiet. You don't need any squeaks, squawks, honks, rattles, or hums from your gear ruining your big day. Bring plenty of extra strings, sticks, heads, reeds, or whatever pertains to your instrument so you don't slow down the recording process if you have an issue. Your instrument is the only thing that should make sound.

Once the engineers have set your microphones in place, don't move them. If you have to do so for some reason, make certain that you let the engineers know immediately, because it will cause inconsistencies in the recording levels of your instrument. If you are punching in, be very consistent as far as microphone levels and playing are concerned.

On more of the studio etiquette side of matters, it is totally uncool to have your phone go off in the middle of the band laying down the perfect take. Some ringtones are so loud they bleed straight through the microphones and get on tape—this is not the way to get on the producer's good side. Turn the phone off!

Be respectful and avoid making noise between takes; jamming on your instrument can be highly disruptive and might instigate a full-blown jam session. This isn't high school stage band; you are being paid good money to get the job done in the quickest timeframe possible.

> *Music is a higher revelation than philosophy.*
>
> —Ludwig van Beethoven

Just about every recording session I have ever done has gone longer than originally planned, and most everything takes more time than you would like. Bring along something to do, such as your laptop computer or a book, so you won't be bored out of your mind.

Even though the producers of most professional sessions will send runners out to pick up food if the session runs long enough, I always bring healthy food with me. This prevents me from experiencing the horribly sluggish feeling that comes right after eating junk food—I need to be sharp, and eating right is one of the secrets to giving my best performance. I also bring additional healthy snacks that I can down real quickly when I feel my blood sugar levels begin to drop. This keeps me from running out of steam when I need it most.

> *One important key to success is self-confidence.*
> *An important key to self-confidence is preparation.*
> —Arthur Ashe

Finally, concentrate hard on playing the music without being nervous or tentative. Get into that zone or mental state in which you know you excel. Even though seeing that little red recording light come on can increase your heart rate, you must exude a calm, cool, and collected sense of confidence and play with gusto. This is all a mental exercise, of course, so make a conscious effort to stay positive and have a good time! After all, you're making music, which is what you love to do, and why you're there in the first place.

SESSION MUSICIAN REQUIREMENTS
I'VE GOT SO MUCH TO GIVE

- Residence in one of the major music recording markets
- Established relationships with key players, producers, contractors, arrangers, and engineers
- Membership in a local union of the American Federation of Musicians (AFM) or the American Federation of Television and Radio Artists (AFTRA) if you are a vocalist

- Highly skilled and versatile playing ability
- Proficient sight-reading skills
- An intuitive sense that enables you to respond to and improvise over what you're hearing
- A good ear and an ability to quickly memorize musical passages and parts
- Familiarity with the latest technological trends in music production
- An enormous and well-rounded musical repertoire
- Quality musical equipment that will achieve the popular sounds
- A willingness to serve the music, producer, and artist
- Nerves of steel and a resilient attitude
- A calm demeanor, flexible nature, and patient disposition

A man's gift makes room for him,
and brings him before great men.
—Proverbs 18:16 (NKJV)

THE AMERICAN FEDERATION OF MUSICIANS (THE MUSICIANS UNION)

LOOK WHAT YOU DONE FOR ME

Two professional organizations advocate for musicians and vocalists to ensure fair compensation and appropriate working conditions. The American Federation of Television and Radio Artists (AFTRA) was founded in 1937. It is the union that represents singers, actors, announcers, and news broadcasters in sound recordings, radio, television programs, and commercials.

For over 100 years, the American Federation of Musicians, better known as the AFM, has represented musicians in the recording industry and been dedicated to raising industry standards for musicians. If you happen to sing back-up vocals on sessions in conjunction with your main instrument, you will most likely go through AFM.

The sole purpose of these unions is to advocate better work situations for their members by using collective bargaining power. They serve a number of functions that benefit the independent musician, such as negotiating contracts, securing health care and pension benefits, as well as lobbying legislatures for laws that protect the interests of independent musicians.

The AFM is made up of more than 250 branch offices called "locals" in various cities throughout the United States and Canada. They are the largest and oldest entertainment labor organization in the world representing the interests of professional musicians. The AFM governs basic wages and pay scales for all professional recording work.

The three biggest locals are the Professional Musicians Union Local 47 of Los Angeles, the Associated Musicians Local 802 of Greater New York City, and the Nashville Musicians Association Local 257 in Nashville. The lion's share of major label recording sessions that are commercially released are filed by these three locals.

UNION RECORDING SESSION WAGES AND SCALE STRUCTURES

MONEY (THAT'S WHAT I WANT)

Sessions are categorized by the union in a few different ways, including the intended end-use of the music and the time allowed on the job. It all gets very technical, but there are basically four pay scales: the Sound Recording Master Scale, the Low Budget Sound Recording Scale (Non-Symphonic), the Limited Pressing Recording Scale, and the Demonstration Recording Scale.

A session player is referred to as a side musician, a leader, or a contractor, and each has a specific pay scale. If you are the leader or contractor playing on the session, you get double what a side musician (any player who is not the leader or contractor) would earn. The role of the leader or contractor is virtually the same. The leader is always hired to play on the session and is designated as the one in charge of the rest of the side musicians. He or she represents the players' interests with the producer. A contractor may or may not play on the session, but still represents the musicians hired on the session.

A basic session typically lasts three hours, with a union stipulation that a maximum of only 15 minutes of recorded music can be released as a result. There are a plethora of other specific hourly arrangements, as well as half-hour and quarter-hour overtime segments. The formula is based on a predetermined amount of music that is allowed to be recorded during the session, ranging from as little as five minutes to as much as fifteen minutes.

> *A business that makes nothing but money is*
> *a poor kind of business.*
> —Henry Ford

The pay scale also coincides with the intended end use of the recorded music for each particular type of session, including basic session scale, special session scale, premium session, double time, and so forth. Sessions are broken down into various hourly increments and classified by the time of the day or night the session takes place. For example, a double time session is a recording that takes place on recognized national holidays, such as New Year's Day, Christmas Day, or Thanksgiving. When you work these holidays, you get paid double what you normally would for the same exact type of session. Another example would be a three-hour Premium Session, which takes place between midnight and 8:00 a.m. Because of the late hours, the pay scale for this type of session is 150 percent of regular scale.

There are a host of other considerations and very specific details pertaining to union pay scales, and since the rules are subject to change and often fluctuate, your best bet is to visit the American Federation of Musicians website at www.afm.org and find the contact information for the union closest to you. They can supply you with the latest rate sheets for each type of session. These rate sheets will not only include the pay scale rates, but also rules, regulations, and a wide variety of other pertinent details. If you have specific questions that are not covered, you can always call the office. That's what they're there for!

Being a member of the union has many benefits. In actuality, you cannot do any major professional recording sessions without being a member of the union, because most major labels have agreements in place with the AFM and are required by law to hire only union musicians.

Record companies that have agreements with the AFM are called "signatories," and before you commence recording with anyone, make sure it is a signatory company. That means it is in good standing with the AFM and has a good reputation for paying musicians in a timely fashion.

DEMO SESSION RATES
NIGHT AND DAY

Since demos are not intended for commercial release or usage, demo sessions almost always pay less. The musicians union refers to the pay structure for these sessions as "Demonstration Recording Scale." If a demo session uses union musicians, they are paid the appropriate scale for that kind of session, which is always about half of the standard full Sound Recording (Master) scale. If the company/producer opts to release the demo to the public at a later time, the musicians must then be paid the full Sound Recording (Master) scale.

If you participate in a demo session that is not governed by the musicians union—in other words, they hire non-union players—your fees are negotiable. The financial arrangements can vary greatly and will depend on many factors including budgetary concerns, geographical location, and level of musicians hired. Sometimes you will be paid on a per-song basis, while other times it will be a flat fee for the length of the session, an entire day's work, or even the whole project, which could span several days.

> *Music is the only sensual gratification which*
> *mankind may indulge in to excess without injury*
> *to their moral or religious feelings.*
>
> —Joseph Addison

UNION BENEFITS
I LOVE YOU MORE THAN YOU'LL EVER KNOW

Besides helping to make sure musicians get paid for their work, the AFM also offers access to licensed signatory booking agents and discounted legal advice. The union's legal department is there to help you recover unpaid fees from those who have tried to stiff you. They also offer a variety of insurance coverage including medical, life, disability, accident, and even equipment insurance in the event your equipment is damaged or stolen. Their newly developed GoPro program offers everything from buying and selling instruments and listing your band on the AFM live music referral site, to music lessons, and even website hosting.

Each local AFM office is run autonomously, so fringe benefits will vary to some degree. Your eligibility for these benefits depends on many qualifying factors, particularly how much recording work you are doing. Check with your local union to see what their stipulations are. Being an active member in your local union is a great way to network and meet more experienced musicians in the business.

SOUND RECORDING SPECIAL PAYMENTS FUND (SRSPF)

YOU WERE THERE

Along with being paid the appropriate scale for recording sessions filed through your local union of the AFM, studio musicians are eligible to receive additional funds from the Sound Recording Special Payments Fund (SRSPF). A friend and ally to all working studio musicians, this important fund was established in 1964 and was formerly known as the Phonograph Record Manufacturers' Special Payments Fund. Committed to establishing residual payments on the sales of phonograph records for musicians, this collective bargaining agreement required participating record companies to formalize an equitable plan that would pay eligible musicians a residual.

The Sound Recording Special Payments Fund provides a great service to eligible session musicians. It helps give them a small residual income from the records that are sold around the world that employed union musicians when recorded. When I get these checks in the mail, they always come as a pleasant surprise and make me feel a little bit more valued within my industry. For more information, just go to their website at sound-recording.org.

The credit belongs to the man who is actually in the arena; whose face is marred by dust and sweat and blood; who strives valiantly; who errs and comes short again and again; who knows the great enthusiasms, the great devotions, and spends himself in a worthy cause; who at the best knows in the end the triumph of high achievement; and who at the worst, if he fails, at least fails while daring greatly.

—Theodore Roosevelt

THE ART OF TOURING
THE BUSINESS OF LIVE CONCERTS

No one can whistle a symphony.
It takes a whole orchestra to play it.

—Halford E. Luccock

I had just finished doing a show in Monterey, California, and headed straight back to the hotel. The band had an early flight to catch for Hawaii the next morning. Totally exhausted from hitting it hard on the road for quite some time, I made sure to call the front desk and set a 5:30 a.m. wake-up call; I didn't stand a chance of getting up at that hour on my own.

The next morning, my wife called at 5:45 a.m. to speak with me about something important, but my line was busy. She tried several more times and kept getting a busy signal. "Who the heck could he be talking to for so long at this ridiculous hour?" she thought.

After numerous frustrating attempts to connect with me, she finally called the front desk and asked them to cut in on my phone call. She knew I had an early flight and didn't want me to miss it. When the hotel operator cut in on the line, they heard me snoring in the background. Evidently I'd gotten my wake-up call and fallen back asleep with the phone in my hand. Talk about being out of it!

I had never fallen back to sleep after receiving a wake-up call, so I must have been in a deep "dead to the world" coma. The hotel had to send someone to pound on my door in order to get me up. When I finally woke up and realized how late I was, I panicked and frantically threw all my belongings into my suitcase like a madman. I made my flight—barely! From that time on, I always made sure I was completely packed the night before a travel day. That way if I ever missed a wake-up call and happened to be running late, I could be up and ready to go in seconds. That strategy has paid off many times since then.

http://4wrd.it/A.BG13

THE PATH TO TOURING GIGS

I CAN DREAM ABOUT YOU

Like most other aspects of the music business, securing work as a touring musician comes mostly by word of mouth recommendations. Yes, it's true that responding to ads placed by producers, managers, and agents—and even advertising your own services—with the musician's union can lead to some live work, but for the sideman, most work opportunities come through the musicians' grapevine. In fact, a big-time manager couldn't get you a gig with a top recording artist no matter how much clout he or she has. Anyone who is heavily connected can certainly apply a little pressure on your behalf and convince someone to give you a shot, but you still have to win the approval of the artist and touring band and beat out your competition in order to land the gig.

Another huge misconception is the whole "agent fantasy." I haven't had an agent who specialized in booking me work as a sideman in my entire music career, and neither have 98 percent of the top recording and touring musicians I have known—and I know an awful lot of them. Some have had managers, but they were primarily for negotiating fees, handling business deals, working out endorsement agreements, and setting up clinics, master classes, and workshops.

Landing work as a touring musician is based on your skill and established reputation, not on the wheelings and dealings of an agent. Artist management companies can be helpful resources, though. Call them routinely to see if any of their acts need musicians or are holding auditions for upcoming tours.

Another link to the vital information highway is the road crew for touring artists. Stage technicians and road managers, in particular, play musical chairs as much as the musicians do, and the good ones work for several bands. Today's advanced production considerations often dictate that the road crew is contracted to work on a major tour before the musicians are even hired, so they tend to hear about playing opportunities prior to anyone else. For instance, they may find out an artist has just fired his or her percussionist and will be holding auditions at a specific time and place. Roadies can be a tremendous source of many potential leads, so it is wise to befriend them.

I think luck is the sense to recognize an opportunity
and the ability to take advantage of it.
—Samuel Goldwyn

While I was preparing for major tours in Los Angeles, I would often hear about auditions at some of the well-established rehearsal studios such as Third Encore and Center Staging and Studio Instrument Rentals (SIR), where many of the big-name acts rehearsed. Unfortunately, most of the time the information was of no use to me because I was already rehearsing for a good gig, but you can best believe I called all my qualified friends right away.

Inside information like this is only available to the privileged few. Reaction time is everything—once word gets out on the street, the entire music community will hear about it in no time. By then it will be too late; the position will most likely already have been filled. On numerous occasions, I found out about an opportunity a split second too late to get an audition for the gig.

MAJOR CONTACTS THAT LEAD TO TOURING GIGS
BACK IN THE HIGH LIFE

- Musicians
- Musical directors and band leaders
- Contractors
- Stage technicians and road crew
- Road managers
- Managers and management company personnel
- Producers
- Trade papers and publications
- Agents
- Musician referral services
- Professional rehearsal studios (applicable only in key major music industry cities)
- The Internet

TYPES OF TOURS

THE LONG AND WINDING ROAD

Within the realm of live road work is a variety of touring situations. The type of work artists pursue depends primarily on what kind of acts they are, what options are open to them based on demand, and what stages they are at in their careers and personal lives. The road is an extremely difficult lifestyle to endure on a regular basis, so it's important to know what to expect from each of the following scenarios and learn how to make the best of each of them.

THE ONE-NIGHTER

WORKING FOR THE WEEKEND

The infamous "one-nighter," also called a "one off," is a one-night engagement with no other gigs booked before or after it. One-nighters frequently occur on the weekend, but can happen any night of the week. Even though they are contractually one-night commitments from the artist's point of view, they almost always eat up about three days: you usually travel to the location the day before the gig to get settled, do the concert the following day, and then travel home the day after that. If the gig is in close enough proximity to where you live, you can cover it all in one day, but that is rarely the case. Three days is pretty standard—so much for the one-nighter actually taking one night!

THE SHORT STINTS

TIME IS ON MY SIDE

A short stint can last anywhere from a couple of days to a few weeks; it can even be considered a mini-tour if it lasts more than two weeks. During the designated period of time, you could have a few gigs or an engagement for each night of the tour.

In large part, the number of engagements depends on the status of the artist. An established artist might work a few nights a week, but if he or she is in a career-building mode—or is a workaholic—the band could gig every single night. In the end, it's all about profit margins. It's expensive to be out on the road, so it's important to look at overhead versus actual take-home pay.

Everyone dies, but not everyone fully lives. Too many
people are having a near-life experience.

—Unknown

THE MAJOR TOUR

GOT THE WORLD ON A STRING

A major tour is comprised of a series of concert dates with big-name artists who play larger venues such as arenas, amphitheaters, or stadiums. Sometimes they will also play larger clubs and theaters as well as colleges and universities.

There are two reasons to put together a major tour: to support a new release, or when an artist already has a plethora of hits and a well-established fanbase in place. Major tours last anywhere from weeks to months and can be regional or cover the entire country.

THE MEGA TOUR

IT WAS A VERY GOOD YEAR

The key difference between a major tour and a mega tour is the duration. Mega tours are with big-name artists and typically include domestic and international dates. Obviously, one of the prerequisites for a mega tour is healthy public demand to support the artist in concert, a demand that is usually prompted by an explosive recording with huge worldwide sales, or by some other marketing effort that increases the artist's popularity.

If the artist is red-hot, mega tours can last as long as two to three years with designated breaks between each leg of the tour. A "leg" is an industry slang term that refers to a particular segment of the tour; it might be the European, Asian, South American, or North American leg of the tour. On these engagements, you might play massive coliseums, stadiums, or outdoor summer festivals with crowds too enormous to squeeze into a normal stadium or concert venue.

TOURING SALARY RANGE

YOU KEEP ME HANGIN' ON

It's really the Wild West when it comes to negotiating fees for tours, because there is no industry standard. The American Federation of

Musicians can help you get paid appropriately when you record a live album or appear on TV shows with artists while you're on tour, but they have no control over what those artists pay members of their touring bands.

Despite those uncertainties, there are ballpark figures you should be aware of for various types of touring gigs. The best tactic is to do some investigative work and find out what other musicians are getting paid. Keep in mind that everything is negotiable and depends on a great many variables, all of which you should take into consideration.

Most major touring work is structured around the weekly salary. Compensation for live touring work can range anywhere from as low as $250 per week to as much as $25,000 per week. The average salary for working with a name act is roughly $1,500 to $7,500 per week. Yearly averages for touring musicians range from $20,000 to $350,000 per year. Earnings depend upon the marquee value of the artist and the tour's budget.

As a sideman, much of your compensation will depend upon your name value as a player, how much you are in demand, if you have a guaranteed salary, and how many weeks you have been able to find touring work throughout the year.

> *Starting out to make money is the greatest mistake in life. Do what you feel you have a flair for doing, and if you are good enough at it, the money will come.*
> —Greer Garson

Earnings vary greatly from year to year. One year you might make $20,000 and the next year top off at $150,000. Top dogs can make well over $150,000 a year—sometimes as much as $250,000 to $500,000—but very few are able to reach the half-million mark.

The reality is that there are only a few major gigs that pay big money, and only a few players deemed worthy enough to get it. I know of a few artists who paid a flat fee of $1 million to certain top sidemen for a mega tour, which was a one- or two-year commitment. That is the sideman's equivalent of hitting the lotto, and, as you know, there aren't a lot of lottery winners. But it does happen!

Salaries also vary between musicians who are on the same gig. One player may get $4,500 per week, while another player might get half that for the same gig and work schedule. The only difference is what instrument they play. The discrepancies are based on things like seniority, how much name recognition you have, your ability to negotiate, how badly the artist wants you, and several other factors. In fact, it is not uncommon at·all for there to be several different salary structures in the same back-up band on a given tour.

Incidentally, the musical director customarily gets paid significantly more than the rest of the band—anywhere from one-third more to twice as much—and deservedly so. They work a lot harder and have a much larger scope of responsibility.

Salary negotiations are typically conducted with the road manager, the musical director, the management, or in some cases, the artist may choose to sign up for this task.

> *When I'm getting ready to reason with a man I spend one-third of my time thinking about myself and what I am going to say—and two-thirds thinking about him and what he is going to say.*
>
> —Abraham Lincoln

As the demand for your services increases, your price to tour should naturally escalate. Truthfully, however, there are certain types of artists who will never pay you more than what they predetermine the job is worth. They may have a cap on the gig, and no matter who you are, they won't pay any more than that fixed price.

I have learned that people in this business don't necessarily get what they deserve; they only receive the financial compensation they are able to negotiate.

TOURING SALARY ARRANGEMENTS

IT'S TOO LATE TO TURN BACK NOW

There are several different ways a touring salary can be structured, and I have experienced them all. The following is a breakdown of the most common methods of paying for services rendered.

THE WEEKLY SALARY: This is, by far, the most common structure. Players are paid an agreed-upon salary on a weekly basis for the duration of the tour.

THE PRORATED SALARY: In this case, the weekly salary is divided into a five- or seven-day work week, and payment is made according to how many gigs are done in that pay week. Let's say, for example, that your salary is $2,500 per week. If the tour operates on a five-day workweek proration and you did three gigs that week, you would earn three-fifths of a week's pay. This method of payment is rather complicated and was devised by clever accountants who found a way of not having to pay you a full week's salary.

THE PER-GIG FEE: With this arrangement, players are paid for each gig, say $600 per show, rather than as a salary. This is generally the case with acts that engage in shorter stints of work on a regular basis and are not on a major tour.

THE YEARLY GUARANTEE: A guarantee is generally offered by longtime, established acts that work between 15 and 40 weeks annually on a consistent year-to-year basis. In this type of arrangement, musicians are promised a certain salary in exchange for their loyalty throughout the year. There is no limit to how many engagements will be performed, and musicians are not usually paid extra for rehearsals—artists can rehearse as much as they like. Television appearances and recordings, however, are not included in the yearly salary since they are considered separate engagements. If you a member of either AFM or AFTRA, by law you must be compensated the appropriate union scale for any television show or recorded performance that will be commercially released.

There are a variety of creative ways a guarantee can be structured. The most traditional method of payment is to divide your salary by 12 months and then pay you monthly. If your guarantee is $70,000 per year, you would be paid approximately $5,833 each month or a bimonthly amount of $2,916.50. The advantage of this type of arrangement is that you know what you are going to earn for the whole year, getting a sense of financial security that is rare for the sideman. The disadvantage would be that you are locked in for the year and unable to contractually accept a better offer if one should arise.

Another popular method of payment is to provide a small weekly retainer as base pay, then divide the salary by a five- or seven-day workweek and pay you a prorated salary based on the number of days you perform. You would then be paid the difference of what you have coming in one lump sum at the end of the year. In the $70,000 example above, if you had only made $55,000 by the end of December, you would be entitled to a bonus of $15,000 to equal your guarantee. The advantage of this method of payment is that you get a nice surprise check at the end of the year, which always comes in handy around Christmastime. The disadvantage would be that your checks throughout the year would fluctuate and might not be as big as you'd like if you don't have that many bookings.

BONUSES: Depending on many variables including how well the tour did financially, some artists will give their players a bonus at the end of the tour. This can range from $1,000 to $100,000 or more! Some will even pay for the band and crew and their families to go to some fabulous vacation resort at the end of the tour as a way of rewarding them for their hard work. The amount of the bonus and the type of luxury vacation can vary drastically, and there are no guarantees of either. These choices are really left to the discretion of the artist and are not based on any formula, but rather on the generous nature of the artist. I was fortunate to get really nice bonuses and vacations on quite a few tours, and was pleasantly surprised each time I did.

To avoid feeling like the character of Clark W. Griswold played by actor Chevy Chase in the movie *Christmas Vacation*, I learned never to expect a bonus or vacation. In the film, Clark expected the sizeable bonus he had become accustomed to receiving each year around Christmastime. He planned to build a big swimming pool, but that year his boss decided to cut expenses by nixing the bonus. He enrolled Clark in the jelly of the month club instead—a hilarious scene for sure!

Success seems to be largely a matter of hanging on
after others have let go.
—William Feather

MORE TOURING FEE STRUCTURES
WE'RE IN THE MONEY

There are several other things to consider when it comes to the financial world of live touring. Familiarizing yourself with these kinds of arrangements and terms will better prepare you for each and every possible negotiation contingency.

TRAVEL DAY PAY: These are the days you travel to and from the gig. For example, you might fly out on a Friday morning to play somewhere on a Saturday night, and then fly back home on Sunday. Friday and Saturday would be considered travel days, while Saturday would be considered a gig day or workday.

There are a variety of ways travel days are dealt with from a financial standpoint. Some acts will pay you for the entire three days and consider that three-fifths of a week's pay. Other acts will only pay you for the day of the gig. If that is the case, demand a higher pay rate since you are unavailable to accept any other work for those two days of travel.

Travel days also occur in the middle of an ongoing tour. For example, you may be on the road for three months straight without coming home. During that 90-day period you play 50 shows; all the other days would be considered non-show or travel days. In most cases, you are paid a continuous weekly salary so it doesn't really matter if you are playing or traveling. Getting paid for travel days is a huge point of contention with artists who are playing shorter stints or a string of consistent one-nighters.

REHEARSAL PAY: On most major tours, artists pay only half to two-thirds of the regular salary of their musicians during the rehearsal phase. Their logic for doing so is that no concert revenue comes in until they hit the road. Oddly enough, you work a lot harder in rehearsal than you do once you get out on the road. The rehearsal period prior to embarking on a major tour can be anywhere from two weeks to two months depending on the artist's comfort level and the complexity of the music and production. Acts that don't employ you on steady basis may pay a flat per-day rehearsal rate, say $200 per day, or an hourly wage such as $50 dollars an hour for a two- to eight-hour block of time.

RETAINERS: A retainer is a weekly salary that is at a lesser amount than your regular salary. They are most commonly found on major tours where there is good consistent work booked for a long period of time. An 18-month tour might be broken into five separate legs. In between, there will be a short break; it may be as short as a day or two, but it is more commonly from one week to one month. During the active portions of the tour, players receive their full weekly salaries, but during break time they may be put on a reduced rate, otherwise known as a retainer. This is typically around 50 percent of your regular salary. Depending on how you budget your living expenses, you can certainly survive on the retainer for the short period of time that you are usually on one.

The purpose of a retainer is to insure your availability so the artist doesn't have to look for new musicians when it's time to go on the road again. If there is a long enough lag in between legs, most musicians look for other paying gigs because their bills won't wait. A retainer is designed to secure loyalty and lessen the hassles of having to replace players in the middle of an ongoing tour.

Retainers can last from weeks to years, which means you get paid regularly without having to do any work at all. But when the boss calls, you'd better make sure you drop everything and are ready, willing, and able to do what's required. Retainers paid out for extremely long periods of time are usually done only by the mega stars who really want to take care of their players. In some cases, an artist may only offer a retainer to his or her musical director or certain players who are integral parts of the live sound, and then look for new players to fill those other positions when it's time to hit the road again.

Music leads every change, for it is the first order
and power before all learning.

—Aristides Quintilianus

PENSION PLANS: Some of the more established artists may offer you the chance to be a vested partner in a defined benefit pension plan, also known as a 401(k). Most of the time this doesn't happen until you are with them for a few years. A 401(k) is a great financial opportunity if you have the good fortune to be part of an organization that offers such employee benefits; in the world of sidemen, this is as close as you get to the benefits most people receive with a corporate job.

If the artist sets up a retirement plan for his or her own corporation and you are considered an employee of that corporation, then, by law, you must be offered the plan, too. In our line of work as freelance musicians, there are relatively few work situations that allow for the possibility of pension plans. If you can be part of a pension plan, it will be a good business move and you should jump on it.

TELEVISION PAY: This is in regards to playing on national and international television shows as a sideman for an artist appearing on the show. In the U.S., this includes talk shows such as the *Late Show with David Letterman, The Tonight Show with Jay Leno, The Ellen DeGeneres Show, LIVE! with Regis and Kelly, Good Morning America, Late Night with Jimmy Fallon, Today, American Idol, Jimmy Kimmel Live!,* and *Dancing with the Stars.* It also includes special event programs such as the Grammy Awards, The American Music Awards, the Academy Awards, the Emmy Awards, the MTV Video Music Awards, and any other similar award shows that feature live performances from recording artists.

Every television show has a slightly different pay scale whether it is live or lip-synched. The range usually varies from $200 to $1,000 for a single one-time airing. The bandleader or musical director, who is considered the contractor on the show, usually gets double. Freelancers are generally paid a scale that is in compliance with the AFM for most television shows in the U.S. The union will process your check, although not always; sometimes the money will come straight from the production staff of the TV show or a separate company that handles their payroll. If you are a singer, you will most likely be paid through AFTRA. Whether you are a vocalist or a player, you are typically only allowed one TV performance before it becomes mandatory to join one of these unions.

You will also get residuals each time your episode is rerun, but it will usually be a lesser amount each time it is played. Without being a signed recording artist, songwriter, or author, this is as close as you get to receiving royalties, only in this capacity they are called "residuals." I have made quite a bit of extra money playing on TV shows with the artists I have worked with while simultaneously being on tour. It's always nice to find a check in the mailbox written out to you for work you did a long time before.

Each television appearance you're booked on while touring with the artist requires an entirely separate fee from your road salary. Your road salary should never include any other kind of performances such as television, studio recordings, video performances, live albums, or in-concert DVDs. Road pay is for live concerts only. A recording of your performance in any way, shape, or form entitles you to extra compensation. Television shows are obligated by law to pay you, so there is usually no problem there, but some artists and managers will try to get you to perform on their videos or on a live DVD or album without paying you extra for that work, and that is flat-out wrong. Make certain they understand that your road pay is not all-inclusive and then make contingencies for those additional services.

> *There are but three events in a man's life: birth, life and death. He is not conscious of being born, he dies in pain, and he forgets to live.*
>
> —Jean de La Bruyère

VIDEO SHOOT PAY: There is a big misconception about what music videos really are. They are not like records where the artist and writer get royalties each time it is aired on television. It would help to think of them as advertisements. Artists are not raking in the bucks just because their video may be in heavy rotation. In fact, it costs an artist a tremendous amount of money to produce each video, and if it is paid for by their record label, the cost will eventually be deducted from their future record royalties. This is what's referred to as "recoupable money." It means the record company loans the money to the signed artist just like a bank, but the label always pays itself back from the first sales of your record before the recording artist sees a penny.

Videos are promotional tools that can help establish an artist in a variety of ways and further their revenue-making opportunities. For example, when a video gets heavy rotation and becomes hot, it can help generate record sales, significantly boost concert attendance, and increase merchandising profits and product endorsements from which the artist does make money. Videos also create demand for more TV appearances, so, indirectly, they do help to generate income, but only if they are highly visible and create a legitimate market for those other forms of revenue.

Where does the sideman fit into all this? Well, we will generally get a one-time fee for the video shoot and that's it, end of story. This "buyout" fee can range anywhere from $200 to $1,000, but many slick managers for artists will try to get you to do the video shoot for nothing if you are in a touring band.

LIVE CONCERT DVD PAY: This is when you are on tour with someone and they decide to shoot footage of the live concert to release on DVD or to sell to VH1, MTV, an A&E documentary, or any other broadcast purpose. The pay structure varies greatly depending on the strength of your negotiating skills and your name. The bigger the name of the player, the more you can demand for your performance fee.

There are really only two deals to be made: you either do a buyout, or the artist's management can offer you a lesser one-time performance fee and a small royalty. I have always opted for the buyout without regret. Money that is in the bank is better than money that may never be seen. There is no way to know how many units were sold and how many other places the show was licensed for broadcast. In other words, there is no way to ever really know if you're being ripped off or not if you opt for the small royalty deal.

PER DIEM: Also referred to as PD, "per diem" is a Latin phrase meaning "per day" or "for each day." Per diem represents the daily food allowance players are given for the time that we travel. It can range from $20 to $250 a day, depending on which country you are traveling in and the budget of the tour. For domestic tours, the PD averages between $35 and $75 a day. In Europe, Asia, Australia, and most other continents, it will be more—between $75 and $250 a day—because it is more expensive to eat abroad than it is at home.

A good road manager will provide your PD on your first day of the tour, but the lame ones will make you wait a few days for it. It's always a good idea to bring plenty of cash with you when you embark on a road trip, just to float yourself until the road manager hands out PD to everyone. Even though you can use a debit or credit card at most places, you will still run into situations in which cash is king (like street vendors), and you'll want to have some of this royal currency on you at all times.

> *Being defeated is often a temporary condition.*
> *Giving up is what makes it permanent.*
>
> —Marilyn vos Savant

GENERAL TOURING INFORMATION AND DEFINITION OF TERMS

FARTHER UP THE ROAD

The following is list of industry-standard terms that are synonymous with the world of the touring musician. Familiarizing yourself with them before a tour will help you navigate and keep you from looking like a deer in the headlights.

INCIDENTALS: These are hotel charges that are not picked up by your employer as part of your lodging expense. Incidentals include room service, personal phone calls, laundry, mini-bar charges, gift shop purchases, massages, in-room movies, and anything else deemed personal that you charge to your room.

DARK STAGE: A term used to describe the time when no one is allowed onstage to do absolutely anything. It has to do with union regulations and codes enforced in certain cities. For example, at the famous Radio City Music Hall in New York City, you may have a sound check that runs from 5:00 to 6:00 p.m., but from 7:00 to 8:00 p.m. the stage is "dark."

Don't even think about going onstage when it's dark to mess with your gear. I know it sounds ridiculous, but this is part of dealing with union rules and regulations, and they're absolutely serious about enforcement. I always wanted to be up on the dark stage practicing my drums when everyone else was gone, but had I done so and been caught, the group would have been slapped with a big fine.

CONCERT RIDER: This is the performance agreement between the artist and promoter of the event. In short, it is a detailed contract several pages in length that specifies exactly what is expected and agreed upon by both parties: the artist or "employee" and the promoter or "employer."

The contract is quite extensive and covers a lot of ground. It lays out all the production requirements such as staging, lighting, sound, and special effects, and stipulates which travel expenses are to be covered by the promoter and which ones the artist will cover. It includes things like what musical equipment the promoter will rent, what the artist provides, the time and length of the show, opening acts, and food and dressing room requirements.

The most important thing the rider covers is the guaranteed fee the artist is to receive and what percentage of the house he or she is entitled to above that if the show is a sellout. (This is only applicable if it is a regular concert date. Private corporate functions always pay the artist a flat fee for an appearance since no tickets are being sold for the event. The concert event is usually offered to all of the employees of the corporation for free or it's a perk to only a select group of the company's top employees and or executives.)

COMP TICKETS: This is an abbreviation for the complimentary tickets that are allotted to the artist, band members, and touring personnel. Most people don't realize that the promoter holds back many of the best seats in the venue to sell to the artist, record label, band, and any other industry people affiliated with the artist or show. These seats rarely go on sale to the general public. The whole comp ticket scene depends greatly on the city you are playing in, the demand for tickets from other band members, and how many are allotted in the artist's performance contract. In some cities you can get all the comp tickets you want, but in other cities—forget about it!

In most cases, there is no set allotment per person. The concert rider may state that the artist is to be given 20 comps per show. The star of the show has first dibs on the tickets, and the rest are divvied up between the management, band, and crew.

Any time you play in a major city like Los Angeles or New York City, the guest ticket scene gets ridiculous. The problem is that in those towns everybody is important, and all of your friends want free tickets. Unfortunately, the artist, their management, and the record label tend to eat up the majority of the comps. In the past, I was usually able to finagle at least two comps in most major music markets, but that is no longer a sure thing. These days, promoters and venue owners crack down on comp tickets for major tours and are no longer as generous as they once were. Many times I have even had to purchase extra tickets at full price to take care of all the people I wanted to get in the show, but at least I was guaranteed they would be good seats.

> *Snowflakes are one of nature's most fragile things, but just look at what they can do when they stick together.*
> —Author unknown

Band members oftentimes make deals with one another. For example, if I was on tour and we were playing in Portland, Oregon, I would have had a lot of family members in the area to accommodate for the show. I would simply trade comp tickets with other band members for this show in return for giving them mine in another city. This arrangement of helping each other out always worked great for all concerned parties.

BACKSTAGE PASSES: When it comes to backstage passes, most people are unaware that there are actually several types of passes, with each allowing a different level of access to the backstage area. The first one is the pre-show pass, which allows guests to come backstage just prior to the show, but will not allow them to come back again after the show. These passes are often used for a "meet and greet" session with the recording artist. A meet and greet is a controlled promotional event for a specified number of fans who win the opportunity to meet the artist through radio or television station contests. Some of these contests are promoted nationally by the record company in conjunction with one of the sponsors of the tour like Pepsi, Coca Cola, Home Depot, or Wal-Mart.

Management limits access backstage after the show because the area is usually bustling with people who know the artist, band, crew, or management personally, and that time is reserved for them.

Next, there is the after-show pass, which allows guests to come backstage directly after the show, but not prior to the event. This pass allows them access to the "green room," the industry term for a room designated for social gatherings with friends of the artist, management, and band only. The after-show pass does not allow guests access to the stage or dressing rooms. Pre-show and after-show passes are usually made of a type of cloth with an adhesive back to be applied visibly.

The most coveted of all passes is the all-access backstage pass, a laminated card on a lanyard that is generally given out to management, band, and crew only. All-access passes may feature the person's photo and his or her position on the tour. This most privileged of all passes allows you access absolutely anywhere backstage, including the green room, dressing rooms, and onstage. The road manager usually has extras made for spouses or children of the artist, management, band, or crew and some VIPs (Very Important People) or notable celebrities. Generally speaking, new passes have special artwork that is created for each tour.

WARDROBE: On most major tours, the purchasing of stage clothes and the cost to dry-clean them is usually taken care of by the artist. Day-to-day street clothes, however, are completely your own responsibility. On lower-budget gigs, you may have to spring for your own stage clothes, as well.

TRAVEL ARRANGEMENTS: Any form of transportation that has to do with getting you to and from the gig is usually picked up by the artist for whom you are playing. This includes tour buses, flights, trains, taxis, car rentals, tolls, and parking. Some artists will even pay for you to get from your house to the airport and then back home again.

EQUIPMENT EXPENSES: On a major tour, management may offer to buy everything you need to do a get the job done, including major equipment purchases and tour supplies such as drumsticks, heads, reeds, or strings. On smaller tours, you may be expected to supply everything at your own expense. This is one of those gray areas.

LOBBY CALL: The time you are expected to meet down in the hotel lobby for any form of departure. An example would be going to the venue or to the airport.

ITINERARY: A highly detailed booklet that lists all of the pertinent information pertaining to a tour. On long major tours, the itinerary will be produced as a slick, spiral-bound notebook with each concert date listed in chronological order and a page for each day of the tour. If the tour has several legs to it, a separate itinerary booklet will be available for each leg. On shorter engagements or one-offs, you may just be given a day sheet, which is a one-page mini itinerary that lists all of the necessary information.

The itinerary will include a day-to-day performance schedule, mode of travel, hotel information, departure times, lobby calls, and sound check times. It will also state whether or not you are leaving directly after a gig for the next city or staying overnight. If air travel is involved, the itinerary will list flight numbers and departures as well as expected arrival times for everyone's flights.

It will also specify the times for each of the day's duties, the name, address, and phone number of the venues, show times for all the acts on the bill, and contact information for everyone on the tour.

> *A strong passion for any object will insure success, for*
> *the desire of the end will point out the means.*
> —William Hazlitt

OPENING ACTS VERSUS HEADLINERS

ON THE ROAD AGAIN

Over the course of my career, I have played behind artists who were opening acts and others who were headliners, and I've seen first-hand what life is like on both sides of the tracks.

I've learned that it's never a good idea to get too comfortable with status. If you play music long enough, one thing is for certain: change. Be prepared for anything, and enjoy the good times when you're riding high, because they are few and far between.

ADVANTAGES OF BEING THE OPENING ACT

STREET OF DREAMS

- You get out of the show earlier (as early as 8:30 p.m.), leaving the rest of your evening free.

- You may get a chance to be heard by the headliner. I have known musicians who have landed major gigs as a result of being heard by the headlining act.

- You won't be stuck in traffic after the show lets out like the headliner will.

- You will have the underdog's "eye of the tiger" attitude that gives you the psychological edge on performing your best. Headliners often lose their edge because they have gotten too comfortable. It's not uncommon for people to leave a show feeling like the opening act was better than the headliner.

DISADVANTAGES OF BEING THE OPENING ACT

I STILL HAVEN'T FOUND WHAT I'M LOOKING FOR

- You may get a lame sound check, if you get one at all.

- The room might be half empty.

- You may have to play on rental equipment rather than your own personal gear.

- The audience doesn't pay attention to the band and you have to work extra hard to win their attention.

- You have a lousy dressing room, if any at all. (Some more modern venues have plenty of dressing rooms to facilitate the needs of both the opening and headlining acts.)

- You may have to tear down your own gear right after the show, which is neither fun nor glamorous.

- You may not have time to adjust your monitors properly.

- You are often not treated with as much respect as the headliner.

While there are pluses and minuses to each scenario, I have never given anything less than my personal best to the artist who is paying me for my services, no matter what their billing status. You never really know what notable musicians may be in the audience, and by giving every gig my absolute best, it led me to other offers when I least expected them.

In order to be irreplaceable one must
always be different.

—Coco Chanel

ADVANTAGES OF BEING THE HEADLINING ACT

SOME GUYS HAVE ALL THE LUCK

- The whole venue caters to you—you're the star of the show for that night, and it is your turn to shine. The entire production revolves around pleasing you.

- The majority of the audience is there to see you!

- You are treated with the utmost respect.

- You generally have your own crew to meet all your specific needs.

- The sound is completely dialed up for you to give your best performance.

- You are playing on your own equipment and it is perfectly set up to your specs.

- You always get plenty of time to check your monitors.

- You usually have ample time to jam after your sound check.

DISADVANTAGES OF BEING THE HEADLINING ACT
LATE IN THE EVENING

- You are the last act to leave and have a longer night. Even though you go on last, you still need to arrive at the venue fairly early to ensure there won't be any problems starting the show on time.

- If you are on a multiple act show and you're the headliner, the audience may already be exhausted by the time you play, therefore giving you less of their energy.

- Most often, the opening acts are gone when you hit the stage, so there aren't as many musicians checking you out as there would be if you were playing in one of the earlier slots. It's good to be heard by as many musicians as possible, because you never know where your next gig will come from.

- More pressure is put on you for a great performance because you are the main reason people dropped a lot of coin. The public is not very forgiving of a bad performance, so you always have to be your best.

- Unless you are the actual star of the show, you may not be able to leave immediately after the show. That means your tour bus will be stuck in traffic with the rest of the audience since everyone ends up leaving at the same time directly after the last song.

The key elements in the art of working together are how to deal with change, how to deal with conflict, and how to reach our potential...the needs of the team are best met when we meet the needs of the individual persons.

—Max De Pree

14

THE ART OF ADVANCEMENT
MAKING THE MOST OF THE ROAD

The amount of satisfaction you get from life depends largely on your own ingenuity, self-sufficiency, and resourcefulness. People who wait around for life to supply their satisfaction usually find boredom instead.
—William Menninger

Some hotel properties are so sprawling it feels like you need a map, an Indian guide, a couple of horses, and a canoe just to get to your room. After a long day of travel, all you want to do is crawl in bed for a quick catnap before you have to be at sound check. As you wander around the place you're ready to explode, because you haven't used the bathroom since arriving at the airport. Then, once you're finally standing cross-legged in front of your door, you discover that your electronic keycard doesn't work. You and your Sherpa start the Lewis & Clark expedition in reverse as you backtrack to the front desk.

Once you are finally in your room, you're ready to check out on the world for a little while, so you hang the "do not disturb" sign on the door knob and nestle in your cozy bed. Sadly, the hotel maid abruptly knocks on your door and disturbs your slumber—why do they bother giving you the stupid sign in the first place when most hotel maids seem to disregard its once highly reverenced instruction?

Truth be told, any kind of travel on a frequent basis is grueling and utterly exhausting. Sure, it's great once I get to Paris, Rome, or London and I'm there for a week, but with the flight delays and cancelations that are all too common these days, getting to your destination is the most painful part of the process.

Sometimes when I'm in the middle of nowhere interesting I think to myself, "What else could I do for a living?" Still, as difficult as traveling is, I have learned to maintain a positive attitude and make the

http://4wrd.it/A.BG14

most of every opportunity, experience, and challenging situation I am presented with, and that mindset has helped me not only survive, but also to flourish in spite of it all.

ROAD LIFE

BAND ON THE RUN

Life on the road is very much like being a circus performer. In fact, the production of any major music show is exactly like setting up for a circus; it is a 24-hour revolving cycle of responsibilities.

Something is always going on behind the scenes before and after the show. While the band is in the dressing room changing back into their street clothes after the concert, stagehands are methodically tearing down the show and loading the gear onto waiting trucks. While the band is sleeping, truck drivers are transporting the equipment to the next town. When the crew bus pulls into the next town in the wee hours of the morning, they go to work like an assembly line setting up the stage, lights, sound system, and instruments. At the same time, the road manager is tending to the many needs of the artist, band, and production crew.

Back on the home front, management is working with the record label, booking agent, publicist, and promoter doing whatever is necessary to keep the show running like a well-oiled machine.

> *I not only use all the brains I have,*
> *but all that I can borrow.*
>
> —Woodrow Wilson

Those in attendance enjoy a concert due to the tireless efforts and talents of a great many technical and creative people, not just the performers. The band, management, and crew work together like an Olympic relay team, passing the baton to one another in total synchronicity with one mutual purpose: the show. If there is a place where teamwork is an essential ingredient for a successful outcome, it is surely in the world of live music shows.

While it is important to show respect to everyone involved in the process, as a musician you will deal most directly with the road manager, the musical director, and the monitor mixer. Work hard at getting along with each of them because they have the greatest influence on your life on the road.

MAKING THE MOST OF YOUR OPPORTUNITIES

LET'S GET PHYSICAL

Though the long and winding road can be a difficult place along which to navigate, having foresight can make the difference between just having a job on the road and advancing toward a long-term career in the music industry. A classic joke has circulated around the professional musician circuit for a very long time: "How do you get a musician to complain?" The answer: "Get him a gig." What makes most jokes funny is that there's always a little truth to them.

> *Making a success of the job at hand is the best step*
> *toward the kind you want.*
> —Bernard M. Baruch

As musicians, much of our lives are spent waiting for doors of divine opportunity to open. Rather than trying to make the most of their good fortune, many musicians whine and complain incessantly and fail to use golden opportunities to advance themselves. They fail to see the potential in every work situation.

There are some musicians, on the other hand, who go on to much bigger and better things as a direct result of how hard they work their gigs. They focused on the positives, not the negatives. It's to your advantage to make the most of every gig and see its potential. Sometimes those pluses are hard to see, but if you make a list of all the positive things about the gig you're on, you'll always find something of value that can be gained if you look hard enough. Most people miss those subtle advantages because they are too busy complaining.

If you want to build a skyscraper of success in your life, then you must be willing to go underneath. The height of a skyscraper is determined directly by the depth of the supporting beams. If you want to go a mile high into the sky, then you must be willing to go a mile deep into the earth. Most people want the skyscraper of their lives to be spectacularly tall, but they are unwilling to work underground for the years it takes to support their vision.

Many of us never notice the excavation and preparation that occur behind the scenes when a tall building is erected, because it's the low-key and unglamorous part of the construction. We all notice when the beautifully designed building suddenly goes up, but quickly forget the ground work that had been going on for years. If you want to go up, you have to be willing to go down and do the dirty work.

> *This is the true joy in life, the being used for a purpose recognized by yourself as a mighty one; the being thoroughly worn out before you are thrown on the scrap heap; the being a force of Nature instead of a feverish selfish little clod of a ailments and grievances complaining that the world will not devote itself to making you happy.*
> —George Bernard Shaw

GLEANING FROM OTHERS

WILLING TO LEARN

No matter what the work situation, there will always be somebody who possesses knowledge that you don't, and it's to your benefit to acquire as much of their knowledge as possible. It could be a guitar player who knows more about country music than you do, a bass player who is well versed in rhythm and blues, or a musical director who is especially gifted at arranging and reading music. You have immediate access to people who have a wealth of knowledge to share, and the road is a great place to glean that information.

Make a list of what you can learn from other personnel on a gig. Since you're stuck with them for as long as you're on the road anyhow, you may as well learn as much as you can from them. This is just one of many ways you can take advantage of a gig regardless of how much money you're getting paid.

Don't limit your intake to just musically oriented information; go deeper and be willing to learn absolutely anything that could benefit your life in some way. Over the years, I've learned a tremendous amount on a variety of subjects—everything from financial investments and politics to marriage and raising children—from people I've gotten to know on the road. Similarly, there is a vast amount of useful knowledge surrounding you on a daily basis, but you have to cultivate the earnest desire to acquire it.

> *If there is any one secret of success, it lies in the ability*
> *to get the other person's point of view and see things*
> *from that person's angle as well as from your own.*
> —Henry Ford

Even though we're all surrounded by brilliant people, we often don't see their genius because it doesn't look like what we pictured. We miss wonderful opportunities to learn from others because we judge people based on outward appearances. Just because a guy has a weird-looking beard, earrings, and tattoos all over his body doesn't mean that he doesn't have deep insights to share with you! It's a tragedy to be surrounded by such possibilities for growth yet remain unmotivated, unchallenged, and thus unchanged. Always stay open to those teachable moments.

SEIZING THE MOMENT

BABY COME TO ME

There are a number of additional advantages to being on tour. When I was actively pursuing endorsement deals at the onset of my career, I contacted the artist relations representatives at companies with which I was interested in developing a relationship. Before departing for a tour, I always looked at my itinerary to see if I would be traveling to any of the cities where these companies were headquartered. Many mutually beneficial relationships were first established by taking advantage of the fact that I was on the road.

Another fringe benefit to being on tour is that you are afforded an opportunity to see some incredible sights. Throughout my travels around the world, I always made it a point to bring my camera along. I love taking pictures and have amassed a huge collection over the years. However, there were also plenty of times when I missed some amazing photo opportunities because I thought, "I can take a picture of that amazing sight tomorrow because we'll still be in town." It never failed; even though we were still there the next day, something inevitably arose that prevented me from capturing that photo, and the opportunity was lost. I didn't seize the moment. Never put off until tomorrow what can be done today.

Since then, I've made it a point to act in the moment. Whether it is sightseeing possibilities, potential business dealings, or personal interests, I no longer let moments pass without taking full advantage of them for every possible positive outcome. For the most part, the opportune moments in life that we let slip by never come back; you have to discipline yourself to act now, because now is all you've got. Missed opportunities equal regrets.

> *Conditions are never just right. People who delay action*
> *until all factors are favorable do nothing.*
>
> —William Feather

A while back, I hooked up a musician named Gordon with an audition for a big-name artist. He was offered the gig and the two of them quickly developed a good working relationship. Before long, Gordon advanced to the position of musical director, and from that position of influence, he wrote and produced two hit songs on the artist's hugely successful album.

As a result of his hard work, talent, and dedication, Gordon made an enormous amount of money and became a sought-after producer in the process; all because he made the most of his situation and was willing to seize his moment in the sun. Gordon could have whined about every aspect of the gig like many of the other musicians on the same gig—but instead, he saw the gold in it and mined it for himself.

MAKE NEW CONTACTS

WHY CAN'T WE BE FRIENDS

Another way to take advantage of all the traveling is to make a concerted effort to meet new people in each town. There are virtually endless possibilities for networking as you travel around the world. My personal list of contacts has grown incredibly over the years, and although it takes quite a bit of effort to develop those relationships, all the work has been well worth it. Now I have friends in just about every city in the country and many around the world.

> *One secret of success in life is for a man to be ready for*
> *his opportunity when it comes.*
> —Benjamin Disraeli

Since most musicians will spend some time on the road over the course of their careers, it's wonderful to have friends to hang with when you're in their neck of the woods. Taking advantage of the opportunities that traveling affords involves thinking ahead. Road managers advance concert dates all the time, which means they are constantly setting up the production details of every gig long before the actual date of the show. For a musician, this translates into thinking about what can be accomplished in the cities you'll be visiting ahead of time.

I had aspirations to put on drum clinics, so I made it a point to meet with college percussion instructors, music store managers, and drum shop owners to establish relationships that would allow me the opportunity to put on a clinic the next time I was in that city. Simple as it seems, foresight plays a significant role in making the most of the road.

> *I've found that luck is quite predictable.*
> *If you want more luck, take more chances.*
> *Be more active. Show up more often.*
> —Brian Tracy

USE YOUR TIME WISELY

SOMETHING SO RIGHT

The road is the road, whether you're traveling with a cover band, original band, or touring with a major pop star around the world. Though the style in which you travel does differ, the bottom line is that you're away from home and unable to follow your normal routine.

The majority of a musician's time on a road gig is spent going from place to place. It's a lot of "hurry up and wait," which at times can be totally boring. One of the most challenging things about being on the road is dealing with all the idle time on your hands. But instead of withering away, you can use your free time in a variety of positive ways.

Regretfully, most of the musicians I have toured with failed to make the best use of their time, and before they knew it, there went five, ten, or even twenty years of their lives. Most people in the corporate working world would kill for the extra time that many touring musicians have on their hands. Take the average person who works eight hours a day, for example. By the time he or she drives back and forth to work, eats dinner and does all the other domestic mumbo jumbo that we all have to do, there is very little time or energy left to invest in other interests.

> *Far and away the best prize that life offers is the chance*
> *to work hard at work worth doing.*
> —Theodore Roosevelt

Musicians who squander their time on the road often have to succumb to day jobs when live work is scarce. Lack of planning and laziness are the key culprits. Because they don't play their cards right, many will never get another major gig—a real shame because there is plenty of opportunity for advancement within the music field. For the most part, those who use their time wisely are able to advance their careers and continue to sustain a living within some area of the industry. Isn't that the goal of every professional musician?

I have even worked with a few musicians who were so discontented with the music business and tired of all the traveling that they started completely new careers that had nothing to do with music. They prepared for these new professions during all their down time on the road: the hours spent sitting at the airport, in hotel rooms, on tour buses and planes, etc. They schooled themselves for entirely new careers while they were getting a paycheck—very resourceful.

Principles for Defeating Idleness
SYSTEM OF SURVIVAL

- Work on a constructive project
- Bring plenty of reading and study materials
- Work out in the mini-gyms at hotels
- Take a private lesson from notable teachers in cities where possible
- Make new friends wherever you go
- Network with people you already have relationships with in each city you visit
- Schedule meetings with instrument manufacturers you would like to endorse
- Practice your instrument as much as possible
- Learn some beneficial computer programs
- Spend time listening to and studying new music
- Develop a new skill that you wouldn't have time to work on at home
- Acquire knowledge from those with whom you are traveling

*Shun idleness. It is the rust that attaches itself
to the most brilliant of metals.*

—Francois Voltaire

WISDOM FOR THE ROAD
FINALLY GOT MYSELF TOGETHER

PHONE CHARGES: Never use the hotel phone directly, especially while in a foreign country. Make all calls from a cell phone or use a service such as instant messaging, Skype, or iChat. Generally speaking, the more luxurious the hotel, the more it will charge you for the use of a phone line.

LUGGAGE: Purchase good-quality luggage; in the long run, it's much more economical than buying several sets of cheap luggage.

FREQUENT FLYER CLUBS: Join all frequent-flyer and hotel frequent-stay programs, and use your numbers on your reservations.

TAX DEDUCTIONS: Save all your receipts that pertain to your travel expenses and equipment purchases so you can deduct those expenses from your taxable income when it comes time to file your personal income taxes.

HEALTHY SNACKS: Pack protein bars, nuts, fruit, and other healthy treats so you don't succumb to junk food when you're stuck in transit and starving.

HOTEL CHARGES: Pay for your hotel incidentals the night before your departure to avoid massive lines in the morning when everyone else is checking out. Better yet, use the on-screen checkout option when available. You won't even have to stop by the front desk.

CURBSIDE CHECK-IN: Whenever possible, use curbside check-in at the airport (and tip generously) rather than standing in long lines at the check-in counter.

SAVE MONEY: Your most expensive days on tour are your days off. Out of sheer boredom, musicians end up shopping for all manner of needless stuff. It's very easy to blow a lot of money on senseless purchases, so exercise self-control. Save as much of your "road" salary as possible; after you get home, it might take a while to get back into the groove and land another gig.

Success does not consist in never making mistakes but in
never making the same one a second time.

—George Bernard Shaw

MEALS: If you should be fortunate enough to stay at a luxury hotel, you might want to avoid eating all your meals there. Stay for breakfast, since that's generally the most affordable meal at a hotel restaurant, but grab lunch and dinner somewhere else. Five-star hotels always have five-star prices, but not necessarily five-star quality. The irony of staying at first-class hotels is that you often can't afford to eat at their restaurants with your per diem and have to dip into your salary to pay for the meals. Dinner is usually catered on show nights. If there is no backstage catering, you'll be given an additional $15 to $35 to get dinner elsewhere.

FOREIGN CURRENCY: When traveling in foreign countries, use an American Express, MasterCard, or Visa credit card to charge all your meals and purchases instead of exchanging currency all the time. This will save you the hassle of having to go to all the banks or getting ripped off by the extremely high hotel exchange rate. The trick is to make sure you account for the money you charged on the credit card, so that when your next statement comes, your breath isn't taken away by the hefty balance. Of course, you'll still need a little cash for taxis, fast food places, and street vendors, but just don't exchange very much if you don't have to.

When I toured throughout Europe and South America, I ended up losing money. Not only did I have to pay a transaction fee, but I also got the worst exchange rates at the little "bureau de change" places. I also seemed to end up with leftover foreign currency when I left each country. Then, when I returned to the good old U.S. of A. and attempted to change all this world currency back to U.S. dollars at my little old local bank, the exchange rate was so pathetic that I might as well have donated that money to a worthy cause abroad. If you have coins, it's even worse; you may as well start a coin-collecting hobby because you're stuck with them.

TRAVEL BOOKS: If you want to make the most of international travel, buy some guidebooks on the cities or countries you'll be visiting. Eyewitness Travel Guides, published by (DK) Dorling & Kindersley publishing, are my top recommendation. They are incredibly insightful and feature gorgeous full-color photography, which helps me choose what I want to see in advance. Due to a lack of foresight in the beginning of my career, I ended up missing out on once-in-a-lifetime opportunities to take in great sights, culture, food, and events. Eventually, I learned to set up sightseeing tours through the hotel concierge to make sure I at least got the highlights of a particular location. I did the tourist thing on days off or got up early in the morning for a day trip and was back before sound check.

I have taken in some pretty amazing sights by doing a little advanced research in these guidebooks, and I never regretted making the extra effort or spending the extra money for the experience. Take in everything you can; people save money all of their lives to go to destinations that touring musicians have the opportunity to travel to for free. Don't take that free ride for granted.

> *The U.S. Constitution doesn't guarantee happiness, only the pursuit of it. You have to catch up to it yourself.*
> —Benjamin Franklin

MAKING THE MOST OF AIR TRAVEL
COME FLY WITH ME

Today, there are more people flying than ever, and the days of having a whole row to yourself seem to be long gone. Airlines have consolidated schedules to save money, and with fewer flights available to each destination, the planes are often oversold and jam-packed. It might be just my imagination, but some of the new planes feel like they were designed for miniature, rather than normal-size people. Whoever is designing these flying machines assumes none of us have knees either. When your tray is down, you're essentially trapped—there is literally no room to do anything except maybe cry.

To combat these traveling blues, I have put two policies in place. First, I always try to use the restroom at the airport before I get on the flight or go on the plane before anyone eats. Second, I refuse to eat plane food. I'll eat almost anything at the airport rather than having to choose between the warthog hoof casserole or the genuine simulated meat loaf that the airlines so proudly serve. Now that I no longer eat plane food, I'm not trapped by that stupid food tray. Ah—freedom, freedom at last, it's a beautiful thing.

On a more positive note, even though it is difficult to navigate in such close quarters, I take advantage of time in the air to read, do research, or get some work done on my laptop. The time goes by much more quickly, and I don't feel like the day has been a total waste.

> *Work never tires me. Idleness exhausts me completely.*
> —Sherlock Holmes

Travel is exhausting, particularly for touring musicians. Your sleep is always being broken up by an erratic schedule; you get two hours here, three hours there, and some catnaps on the plane. but you rarely get a solid eight hours all in one shot like most normal folks. You constantly feel beat and sluggish, even though you may have not done much of anything. Travel—we love it and we hate it at the same time.

If you're used to doing this for a living, it gets hard to adjust to a different lifestyle. I have friends who quit the road to settle down for some kind of day job that keeps them in town, but after a while, they admit they get the urge to be on the road again. It's total craziness; you can't live with it, and you can't seem to live without it. Once you're a performer, it's always in your blood.

> *Keep on the lookout for novel ideas that others have used successfully. Your idea has to be original only in its adaptation to the problem you're working on.*
> —Thomas Edison

ROAD RULES FOR AVOIDING TROUBLE
WALK THIS WAY

BE PUNCTUAL: Be on time for all scheduled departure times, including flights, bus call (the time everyone is supposed to get on the tour bus), and lobby call (the time everyone meets in the lobby to go to the sound check or gig). Bring a portable alarm clock, or program your cell phone to make sure you're always up on time. I always use both and ask for a wake-up call as well; this way I can't possibly blow it when it comes to being on time.

KNOW WHERE YOU ARE: Upon arrival at your hotel, grab a business card at the front desk and keep it on you whenever you leave the premises. It's not at all uncommon for those who frequently travel to leave the hotel only to realize they have no idea where they are staying when it is time to return. This way you can just hand the card to the cab driver.

GET A RECEIPT: When you check out of the hotel and pay your incidentals, make sure you get a statement so there are no disputes over the billing later.

CARRY YOUR TRAVEL INFORMATION: Without exception, travel at all times with an itinerary and a contact sheet of all the personnel, including the travel agent. It's wise to enter all the information into your cell phone, but I always travel with a hard copy just in case I don't have my phone, lose it, the battery dies, or I accidentally delete the information. One day this could really get you out of a bind.

I have checked in and out of countless hotel rooms in my life, and one of the greatest challenges is remembering my room number. Since most room keys are now electronic and have no room number printed on them for security purposes, jot down your room number on something or commit it to memory once you check in.

DON'T PROCRASTINATE: Always pack the night before a trip so you're ready to leave at a moment's notice. Doing so will lessen the pressure if you're ever really in a time crunch and running late.

Somehow I can't believe there are many heights that can't be scaled by a man who knows the secret to making dreams come true. This special secret to me, can be summarized in four C's. They are Curiosity, Confidence, Courage and Consistency, and the greatest of these is Confidence. When you believe a thing, believe it all over, implicitly, and unquestionably.

—Walt Disney

15

THE ART OF SELF-MANAGEMENT
TAKING CARE OF BUSINESS

Rose-colored glasses are never made in bifocals.
Nobody wants to read the small print in dreams.

—Ann Landers

Theatrical rock legend Alice Cooper once attended a concert I played in Phoenix, Arizona. While he was backstage, I had the pleasure of talking with him for quite a while. I learned that he was all about the business; that doesn't mean he doesn't love performing, but he understands that if you don't take care of business, you won't have the luxury of making music for a living for very long.

At the time, he generally did about five shows a week when he was on the road. The first three shows paid for the cost of the tour, and the last two shows were gravy. While he has a rather flamboyant stage presence, at the core Alice Cooper is a businessman, plain and simple.

This is the case of many famous rock stars. Classic rock groups like KISS may have appeared to be wild and out of control, but when they were offstage after the show and the make-up was off, they focused on running a highly successful enterprise.

Contrary to his rock 'n' roll bad boy image, Gene Simmons, the founder of the band, is a shrewd businessman who continues to reinvent himself and effectively market the KISS brand. Behind the stage show and illusions there's a lot of money changing hands. How much ends up in your pocket depends on how good a manager you are.

The same management principles apply to sidemen, only with the independent musician you are dealing with a lot less money. In the music industry your image may be one thing, but how you conduct business shows how serious you are about what you do. Image is the show business side, but the way you handle your personal affairs is the business behind the persona. It's just like a coin: there's an image on one side, but if you flip it over you will see a completely different picture.

> *Make no little plans. They have no magic to stir*
> *men's blood and probably themselves will not be*
> *realized. Make big plans. Aim high in hope and work.*
> *Remembering that a noble, logical diagram once*
> *recorded will not die.*
>
> —Daniel H. Burnham

TAKING CHARGE OF YOUR CAREER

THE END OF THE INNOCENCE

Playing your instrument is only half the job of being a musician. With very few exceptions, the other half is managing your affairs. After you have developed your musical skills and have the goods to deliver, it's time to begin selling your services to recording artists, producers, musical directors, and other working musicians.

What? You thought your manager or agent was supposed to do the selling? Think again! Most sidemen do not have anyone representing them, and even those who do soon discover that most representatives, whether a manager or an agent, do not have the time to dedicate solely to their careers. Eventually, you'll come to the realization that no one is more interested in your success than you are, and no one will push you harder than you will push yourself.

> *It is my belief that talent is plentiful, and that*
> *what is lacking is staying power.*
>
> —Doris Lessing

Professional managers focus on recording artists and bands for a reason—to make money. Unless you are already earning substantial sums or show incredible financial promise, you won't attract the attention of a world-class manager. Those who are interested in handling unknown players are often inexperienced, lack the desperately needed connections, and have little or no clout in the industry. Working with them will do little to boost your career and is often a big waste of time. Worse, if you do accept an offer from an unproven manager to handle your affairs, and then discover that person is incompetent, getting out of your contract can be very sticky.

Generally speaking, only sidemen who become recording artists, songwriters, producers, or members of signed bands can afford to employ a support team. This team typically includes a personal manager, booking agent, business manager/accountant, and an attorney.

A personal manager's role is to oversee the artist's entire career, whereas an agent's primary responsibility is to secure gigs. Unfortunately, there are very few agents who work with independent musicians, and even fewer who do so successfully. I know a couple of agents in Los Angeles who specialize in getting sidemen work, but they have a lot of musicians on their rosters. So, when they find out about an audition through a record label, they send all of their musicians—they don't really care which one of their clients gets the gig as long as they get their cut. Whoever lands the gig has to give up anywhere from 15 percent to 25 percent of the income they earn. Whose interest do you think they are serving? Theirs!

> If you are successful enough to hire a management team, you're probably no longer considered a sideman.

If you are successful enough to hire a management team, you're probably no longer considered a sideman. Jazz guitar legend George Benson is a great example of this transformation. His career evolved from being a young, hard-hustling freelance jazz musician backing up famed organist Jack McDuff for several years, to an in-demand sideman on recording sessions for other notable jazz artists, to a bestselling recording artist himself. For sidemen, there just isn't enough money to be made to warrant hiring a team of high-level industry professionals to manage your business until you morph into a producer, songwriter, or recording artist.

Besides, if you have a manager too early in your career as a sideman, you'll come across looking like a prima donna and risk being shunned by other musicians. The truth is, most recording artists and their management don't want to deal with freelance musicians who have their own personal managers. They like to negotiate with sidemen directly and will only make an exception if you are a top-notch, A-list player who is really in demand, or a newcomer they desperately want to work with.

I've had a personal manager twice in my career. The first time was during the early days of my career in the mid '80s. He was initially very zealous about what he could do for me, but in the end, he was all talk and didn't have the necessary follow-through to see things to a profitable conclusion. I finally made the decision to terminate our agreement and was disappointed, as well as frustrated, when I realized I was back to managing my own career. It's unglamorous, grueling work.

Life is a grindstone. But whether it grinds us down or polishes us up depends on us.

—Thomas Holdcraft

Then two decades later, under somewhat different circumstances, I hired another personal manager. The second one was even worse than the first! This guy liked the idea of looking like a manager, but when it came down to really digging in the trenches when the going got tough, he couldn't handle the combat. A good manager has to be able to withstand rejection and continue to do battle for you.

I learned from these two experiences that if you want the job done right, you have to do it yourself. In the end, I found out that nobody is more interested in my success than I am.

TOP REASONS FOR BECOMING YOUR OWN MANAGER

MY WAY

- Because no one is more interested in your success than you are
- Because you know the job will get done
- Because you can trust yourself

- Because you will have total artistic control over your career
- Because you will work hard for your money
- Because most worthwhile managers won't manage you until you have a big name
- Because if you really want to make it you don't have any other choice
- Because no one else will do it

Virtually every successful independent musician I know has self-managed for a good portion, if not all, of his or her career. Unfortunately, most players don't have a clue how difficult it is to be an effective manager. You need a thorough understanding of the inner workings of the music business and the fundamentals of marketing to propel and sustain your career. Just as there are "one-hit wonder" recording artists, the same is true for backup musicians.

> *It has been my observation that most people get ahead during the time that others waste time.*
>
> —Henry Ford

Perhaps being a manager is not what you had in mind when you said you wanted to be a musician. The truth is, however, if you want to score the big gig—and then stay on the big stage—you'll have to learn how to manage and market yourself. Many musicians tend to lean toward their artistic natures and put all their efforts into practicing and performing but neglect the selling and promoting aspects of the business. The truth is that you need to do both. Understandably, most musicians just want to invest their time in playing music, but if you hope to make a living in this industry, you have to learn how to conduct business on all levels.

Being your own manager requires a variety of skills. The following is a list of essential components you'll need in order to successfully manage your career. We will go into more detail about each in upcoming chapters.

ESSENTIAL SKILLS NECESSARY TO BE AN EFFECTIVE MANAGER

I GO TO EXTREMES

- Business (negotiating, financial planning, and accounting)
- Networking (relationship building, correspondence, social networking, word processing, and computers)
- Marketing (publicity, advertising, presentation, photography, printing, graphics, writing, and endorsements)
- Multi-tasking (the ability to keep many things moving forward simultaneously)

LEARNING TO NEGOTIATE

WHAT A FOOL BELIEVES

One of the most unpleasant aspects of managing yourself is negotiating money. In your journey to the musical Land of Oz, you will surely run into just as many obstacles as Dorothy did—wizards, wicked witches, and a gang of flying monkeys that are really just snake oil salesmen trying to get you to do something for nothing. Taking advantage of the fact that you just love to play your instrument, some managers of recording artists will prey upon your inexperience when conducting business. If you let them, unscrupulous ones will nickel and dime you to death.

> *Information and communications technology unlocks the value of time, allowing and enabling multi-tasking, multi-channels, multi-this and multi-that.*
>
> —Li Ka Shing

Let me share an experience that illustrates just how this money game is played at the top levels of the industry. At this time in my career, I had already built a name for myself and played with many big-name recording artists. In other words, I wasn't a novice. In this particular scenario, I was promised a certain amount of money and a "point"—a small percentage of the record sales—on the album we would be touring to support. The manager of the act presented this arrangement as a rare business opportunity, which indeed it certainly was.

Time passed and we were well into rehearsals for the upcoming tour. Still, an agreement had not yet been solidified. While I continually reminded management about the compensation deal they had promised, they continually dragged their feet. Finally, after going around and around with these guys for weeks, they sent me a ridiculous contract. When my attorney looked it over, he thought it was a joke.

> *Experience is a hard teacher because she gives the test*
> *first, and the lesson afterwards.*
> —Vernon Law

Suddenly, I knew in my gut that management had just dangled the point in front of me like a carrot to get me to join the tour. In actuality, they were trying to get me to take a lesser salary by seducing me with the promise of a point—the allure of long-term revenue.

From personal experience, I knew that even if the contract was legit that it wasn't worth the paper it was written on—their offer was really all smoke and mirrors. They could still find a million and one ways to get out of paying me the point. In order to be certain I wasn't cheated out of my percentage, I would need to have the record company and management audited, because clever accounting, for which the industry is notorious, would ensure I got nothing. Chasing down my money after the tour was over would be far too exhausting, expensive, and time consuming. Besides, if I got a reputation for auditing the groups I worked with, eventually nobody would want to work with me.

Based on how they had conducted business in the past, I didn't trust any of these guys as far as I could throw them. After giving the offer some serious thought, I decided to renegotiate my deal. Time was running out; the tour was getting close to starting and the concert dates were already booked. As much as I wanted it, and as good as it might have been for me financially, I opted to nix the idea of getting the point. After thoughtfully considering what I felt I was worth, what I brought to the table, my level of experience, and what the competitive rates were at the time, I presented my offer to management. I asked for a hefty salary—one that would cover the point I'd been promised.

To put it mildly, they f-r-e-a-k-e-d!!! They said it was a ludicrous amount, which just proved to me that they had never intended to pay me that point at all. Now, keep in mind that managers almost always scream highway robbery; it's their favorite intimidation tactic. They rant and rave so you will feel like you are asking for way too much. It works on most musicians because they are just happy they got the gig, which allows unscrupulous managers to take advantage of them. I had bought that jive hook, line, and sinker in the past, but it wasn't going to work this time.

Even though it was one of the hottest tours going, with sold out shows around the world, it still wasn't worth getting an ulcer. My peace of mind at that tumultuous time was more important than the gig, so I quit.

I went away for a while to my mother's house in Seattle, a place I was sure no one could possibly track me down. I needed some time to lick my wounds and figure out my next career move. The whole experience had been a real drag; I didn't know I'd have to pull out my Louisville slugger baseball bat just to play the drums. I felt pretty down.

> *Success is how high you bounce when you*
> *hit rock bottom.*
> —General George S. Patton

Much to my surprise, the artist's manager actually located me; he must have really wanted to find out where I was, because I had never given out my mother's contact information. He pleaded with me to come back and he told me how much the artist wanted me, that I was the only guy for the job, and all kinds of other flattering and insincere malarkey. I knew he was just trying to give me a snow job, tickle my ears, and feed my ego, but at this point I couldn't possibly care less. I told him to leave me alone. I was really hurt.

Now, you're probably thinking I should have had my head examined. Everyone wants the big gig, right? That's what I was being offered— being begged—to do. How had I gotten to the point that I was telling one of the most powerful managers in the business to buzz off? In truth, I had accepted the fact that I was off the gig and no longer cared one way or another. In this situation, that proved to be an advantage for me.

The manager called again and again for a couple of weeks. I knew they were auditioning other drummers for the job and were having trouble finding someone who could make the artist happy. Not that I was irreplaceable by any means, but when an artist likes a musician, and that player is an integral part of their sound, they're not always willing to make a change. They may even audition players that are far better but don't have the eleven secret herbs and spices that makes the chicken "finger lickin' good!"

You get my drift—in this case the chemistry wasn't right and they were running out of time to get a drummer in place before the tour started. That put me in a much more favorable position. Finally, I agreed to negotiate with them one last time.

> Take time to deliberate, but when the time for action
> has arrived, stop thinking and go in.
>
> —Henry Ford

I told them how much money I wanted to do the tour, but this time I added a new stipulation; I wanted the entire amount in advance. He used some very colorful four-letter words in response. "This is unprecedented! In all my years in the business we've never done that for anyone, and we're not about to start!"

Still, I stuck to my guns; after all, they were the ones calling me. I was in the midst of a transformation of sorts; I was tired of the jive and was appalled by their business practices. I thoroughly enjoyed telling them what every other musician on the gig wished they had the guts to say. I had nothing to lose; I became the vigilante, a revolutionary, and the ambassador for all mistreated musicians around the world— and I loved every minute of it.

With the attitude I gave them, I expected them to write me off, but they miraculously persisted. They presented a counteroffer: they would meet my salary demands, but would not pay me in advance for the entire tour. In my mind, however, that was not negotiable. I could read a calendar—the first leg of the tour was from September through December. I knew when they took a break in January that they might start holding secret auditions and try to find a replacement—just to spite me for having them over a barrel. Getting the money in advance was my insurance policy.

So how does the story end? Drum roll please... I got everything I asked for! I remember driving down to their accountant's office to pick up the biggest check I had ever cashed. All I wanted was to play the music and get what I was promised—a fair deal for the service I provided and for my efforts and loyalty. I wasn't purposely trying to be a difficult prima donna, but I must admit I was quite proud of myself for standing up to those people who would have otherwise sucked me dry.

> *Progress comes from the intelligent use of experience.*
> —Elbert Hubbard

I knew exactly why they gave me what I wanted. It had to do with leverage, timing, and how much money they would lose if they had to extend rehearsals and start canceling concert dates. It certainly wasn't about friendship, honor, or doing the right thing. The bottom line was dollars and cents—in the end, meeting my demands was far cheaper than messing with the calendar.

Unfortunately, several other backup musicians on that tour opted for the point deal and a lesser salary. To this day, not one of them has made a dime in royalties, despite the fact that millions of albums have been sold. That experience reaffirmed my understanding that in this business you don't get what you deserve, you get what you negotiate.

MAKING WISE FINANCIAL DECISIONS

STAYING ALIVE

As I have stated in various chapters throughout the book, the life of a freelance musician is unpredictable and subject to unstable income flow. Musicians have to be very calculating in order to survive financially throughout their career.

Your goal should be to keep as much of your money as possible by making the choice to live well below your means. Lessening your financial pressure will free you up to invest more of your time practicing and networking, which will ultimately lead to better-paying gigs. As an independent contractor, you are on your own when it comes to retirement funds, medical insurance, and a host of other benefits that usually come with more traditional forms of employment.

> *Money is in some respects like fire; it is a very excellent servant, but a terrible master.*
>
> —P.T. Barnum

The following are some tips that can help you make the ride a smoother one. It wouldn't hurt you to learn a little more about money management and financial planning, and there are a myriad of resources out there to become better educated on these all-important subjects.

FINANCIAL WISDOM FOR THE FREELANCE MUSICIAN

I WILL SURVIVE

- Live well below your means.
- Don't be a poser and pretend to live a lifestyle you know you can't afford.
- Stay out of credit card debt.
- Have only one credit card with the lowest interest rate you can find.
- Use an American Express Card. It doesn't charge interest, but you must pay the balance in full at the end of the statement due date.

- Don't borrow money.

- Drive an economical car that gets great gas mileage.

- Sock away a few months' worth of living expenses for times of unemployment.

- Find a good certified public account to manage your taxes.

- Purchase software like Quicken or FileMaker Pro to help you keep an accurate log of all of your expenditures, and save your receipts for tax purposes.

- Put money into a retirement fund of some kind (Roth IRA).

- Shop around for the best cell phone and insurance rates.

- Use Skype, iChat, or instant messaging to cut down long distance phone bills.

- Read informative books on money and finance.

- Stay away from fast-food joints that will cost you in needless medical expenses later in life. Instead, shop at the grocery store when items are on sale and plan out your healthy meals in advance.

- Avoid wasting money on unnecessary purchases.

- Avoid throwing money away on alcohol, cigarettes, and drugs.

- Make wise investsments such as private lessons, good music equipment, and inspirational books to acquire the necessary knowledge to succeed.

DEALING WITH UNSAVORY CHARACTERS

BACK STABBERS

Be aware of the false prophet who offers to lead you to the Promised Land—something that is neither their true intention nor within their power to deliver. Two-bit slime balls, liars, sharks, scumbags, hustlers, cutthroats, back stabbers, and downright ruthless people all make up the cast of unsavory characters that are part of the dark side of this business. I have met and worked with a vast number of these circus freaks, so many, in fact, that the horror stories alone would fill up the pages of an entirely different book.

How can you prepare yourself for encounters with this class of people? Well, you're going to have to sift your way through an awful lot of garbage, but if you hang out in this industry long enough you will learn to read people quickly and decipher their BS.

After being in the game for as long as I have, I can tell in seconds if someone is full of it. Of course you can't always be 100 percent accurate, but in time you will improve your ability to proficiently judge character. It's an important skill to develop; you can spend an awful lot of time chasing after rainbows if you can't discern fact from fantasy and the genuine from the counterfeit.

Be on guard, watch your back, and never be surprised by what a desperate individual is capable of doing, including jealous friends. Because there are so few great gigs and so many hopeful musicians vying for the same jobs, some people will succumb to unethical behavior in an effort to get ahead.

> *You cannot sink someone else's end of the boat and still keep your own afloat.*
>
> —Charles Bower

The competitive nature of this industry often breeds desperate characters that are less than noble and seem to have no heart or conscience. Backstabbers will attempt to tarnish your reputation with false rumors in hopes of lessening your chances of getting a gig, and supposed friends will try to steal your gig or your significant other. It can get ugly.

Try not to take these negative encounters personally, and just realize that this self-serving behavior is exemplified in all industries and really reflects the corrupt nature of the human heart. The important thing is not to turn into one of these lost souls.

Personally, I always felt that if I couldn't make it based on honest, hard work that maybe it just wasn't worth it. I didn't want to purposely burn someone else just to get ahead, because I knew I would still have to live with my conscience. If I did make it, I wanted it to be in an honorable way based on sheer determination and fair business practices.

*Success without honor is an unseasoned dish; it will
satisfy your hunger, but it won't taste good.*

—Joe Paterno

GETTING ORGANIZED

EYE OF THE TIGER

Working with disorganized musicians is just as annoying as working with lazy ones. You know the type—the ones who forget their music stands, don't bring their charts, can't find the songs they are supposed to learn, lose the directions to the gig, or forget what time the gig starts. It's nerve-racking and disappointing to have to deal with such people, and downright embarrassing when we're the ones causing all the commotion.

I am convinced that my strategic approach to my career, which has its roots in organization, was largely responsible for my transition from amateur hobbyist to professional musician in a relatively short time.

Organized people know how to get the job done. I have heard it said that if you want to get something done, delegate it to a busy person. Busy people know how to organize their time to get the most out of it. Ironically, the people who seem to have all the time in the world never seem to be able to get the job done.

Procrastination is the thief of time.

—Edward Young

Music is like any other business; if you expect profitable returns, you have to make sound investments. You certainly can't get something for nothing, at least not something of lasting value. Time is one of your most valuable assets because it is limited; from the second you are born, you are running out of it. Once it is spent, you can never get it back, so use your time wisely. What you do with your time will demonstrate what you value and determine the outcome and productivity of your life.

There just doesn't seem to be enough hours in the day to take care of everything that needs attention, and the older you get, the more obvious this becomes. In an ideal world, it would be great to concentrate solely on musical concerns, but until we live in that utopia, the real world of hustle and bustle remains our home.

Organization is the key to time efficiency. If you lack organization, you are probably wasting valuable time that could be used practicing, networking, writing, or managing family obligations. Remember, time is money.

If you expect to make it in this business, you'll need to learn to be organized and stay on top of things. Make yourself as user-friendly as possible to any potential employer.

FOLLOWING THROUGH

LET'S GET SERIOUS

When I was writing my first book, *The Commandments of R&B Drumming: A Comprehensive Guide to Soul, Funk and Hip Hop*, I had to get permission from more than 40 record labels to use their album cover art in the recommended listening guide portion of the book. It took a ridiculous number of phone calls over several months to get clearance from each label. I couldn't believe the hoops I had to jump through just to give them some free advertising for the titles in their catalogs.

The whole process was a pain in the neck, but if I had not stayed on top of the labels and followed through to the very end, my requests would have slipped between the cracks and the mission would not have been accomplished.

> *Time is our most precious asset, we should invest it wisely.*
> —Michael Levy

Follow-through is the difference between bringing your dreams to life and letting them drift away. Hypothetically speaking, let's say it takes ten phone calls for you to land an audition with a certain music group. Most people will attempt to call at least once, but after a second phone call without a positive response, many just give up and quit. A certain percentage of people are more persistent and try three or four times, and an even smaller number picks up the phone six, seven, or even eight times before giving up. An infinitely smaller percentage of people are willing to make that ninth and tenth phone call, but that's ultimately when you get the go-ahead on an audition.

The point is that you may not know the answer is a definite yes or no until you have made that tenth phone call. When you go the distance, the outcome often changes. Until you make that tenth phone call, you won't know whether or not you will be hitting a brick wall or whether an opportunity will open up.

> *Perseverance is a great element of success. If you only knock long enough and loud enough at the gate, you are sure to wake up everybody.*
> —Henry Wadsworth Longfellow

Many of the people you are approaching are very, very busy, especially those who are in prominent positions, and they have ten thousand things on their minds. One or two phone calls can easily be forgotten overnight, but they might not forget five, six, eight, or ten! They're only going to remember you if you are persistent. Sometimes they'll end up succumbing to your request just to get rid of you!

Now, I'm not saying to be a complete pest—there's a big difference between being persistent and being obnoxious. You're a pest if you call up a management company for a gig and they tell you all of their artists have bands at this time and they do not need anyone, yet you continue to call them up every day anyway. You're going to annoy the heck out of them and lessen your chances when an opportunity opens up down the road.

Instead, check in with them periodically. Keep track of these callbacks in a notebook, on your cell phone, or with a calendar program on your computer. You need some kind of system, whether on paper or computer.

The process of following through can become a real drag. It's tedious, and it takes a lot of hard work, determination, and patience, but there's just no other way around it. Follow through to the very end. Remember, if you never ask, the answer is always no!

*When you get right down to the root of the meaning
of the word succeed; you find that it simply means to
follow through.*

—F.W. Nichol

Obviously, there are only so many hours in a day, so it's impossible to follow up on every lead. But just contemplate for a moment what might result if you followed up on just 20 percent of your intentions— now that takes persistence.

DEVELOPING GOOD CHARACTER

MAN IN THE MIRROR

What character traits do you want people to associate with your name? What images do you want to come to their minds when your name is brought up? If you are flaky and lazy, that's how people will think of you, and that's a tough image to erase. Do as much as you can to rid yourself of bad character flaws that are commonly associated with the average musician stereotype and replace them with the more productive ones outlined next.

*The greatest virtues are those which are the most
useful to other persons.*

—Aristotle

I call them the "Be-Attitudes." The more you adopt these mindsets, the more you have a real shot at a career as a player. Take the time to write down where you think you may be deficient, and then make a concerted effort to improve in those areas. As Jonathan Von Schiller reflected, "He who has done his best for his own time has lived for all times." You will never regret doing that and it will open up possibilities for you in every arena of your life. Look at it this way: taking care of all your business is a sign that you take yourself seriously as a person and musician, and if you don't take yourself seriously, why should anyone else?

THE BE-ATTITUDES

MY EYES ADORED YOU

- Be Prepared
- Be Aware
- Be Informed
- Be Punctual
- Be Reliable
- Be Focused
- Be Strategic
- Be Intentional
- Be Flexible
- Be Tenacious
- Be Consistent
- Be Confident

- Be Determined
- Be Disciplined
- Be Committed
- Be Persistent
- Be Respectful
- Be Sober
- Be Patient
- Be Grateful
- Be Kind
- Be Helpful
- Be Yourself
- Be All You Can Be

He is rich or poor according to what he is,
not according to what he has.

—Henry Ward Beecher

16

THE ART OF NETWORKING
BUILDING WORKING RELATIONSHIPS

*It marks a big step in your development when you
come to realize that other people can help you do a
better job than you can do alone.*

—Andrew Carnegie

Shortly after I graduated from Oregon's North Eugene High School in 1980, I moved in with my older sister Patricia, a successful model in Beverly Hills, California. Still a teenager, I wanted to meet other musicians my own age. Even though I was out of school, I started hanging out at Beverly Hills High to see if I could meet some new people. I had a plan.

You should have seen me. I pimped myself out in a pair of banana-colored slacks and an even brighter yellow silk shirt. To top off the already unforgettable outfit, I popped on some aviator shades and threw on a Panama Jack style straw hat with a yellow sash that ran around it and cocked it to the side for some extra attitude. I was beaming with so much yellow that even *Sesame Street*'s Big Bird and the sun itself were envious.

I brought my drum sticks and practice pad, and I cranked up my huge boom box with some funk tunes of the day and began jamming along in the courtyard during lunchtime. The whole point was to get the attention of some other young musicians and arouse their curiosity. "Who is this new drummer cat? I've never seen him before. Where's this dude from? Can this guy really play or is he all show?"

Unbelievable as it sounds, my preposterous gimmick actually worked! Within minutes, a few intrigued musicians came up and introduced themselves. Right there on that beautiful campus, I began friendships that ultimately led to all of my future success in the music

http://4wrd.it/A.BG16

industry. All of this stemmed from taking a chance and not being afraid to make a fool of myself in public in such an outlandish way.

BUILDING YOUR NETWORK

YOU'VE GOT A FRIEND IN ME

One of the first friends I made on the lawn that day at Beverly Hills High was a guy named Kenny Gordy, who was the son of the legendary Motown Records founder Berry Gordy Jr. Kenny introduced me to Lenny Kravitz, and through Lenny I met four other musicians: Osama Afifi, Vadim Zilberstein, Donn Wyatt, and Richard Allen. Each of them eagerly introduced me to their friends and dialed me into their local networks and inner circles of musicians. They did that for two reasons: because they said I was a better drummer than anyone in their current posse, and because they simply liked me.

At its core, networking in the music industry is very similar to the way multilevel marketing works. Multilevel marketing—also known as network marketing, direct selling, or referral marketing—is more popular today than ever before. It's a business paradigm in which the sales force is compensated for what they sell and for the sales of those they've recruited. In order to achieve success within this marketing strategy, you have to build a solid down line through relationship referrals and word-of-mouth marketing.

> *Don't judge each day by the harvest you reap but*
> *by the seeds that you plant.*
> —Robert Louis Stevenson

The premise of this business model is simple; you earn more money as the number of people in your down line increases because you get a small commission from their sales.

Rather than selling cleaning supplies or cosmetics, a musician's product is his or her skill. Throughout your entire career you will build a down line. You start off with no contacts, then you meet your first friend, this person then tells someone else about you, and it goes on and on until you build a huge network of people who know you and are willing to "sell" your abilities to others. I instinctively built my down line from the word "go," and that chain of relationships has in one way or another led to everything I have done in my professional career.

MAKING CONTACTS FROM A SMALL TOWN

RESCUE ME

Let's say you're not living in Los Angeles, New York, Nashville, Chicago, Atlanta, Las Vegas, Miami, or any of the major cities where opportunities for musicians are plentiful. Perhaps you live in a small town, removed from any semblance of a major music scene. If that's your situation, you're basically in the same position I was in when I started out in Grants Pass, Oregon.

Prominent musicians sometimes pass through smaller communities doing lectures, clinics, seminars, club dates, or college performances. A wonderful woman named Pearl Jones always encouraged me to get out there and meet as many of those musicians as I could. Pearl owned The Music Shop in Grants Pass and was kind enough to allow my mother to make really small payments on my first record player. She also gave my brother Bobby and me the opportunity to pay for the instruments we wanted by doing odd jobs for her—it was a huge blessing since we didn't have the cash.

Pearl was a gem, and through her prompting I did my best to make contact with every credible musician who passed through town and was willing to give me his or her phone number. The hope was that I could call on these musicians if I had an important question about the business or even maybe have a chance to play for them when my skill improved.

Because my hometown was so small, I drove to concerts in neighboring cities and made it a point to meet the musicians who were performing. On some occasions I wrote letters to the drummers of these groups in advance of their shows, stating that I was a fellow drummer and fan and would love the opportunity to meet them. I tried to have the letters delivered to the hotel where the groups would be staying, but if I couldn't find out where that was, I'd give the letters to the sound guys before the shows and ask if they would deliver them to the drummer backstage.

Pearl always told me to do whatever I had to do to get backstage, and I figured if absolutely anyone at all responded, it was worth taking the time to write a little note.

> *All you need in this life is ignorance and confidence,*
> *and then success is sure.*
>
> —Mark Twain

I met one of my favorite drummers this way. Dennis Bradford invited me to the sound check and introduced me to a few of the other musicians on the gig. One of them was an amazing saxophone player named Kenny Gorelick. Not long after I met him, he changed his name to Kenny G, and went on to become one the most successful instrumental musicians of the modern era.

Both Dennis and Kenny were playing with one of my favorite bands, a funky jazz-fusion group called The Jeff Lorber Fusion. Dennis even invited me and my brother, Bobby, to have dinner with the band. I was blown away that these cats I admired would even give me the time of day! You'll never know what the outcome of your efforts will be unless you try.

When a band is on tour, they will occasionally put on a party at their hotel after the concert, or hit the hip nightclubs in town to sit in and jam or just hang out. I met plenty of world-class musicians this way. I have a number of friends who got their big breaks because a famous musician came to the local club where they were playing, was blown away by what they heard, and then later recommend that undiscovered player for some great gig!

> *Nothing splendid has ever been achieved except*
> *by those who dared believe that something inside them*
> *was superior to circumstance.*
>
> —Bruce Barton

But what if you're in such a remote location that none of the situations I just described are even open to you? The answer is the Internet! There are so many ways to network in this day and age that it is mind-boggling. Many musicians have been able to successfully connect through websites such as Craigslist by listing themselves in their particular region and responding to musician want ads. Investigate the possibilities on the Web; get online and do some serious research, and then act on what you've learned.

RELOCATING TO A MAJOR MUSIC INDUSTRY CITY

FLY LIKE AN EAGLE

I stumbled upon one of the most phenomenal bass players I have ever heard while I was in the Mauritius Islands. In case you've never heard of them, look to the east of Madagascar, near the southernmost tip of Africa. That is just about as far south as you can go on this planet before venturing to Antarctica, where there are no gigs—unless you are a penguin.

No, I was not in the Mauritius Islands on assignment for National Geographic Explorer, I happened to be there on tour with French pop star and longtime girlfriend of actor Johnny Depp, Vanessa Paradis. Playing in that island paradise was one of the perks of the tour.

While I was there, I sat in at a local club and was blown away by the bass player. I mean, this dude was ridiculous, and no one in the outside world had ever even heard of him! I guess there wasn't a whole lot to do if you lived down there except practice, and it's obvious this dude did a lot of that.

Unless people are aware of your existence, you'll wind up stuck on Gilligan's Island patiently waiting to be discovered. With no plan in place to get off the island, you may as well get used to sunbathing, surfing, and snorkeling, because that's about all you're going to be able to do.

> *One doesn't discover new lands without consenting to*
> *lose sight of the shore for a very long time.*
>   —Andre Gide

In my world travels, I have discovered that there is no shortage of incredible talent. If you feel you have the skills, it's important to relocate to an area where there is more work for musicians.

One strategy employed by musicians is to make it on a local level first by being the best player in a small town and then making a move up to the next biggest city. There, you can meet players who are better connected and tap into more opportunities. It's not uncommon for an aspiring player to relocate several times before they are musically ready and financially able to make the jump to one of the major music markets and have a chance to score the bigger gigs. This gradual approach has worked for hordes of musicians and is a logical progression.

Strategic maneuvers like these are easiest to execute as a young, single musician. These risky moves are much more difficult to undertake when you have a family. The older you get, the more you are bogged down with responsibilities that make relocating a much more complex proposition. When you're not tied down, you can take chances and bounce back if your gamble doesn't pan out.

GETTING DISCOVERED

COME SEE ABOUT ME

Every accomplished musician has developed a keen sense of hearing, what we refer to in the business as having "good ears." I make it a point to listen to local talent whenever I'm on the road, whether it's at a club or in the hotel lounge. When I play private corporate functions with major acts, I have the opportunity to check out even more local talent because the promoter usually hires a local band as an opening act, and then employs another set of musicians to play after the headliner is finished. Players in the headline act usually stick around to check out the other local talent to see if anyone is really happening. By nature, most musicians are curious about other players.

> *The more you are like yourself, the less you are*
> *like anyone else.*
> —Walt Disney

Regardless of their age, skilled players always command the respect and reverence of other musicians in attendance. What always captures my attention is hearing someone with a great sound who makes the music feel genuinely good in an original way. The best way to get noticed, or "discovered," so to speak, is to develop your playing to the point at which your skill becomes undeniable and excellence seeps in through even the simplest songs. That's really how musicians who are in the position to do something for you will end up noticing you.

MAKING YOUR PRESENCE KNOWN
I'M GONNA MAKE YOU LOVE ME

Let's say that you eventually get the opportunity to go to an industry-related party with some major players in attendance. There are a couple of different ways to operate at the function, and each would have a drastically different outcome. It's quite possible to attend without actually meeting anyone, in which case you're no better off for having gone. Or you can leave knowing you made a serious effort to connect with a few people and that you left a lasting impression.

The second scenario doesn't happen by accident. You have to make it a point to carry on intelligent conversations just long enough for them to remember you, but not too long to overstay your welcome. It is critical to cultivate a charismatic personality that makes it hard for people to forget you (without being totally obnoxious). To connect with people, you need to zero in on common ground and take an interest in them.

> *You can close more business in two months by becoming interested in other people than you can in two years by trying to get people interested in you.*
> —Dale Carnegie

It takes a lot of guts to go into a roomful of people you don't know and boldly insert yourself into an existing conversation, or to walk right up to someone cold with no introduction and try to strike up a conversation. It's easy to walk away thinking, "How can I mingle with these people when I don't know any of them?"

What you should be thinking is, "I don't really know any of these people yet, so let's see how many I can get to know before the night is over. How many can I make aware of my existence?" You must learn to come out of your cocoon in order to become the social butterfly you need to be. You'll end up flying a lot faster and farther if you do. Be the kind of person who is always willing to socialize and refuses to go unnoticed.

HOW TO MAKE A NAME FOR YOURSELF

THE BREAKS

There are a few lucky people who get their so-called "big breaks" out of the clear blue sky without paying any dues. In general, though, a big break happens after a series of little breaks, and by building working relationships over a long period of time. I made it a point to hang out with musicians who were very serious about making it. Not only did these people inspire me, but I also knew if I could stay on the same playing level with them, that eventually they would be able to open some doors for me.

> *Keep away from people who try and belittle your*
> *ambitions. Small people always do that, but the really*
> *great make you feel that you, too, can become great.*
> —Mark Twain

Sometimes it's much easier to become part of an up-and-coming clique of hot players than it is to break into one that already has well-established relationships. There is always a promising generation of young players that become the "new cats." If you can build positive relationships with them as they are working their way up, you'll have a good chance of getting the call when they are in a position of power. You will only succeed as a working musician to the degree that you succeed with people.

When I finished my studies at Berklee College of Music in 1981, I went back to Los Angeles, but I continued to nurture my new friendships with my fellow students. I began to work the local L.A. scene by doing every gig I could do: recording sessions, corporate events, bar mitzvahs, club gigs—you name it, I was there.

After proving myself on a local level by playing in a variety of situations, my name and reputation started to spread around town.

Many of the people I worked with in the very beginning rose to prominence, and since I had strong healthy relationships in place with them, they recommended me for other situations.

A good example is my friend Lenny Kravitz. Lenny always believed in my talents and abilities and in me as a person. As we both worked our way up—Lenny as a young, hip producer, and me as a player—we remained close. He hired me for recording sessions and live band projects and recommended me for every other conceivable opportunity.

One such event was an audition for MCA recording artists The New Edition. As you earlier learned in the chapter "The Art of Reacting," I was fortunate to land the gig, and that put me on a path of working for many major recording artists. I worked extremely hard to build my name, credibility, and solid reputation, and it paid off.

> *I have learned this at least by my experiment: that if one advances confidently in the direction of his dreams, and endeavors to live the life which he has imagined, he will meet with a success unexpected in common hours.*
>
> —Henry David Thoreau

These opportunities came about as a result of paying careful attention to detail, building healthy working relationships with musicians, artists, and other industry people, and by capitalizing on every gig situation. You may get lucky once or twice, but you can't make a career as a sideman based on luck. Skill, experience, and instinct get you the gigs.

As time goes by, your circle of professional relationships should expand. Every style of music has a different group of people associated with it, so if you want to get a variety of work, try to circulate in as many circles as possible.

DON'T BURN BRIDGES

MAKE IT EASY ON YOURSELF

One thing to keep in mind as you are trying to build relationships is never to burn bridges. Don't forget that the people you run into on the way up are the same people you'll run into on the way down. Since none of us has a magic crystal ball, we cannot foresee exactly who will rise to the top and who will not. We don't have the privilege of knowing in advance who will really become our allies and come through for us. In many cases, the person I expected the least from helped me out the most, and the people I expected the most from let me down.

Treat everyone as if he or she is the most important person in your life. Those who are struggling right now may very well become the stars of tomorrow. The people you trample on today could easily end up being the ones who end up in a position to hire you later on. I've seen it happen dozens of times; those who are underestimated end up fooling their doubters all the time. Five, ten, or even fifteen years later they're suddenly in very powerful positions. Life is full of ironies, and there is often more to success than meets the eye.

> *The ladder of success is best climbed by stepping*
> *on the rungs of opportunity.*
> —Ayn Rand

Most of the cats I worked with on various tours started off as low man—or woman—on the totem pole, but years later became record company executives and presidents, hit producers, and songwriters. Some even started their own management firms and became major players in the game.

What you're dealing with here is a good old-fashioned game of musical chairs, a huge part of this business. Prominent positions are constantly being swapped, so you want to make sure you are diplomatic at all times and remain on good terms with everyone to keep your options open. Most artistic people are very sensitive, and as they are working their way up the ladder, they seldom forget those who "dogged" them during their days of struggle. Never burn a bridge; that may be just the bridge you need to cross later.

STAYING CONNECTED

REACH OUT AND TOUCH

As you begin networking and making connections, it's important to stay in touch with the people you meet on a regular basis. Follow up with new contacts very soon after you first meet them and then every two or three months afterwards just to touch base so they won't forget you. Each time you connect, your goal should be to get an update on what they're doing and give them an update on your current activities so you can become better acquainted.

Staying in touch with people electronically is the next best thing to being there and in many cases, even better. People are very busy these days, so if you wait until you see someone in person, you may never develop many strong friendships. Some relationships, especially with friends located in other cities, cannot be built on an in-person basis, so take advantage of phone, e-mail, and Facebook conversations.

> *To be busy is man's only happiness.*
> —Mark Twain

There have been periods of time in my career when I was burned out and didn't bother to stay in touch with a lot of the people I know. When my inspiration returned and I reconnected with people I hadn't talked to in months or years, they often told me about gigs I'd just missed out on. If only I had contacted them a few days earlier!

Fortunately, they would then go on to say they were going to recommend me for something else that was coming up on the horizon. They had forgotten about me—not permanently, mind you—but I was once again fresh on their minds. Because I hadn't stayed in touch, I was "out of sight, out of mind."

This is precisely why you need to stay on top of your networking and correspond with all your contacts periodically. It is hard, time-consuming work, but as you can see, it's totally necessary. To make sure you don't miss out on golden opportunities, get in the habit of returning any form of correspondence quickly and regularly. There have been a few times when I didn't get back to people quickly enough and I missed out on really great gigs—as they say, you snooze, you lose.

On the flip side, there have been many instances when I've called players that I wanted to recommend for good gigs, but they never returned my calls. If I didn't get quick responses, I would pick up the phone and start dialing up the next guys in line. When I'm going out of my way to recommend people, they should at least have the decency to get back to me. Whether they could do the gig or not, it's just common courtesy to respond.

> *The heights by great men reached and kept were*
> *not attained by sudden flight, but they while their*
> *companions slept were toiling upward in the night.*
> —Henry Wadsworth Longfellow

When you leave a message for someone, whether for the first time or if you have not made contact in a while, it's a good idea to leave your number. I've had friends who've lost their phones, had computers crash and hard drives fail and cannot locate my number. Make it convenient for someone to get back to you. I learned that the calls most frequently returned by busy professionals are those that include a phone number. Since time is of the essence, they are naturally going to respond to whatever is easiest; this way they don't have to look up anything or ask an assistant to find the number.

Also, unless you have a very unique first name, be sure to leave your last name on your message. Here is a typical message that someone might leave with my wife if I'm not in.

"Hello, can I speak to Zoro?"

"He's not in right now, can I take a message?"

"Sure, please tell him that John called."

John who? I know about a zillion cats named John.

MAXIMIZING YOUR NETWORKING EFFORTS

ALL THE WAY

When you have the opportunity to connect with someone for a meal, offer to pick him or her up. It's a great idea for a couple of reasons. First, you will have more one-on-one time before getting to your destination. The time you spend bonding in the car can be very productive and personal. People tend to open up more and put their guard down when they are not in a crowded restaurant or club and they have your undivided attention. Riding together guarantees a captive audience.

Second, offering to drive them makes getting together more convenient from your passenger's perspective. If he or she works or lives where parking is hard to find, that might be the one reason to turn down your offer. In cities like Los Angeles, the hassles of driving and parking are enough to discourage almost anyone from making the effort to get together.

> *When a man has put a limit on what he will do, he has*
> *put a limit on what he can do.*
> —Charles Schwab

By the way, if you are given the choice to bring this person into your circle of friends or get together with theirs, I recommend the latter. This is where they are most comfortable, and it will give you an opportunity to make new contacts and expand your network of friends.

CREATING A DATABASE OF YOUR CONTACTS
LET'S PUT IT ALL TOGETHER

Since no one can possibly remember all the pertinent information on everybody they have ever met, take advantage of modern technology and get some kind of computer program that can help you keep track of your contacts.

I use Address Book, a program that comes standard on all Mac computers, and I find it easy to use and extremely useful. Whenever I meet someone, whether at a trade show, conference, concert, or club, the first thing I do when I get home is enter all of their data into my Address Book program while it is fresh in my mind. The entry not only includes the basics like name, address, phone number, and e-mail, it also includes more detailed information. When somebody hands me a business card, I jot down additional information about them on the back of the card such as "plays keyboards for Paul McCartney."

If you categorize your contacts according to what they do, you will have a vast wealth of useful networking information at your fingertips. For example, in my Address Book program I can search for any specific group of individuals that I initially set up. If I need to contact a producer, manager, percussionist, music store, or anything else, I just scroll through my categories and go straight to the one I need and it lists out everyone who is classified under that category. Now I can see every bass player I know with one quick glance.

Starting a database of contacts is a brilliant way to become more efficient and intentional in terms of networking.

> *Wisdom is knowing what to do next; virtue is doing it.*
> —David Starr Jordan

I have thousands of contacts in my database, so I can't possibly remember each person's name. But because I have set it up properly, if I know I met a guy at a certain record label a long time ago, all I have to do is search for the name of that company, and bam! Every person I know at that label pops up. This method of networking has been highly effective and brought about many favorable results. In the end, making things happen is all about who you know, but the challenge lies in remembering who, exactly, you know!

THE SCHMOOZE FACTOR

HOLLYWOOD SWINGING

Social gatherings of any kind have always been the best place for schmoozing in our industry, so try to go to as many as you can. You get invited to parties and various industry functions like music showcases and record release parties by having a network in place. The people who make the most of hanging out are quite often the ones who move up the ladder the fastest.

As you infiltrate the scene in one of the major music industry cities, you will inevitably hear about various social gatherings. I've met a ton of amazing people at parties and made some really good connections, but I've also wasted time with people who turned out to be total flakes. I have run into more of these flakes late at night than I have in my breakfast cereal in the early morning.

To me, most of these gatherings are strictly opportunities to do business. They can tend to be a masquerade ball of sorts, and personally I would rather be at home chillin' out, practicing, or playing a gig than shuckin' and jivin' at some function. However, I learned early on that there is no way to make contacts without getting out there.

> *Our goals can only be achieved through a vehicle*
> *of a plan, in which we must fervently believe,*
> *and upon which we must vigorously act. There is*
> *no other route to success.*
>
> —Pablo Picasso

Always be fully prepared to network at social gatherings by bringing business cards, a pen, and a little notepad to jot down contact info in case people don't have business cards to exchange.

EFFECTIVE WAYS AND PLACES TO NETWORK
ACROSS THE UNIVERSE

- Phone calls
- Texting
- Emails
- Facebook
- Twitter
- Letters
- Cards
- Postcards
- Parties
- Jam sessions
- Clubs
- Concerts
- Conventions and trade shows
- Schools
- Clinics
- LinkedIn

THE COST OF NETWORKING

MONEY HONEY

For those of you who have your playing skills together but still haven't had your big break, it is usually a lack of contacts that prevents you from climbing any higher. Generally speaking, one of the biggest misconceptions about this business is the notion that people are going to come to you with incredible opportunities. You have to take the initiative and get comfortable talking to new people. You had also better get used to the fact that you will be spending a lot of time on the phone and Internet if you want to make things happen. Getting a shot in this business is largely dependent on social skills.

> *You can do so much in 10 minutes' time. Ten minutes,*
> *once gone, are gone for good. Divide your life into*
> *10-minute units and sacrifice as few of them as possible*
> *in meaningless activity.*
>
> —Ingvar Kamprad

You never know what turn of events is going to lead you to success. A lot of success comes from just doing what you do with a spirit of excellence, and as a result of your faithfulness to your craft, many unplanned divine appointments will find their way to you.

Musicians often make it in the strangest and most unpredictable ways. From this person you meet that person, who turns you on to yet another person, who then introduces you to the situation that can change your life forever. You honestly can't know in advance exactly how it's all going to happen. Nobody does. But I can tell you that networking is certainly one of the biggest pieces of the puzzle.

Networking is an investment, and a costly one at that. It costs money to connect with people—parking, gas, cover charges, drink minimums, concert tickets, food, phone service, Internet service—all of these expenses quickly add up. You must be willing to make the investment, or the only thing you can count on happening is nothing.

The first requisite for success is the ability to apply your physical and mental energies to one problem incessantly without growing weary.

—Thomas Edison

17

THE ART OF MARKETING
THE NECESSITY OF SELF-PROMOTION

*Glory gives herself only to those who have
always dreamed of her.*

—Charles de Gaulle

My journey into the world of media initially began as a result of landing my first big-name gig. Due to their extreme popularity, The New Edition, the group with whom I was playing, was featured in all the teen fan magazines on a regular basis. I remember frequenting the newsstands and riffling through each new issue in hopes of seeing a live shot of the group with me somewhere in the back playing drums. Mind you, I wasn't expecting to see a big picture of me, I just wanted proof that I was playing behind this very famous act. I desperately wanted to give my mother something that she could be proud of; she always believed in me so much.

I finally showed up in one of those magazines, but it was hard to tell it was actually me. All I could see was my arm and part of my nose; not exactly the kind of proof I was looking for. How did the independent musicians playing behind famous artists get any notoriety?

By a stroke of good luck, I was asked to do an interview with *Fresh* magazine, one of big fan rags of the day. They wanted to do a feature story on what it was like playing for the most popular teen group of the era and thought I was the perfect person to be interviewed. Widely distributed, the story led to numerous press and marketing opportunities and started the process of building my name within the industry. As a novice to the world of public relations, I knew nothing about media and marketing, but I soon learned how it all really worked.

http://4wrd.it/A.BG17

UNDERSTANDING MARKETING

I GET A KICK OUT OF YOU

One of the chief reasons so many musicians fail in this business is that they don't understand how to present and market themselves in a professional manner. For an independent musician, marketing is crucial to your success.

But before you can develop an overall strategy for your freelance career, you must first understand a few aspects of marketing. An effective campaign will include advertising, public relations, and promotional activities. Each of these essential components is a separate undertaking and should be addressed with slightly different methods.

Advertising is multi-faceted and should encompass a strong Internet presence (YouTube postings and social networking sites, for example) and ads featuring you that are placed by equipment manufactures you endorse. Promotion involves the development of business cards, resumes, biographies, brochures, and promo photos, as well as CD and DVD demos. Public relations has more to do with image development and involves sending out news releases and lining up interviews with various print and electronic media.

The best publicity of all for a sideman is playing behind a big-name artist, because television appearances and possible hit recordings will highlight your playing. Publicity like this will open up a plethora of other marketing opportunities, and some level of notoriety, as well.

In the same way a corporation's incentive is to increase profits for their stockholders, the sole purpose of your marketing efforts is to increase your personal salability, profitability, and net worth. If you can't generate enough money playing music to sustain a living, then it will be very difficult to do so for very long.

Marketing doesn't just mean scoring a magazine interview or signing a major endorsement deal with a musical equipment manufacturer. It is much more than just the idea of garnering publicity. How you conduct yourself, whether as a musician, a businessman, or an employee, is all a huge part of selling yourself. Building a credible reputation from the onset of your career by being reliable and doing the right thing is one of the best marketing strategies you can employ.

Presenting yourself to this industry in the most favorable light is a true art form, and it takes an incredible amount of forethought. The image you portray requires strategic effort and keen insight—it will ultimately determine how people respond to you.

> *Nothing limits achievement like small thinking; nothing expands possibilities like unleashed thinking.*
>
> —William Ward

There are a number of ways you can market your services to potential employers, but there's definitely a right way and a wrong way to go about it. Unlike some other types of independent contractors, plumbers or attorneys for example, straight-up advertising for a sideman is completely ineffective.

To take out a full-page, four-color ad in the yellow pages or *Keyboard* magazine with your picture and a caption stating what a great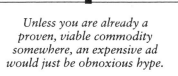

Unless you are already a proven, viable commodity somewhere, an expensive ad would just be obnoxious hype.

keyboardist you are is practically worthless. If you ran the ad long enough, people might eventually know your name, but it's doubtful anyone with hiring authority would respond. Instead, you'll end up making yourself look like a joker or wannabe, and no one will take you seriously. Unless you are already a proven, viable commodity somewhere, an expensive ad would just be obnoxious hype.

The only time display ads like these make any sense is if they are paid for by an equipment manufacturer that you endorse, the publisher of your book, or a record label that signs you. You are better off investing that money into your education and some serious private lessons.

UNDERSTANDING PUBLICITY

FAME

Publicity serves a different function for a signed band than it does for a sideman. The purpose of publicity for a signed band is to generate public awareness to increase the sales of their music through CD purchases and digital downloads. Good publicity will generate increased ticket sales to live events and sell more band merchandise.

It will also open the door for many other sources of revenue, such as product endorsements and commercials.

Publicity is generally handled by a publicist. A public relations expert helps create the image that is being sold and sets up media interviews and elaborate social networking campaigns. A publicist's goal is simple: attract as much attention to the band as possible by creating a massive amount of hype.

For a sideman, one of the main purposes of publicity is to increase awareness of you as a player to other potential employers—producers, recording artists, musical directors, and, of course, other musicians. The goal of this visibility is to broaden work prospects and ultimately raise your fees for performing.

For the freelance musician, publicity has a completely different set of rules than for a signed band. It's not about hype, it's about credibility. You can't realistically boast to other players about how great you are; your musical ability will speak for you, and that comes from the reputation you have established as a player.

> *Desire is the key to motivation, but it's the*
> *determination and commitment to unrelenting pursuit*
> *of your goal—a commitment to excellence—that will*
> *enable you to attain the success you seek.*
> —Mario Andretti

While press for a signed band is generally taken care of by the record label's in-house publicity department or an independent firm that is hired by the band, freelance musicians are responsible for their own publicity. Most of your efforts will revolve around doing interviews with magazines, newspapers, online publications, and other media outlets.

However, there is a common misconception bouncing around in the minds of aspiring musicians that being mentioned in the publications that focus on your individual instrument such as *Modern Drummer*, *Bass Player*, *Guitar Player*, *Electronic Musician*, and *Keyboard* magazines is going to get you a lot of gigs.

Since 1985, I have consistently appeared in major drum magazines throughout the world either as a cover story, feature interview, in reader polls, with articles I wrote, or in advertisements for the instrument companies I endorse. The truth is that I have never landed one gig as a musician as a result of the publicity I received in those magazines. I feel honored to have been featured in them, of course, but in reality, their readers—drummers—don't hire other drummers, and no one has ever hired me because they read about me in a magazine or saw me in an advertisement or on a poster.

Producers, musical directors, and recording artists may have heard of me through various media outlets, but they hired me because they believed I was able to provide a service they needed. My reputation as a player in the inner circles of the music industry is what opened those doors for me. Established recording artists, bandleaders, musical directors, contractors, and producers hire me to play, and unless they happen to be drummers, they don't read drum magazines.

> *You are today where your thoughts have brought you.*
> *You will be tomorrow where your thoughts take you.*
> —James Allen

It's great to increase your profile through publications that celebrate your particular instrument, but generally speaking, the musicians who play your instrument are looking for gigs themselves, so they can't help you too much. This kind of publicity does, however, help boost the amount of respect, recognition, and notoriety you receive within your own instrument community. But remember: respect, notoriety, and recognition alone do not pay the bills.

Where this kind of publicity really does help is in developing an audience and a market for other streams of revenue such as clinics, your own CD as an artist, signature lines of equipment, instructional books, DVDs, private instruction, and a variety of other products.

Your publicity must serve a purpose. I never pursued any kind of publicity until I thought it was warranted. In my case, I waited until I landed a major gig with a big-name artist to pursue any kind of publicity. Until that time, all of my efforts were spent trying to develop into a credible musician.

> *I never wanted to be famous. I only wanted to be great.*
> —Ray Charles

Many famous musicians never initially sought out publicity or fame. Their focus was on being the absolute best musicians possible, and because of the incredible level of artistry and control they possessed on their instruments, they landed great gigs and the press came to them.

WHEN TO LAUNCH A PUBLICITY CAMPAIGN
SOMEBODY'S WATCHING YOU

There is an optimum time when one should engage in publicity efforts, and discerning it can be challenging. Because they are impatient and don't understand its purpose, many players seek serious publicity before the time is right. Establish your reputation as a player first to ensure that your publicity is not a waste of time and money.

Unless a player can back up the attention he or she is getting in the press with proven playing ability, there is no reason to seek that publicity. All that will do is create unrealistic expectations of your playing skills. Don't confuse publicity with reputation; successful sidemen develop very reputable names within the inner circles of the industry long before they begin to hit the publicity campaign trail.

> *If you want to be successful, it's just this simple.*
> *Know what you are doing. Love what you are doing.*
> *And believe in what you are doing.*
> —Will Rodgers

Any sideman can hire a publicist, but there must be something notable to pitch to the media. A top-notch publicity firm is quite expensive and really only worth the investment if you are on a high-profile gig.

Such was the case for the members of Sting's band in the mid '80s during the *Dream of the Blue Turtle* album era. The band hired a respected publicity firm to secure interviews for every sideman in the band, splitting the cost amongst the players. Even though they were all getting paid very well on the gig, it was still a rather costly endeavor. At that pivotal point in their careers, however, the cash outlay was totally worth it. The timing of the media blitz was perfect; Sting was hugely popular at the time, his musicians were some of the best players around, and it was one of the hottest gigs going. It made sense to make the investment then.

This very intentional publicity effort did a great deal to boost the band's profile, which in turned helped to open up more endorsement deals and many more playing opportunities with other notable artists and producers. One of the primary reasons for the investment in their publicity was to raise their value as players and be able to command a higher fee for their time. Keep in

> *A press kit is designed to market your talent and toot your horn so you don't have to.*

mind, of course, that they were already monster players, and that each had a great reputation amongst the inner sanctum of well-respected musicians. This was not their first touring gig either, just one of their biggest in a pop setting. Most of these players had previously focused on heavier, jazz-oriented gigs.

CREATING THE KILLER MEDIA KIT

GIVING YOU THE BEST THAT I GOT

A media kit usually consists of a cover letter, biography, resume, photo, and some press clippings or tear sheets. A media kit is an essential tool for promoting whatever it is you're selling. It is designed to market your talent and toot your horn so you don't have to.

Although having a media kit is not completely essential for landing work as a musician, it will influence how you are perceived by others. I got plenty of work early on in my career without one, but when I finally did put one together it gave me the means to present myself to any organization in a more professional manner. More than anything else, the media kit helped me successfully solicit endorsements and various other business endeavors. I was able to land far more interviews in publications once I was on a string of big gigs and had an impressive media kit.

*When you can do the common things of life
in an uncommon way, you will command
the attention of the world.*

—George Washington Carver

When the time was right to have a media kit, I made sure mine was attractive, inviting, clean, and concise. If I was going to spend the money on it, then I wanted it to stand out, look aesthetically pleasing, and have some kind of impact. Making a first-class effort is just another way you can rise above the mediocrity that permeates much of our industry. This is your business, so learn to treat it like a business.

The time to send out a media kit is when you are making solicitations for an endorsement, an audition, or an interview in any form of media. When you finally have a reason to send one, make sure you always write a grammatically correct and professional cover letter to accompany your package, and state very clearly and concisely what it is you are seeking. The recipient must have a reason to review your materials.

Magazine editors and management firms for artists are inundated with unsolicited press packages, and yours may sit at the bottom of a huge pile on someone's desk for a long time. When I really wanted mine to get noticed, I sent the package by FedEx, which usually made it stand out from all the other padded envelopes. I would also call beforehand and get the name of the office manager or secretary and let that person know that I would be sending the package to them overnight.

These were all strategic efforts designed to increase the possibility that decision makers would actually look at my package. There are no guarantees any of this will work for you, but I had some success with these tactics. Remember your priorities though; there's no sense having a killer media kit if your playing leaves a lot to be desired.

MEDIA KIT COMPONENTS

SHINING STAR

From actors and comedians to recording artists and dancers, most everyone in the entertainment industry usually has a media kit of some kind. What components are in each one can differ depending on what purpose it will ultimately serve.

Your first media kit doesn't have to be anything fancy. Just get a glossy black folder, staple a business card on it, and throw in a one-page resume, a photo, a one-page bio that directs readers to online sites where your performances are posted, and bingo! You have a basic media kit.

Obviously, if you are just starting out you won't have very much in your media kit or probably much money to invest in it, but you can add components as your career progresses and your budget allows. What you look and sound like are the two most important things that anyone would want to know before hiring you.

> *One of life's great rules is this:*
> *The more you give, the more you get.*
> —William H. Danforth

Here are some specific recommendations for what should go in your media kit:

BUSINESS CARD: Professionally printed business cards with all of your pertinent information looks far more impressive than writing your phone number on a napkin like most musicians do. Handing out do-it-yourself business cards printed on a poor-quality printer is like wearing a $3,000 suit with scuffed-up shoes. Be sure to include the obvious bits of information like your name, phone number, e-mail, website, Facebook, Linkedin, and Twitter addresses, and what service you provide. Be specific; don't just put a picture of a music note on your card and make people guess what instrument you play. When I'm at a music trade show, I end up throwing away half of the business cards I'm handed because I can't remember who they belong to or what they do.

Whatever you do, make sure the card is legible. One of my pet peeves is print so stinking small or so fancy that I have to pull out a magnifying glass to read it. I just throw them in the trash out of frustration. If you had a nice, clean logo designed, you may want to add that on your card as well.

COVER LETTER: Accompanying your media kit must be a professional-looking cover letter that states your purpose in the most succinct manner possible. Get right to the point; these are busy people! The letter should obviously be typed on letterhead that contains your contact information. Nothing screams "amateur" like a handwritten note. At the conclusion of the letter, state that you will be following up by phone or e-mail within the next few weeks. That takes the pressure off of them having to respond and puts you in control of the next action of correspondence.

PHOTO: It's always a good idea to put a headshot in your media kit so your intended recipients can put a face with a name. There's no need to hire an expensive photographer; no freelance musician I know has ever landed a gig based solely on a photo. The main thing is for the photo to be in focus and fairly recent. Steer clear of overly artistic or abstract photos like those a recording artist would tend to use—this is not the cover of your solo CD. People just need to see what you really look like.

RESUME: A resume serves two primary purposes. The first is to get potential employers to consider calling you for an audition, and the second is to give them some tangible ways to remember you after the audition is over. When you reach a certain level in your profession, you are expected to have a resume, and having one that is done professionally will give the appearance that you have your act together.

In the corporate world, you wouldn't expect to apply for a really high-powered job without first sending your resume and hoping to be called for an interview. It's not that different in the music industry, except that instead of having an interview after the powers-that-be see your resume, you have an audition.

If you don't have anything substantial to put on your resume, don't panic. Your main credential is your musical ability. Even if you don't have a resume, you'll get hired if you play the music incredibly well.

Here is some other content to include on your resume. You'll need to include your contact information—phone number, e-mail address, website, Facebook, Linkedin, and Twitter profile addresses, and the URLS where videos of you playing can be found online. It's also a good idea to list all the equipment you own, as this can be a plus if you have good gear. It's also a nice touch to get a couple of quotes about you from people with whom you have either worked or studied that speak to your character and ability. Testimonials can go a long way in making up for a lack of content or recognizable names on a resume.

Be sure to list your formal education and the private teachers you studied under, and a personal reference with contact information for each. List the bands or artists you have worked with and in what capacity. But don't put someone on your resume that you jammed with for five minutes, even if they do have a big name. Anyone can falsify or exaggerate playing credentials, and doing so will only make you look like an idiot. It's not that hard to find out whether something is true, and any seasoned professional can tell by hearing you play if the names on your resume don't line up with your playing skills.

Action is the foundational key to all success.
—Pablo Picasso

BIOGRAPHY: A bio is a chronological retelling of the facts contained in your resume in narrative format; a short story of who you are as a person and a player. Your bio should not exceed one page in length, which is about 500 words—for a sideman, the shorter the better—and should highlight your skills and experience. It's a good idea to have short, medium, and full-length versions of your bio tailored for various media purposes. Include the usual pertinent background information such as your date of birth, where you're from, educational background, any awards or notable achievements, the musical styles you specialize in, and any other interesting tidbits of information that set you apart.

If you aren't a good writer, enlist a talented friend to help you put together a killer bio. You might be a great player, but if your bio reads like a fifth-grader wrote it, that might also be the impression potential employers will have of your playing. Make sure your contact info (and logo if you have one) appears at the top or bottom of the page.

MEDIA CLIPPINGS: Also known as tear sheets, media clippings are reprinted copies of media coverage or reviews you have received in newspapers, magazines, or online. It can be as simple as a one-sentence blurb where you name is mentioned in association with any of your musical activities. Don't worry if you don't have any clips yet; if you're really killin' on your instrument and nailing the music, that's all that really matters, and good media will come in time.

If you do have media clippings, scan them into your computer as high-resolution images and then print them out on a good quality copier. Highlight the sentence or paragraph that mentions you so no one has to read through the whole article to get to you. Make it obvious and easy for people to get right to it.

CD, MP3, AND DVD DEMOS: The most effective way to give people the opportunity to hear you play is to provide a CD, MP3 file, or a link to a performance posted online. Make sure whatever you send musically fits the gig for which you want to be considered. Having said that, please don't waste a lot of money paying for studio time and hiring expensive musicians to create a demo unless you are at the stage that warrants such an effort.

With today's technology, it is easy to inexpensively produce a really great reel of your playing. That means you can have a number of demo compilations representing a wide variety of playing examples and styles so you can customize what you send to people for their specific needs. If an artist is looking for a rock 'n' roll drummer, for example, don't send them samplings of your jazz and funk playing. Target your market specifically and send them what they need to hear. If you have something on DVD that is a good representation of your playing ability, you may want to include it in your media kit as well. I would suggest that you keep your demo short and sweet and load it up front with the most engaging performances that will demand immediate attention.

> *It's a funny thing about life; if you refuse to accept*
> *anything but the best, you very often get it.*
> —W. Somerset Maugham

YOUTUBE AND WEBSITE DEMOS: In today's high-tech world, establishing an online presence is imperative. Posting performances on your own website and on YouTube is absolutely one of the most extraordinary marketing tools available. Keep it simple though, and limit the number of videos posted. Too many will dilute your message. Less is more: highlighting a few killer performances is far better than having a bunch of mediocre material floating around in cyber space. I know a few big-name recording artists who recently looked for players on the Web and flew in the ones they liked most to audition for them in person. This is legitimate proof that creating a strong Web presence can open up possibilities to be heard that never before existed.

THE DIGITAL MEDIA KIT: Now you have the option of producing most of the components in your media kit in digital format. Many high-priced publicity firms use digital media kits for the clients they represent. Your bio, photo, and resume can be made available as downloadable PDFs on your website, which makes it easy for people to access and share your promotional materials.

It's still important, however, to have a hard scopy of your media kit available to hand to people in person. Some important decision makers are old school and prefer something they can hold in their hands, and some equally powerful people are more digitally savvy. They would rather click a few buttons on their computers rather than dig through piles of media kits on their desks. Print and digital each have advantages and disadvantages, so cover all your bases and have both options available.

As you create your media kit, treat each component as a stand-alone in the event the pieces get separated. Make sure your contact information appears on every individual item so interested parties can get a hold of you if their interest is piqued. The golden rule in marketing is to make it easy for people to find and contact you.

> *Where success is concerned, people are not measured in*
> *inches, or pounds, or college degrees,*
> *or family background; they are measured by*
> *the size of their thinking.*
> —David Schwartz

18

THE ART OF SPONSORSHIP
UNDERSTANDING HOW ENDORSEMENTS WORK

*I have found no greater satisfaction than
achieving success through honest dealing and
strict adherence to the view that, for you to gain,
those you deal with should gain as well.*

—Alan Greenspan

When I first started playing music, I remember thumbing through catalogs, brochures, and pamphlets of my favorite instrument manufacturers and drooling over the equipment for hours on end. The scent of fresh paper and ink had a distinctive aroma. The shiny chrome hardware, bright colors, and drums captivated me. The visually stunning images that jumped off those pages long ago are just as vivid today. They ignited a fire inside of me and made an indelible mark on an impressionable wannabe drummer.

I used to dog-ear the pages that featured my drum heroes and carefully take the time to circle, highlight, and underline anything I felt was important. We didn't have the Internet back then, so those catalogs were my windows to the outside world. They were the stuff dreams were made of; I read them cover to cover and memorized every bit of text written to describe the instruments I had my heart set on owning someday.

As a young boy, I was fascinated with endorsements and how they worked, but I had no understanding of how the music business operated, how it differed from the instrument manufacturing industry, or how the two might be intertwined. Still, the dream of being in a catalog alongside some of the musicians I idolized kept my young mind endlessly engaged.

When I was 17, I wrote a letter to Vic Firth, the president of Vic Firth, a manufacturer of drum sticks, asking him

http://4wrd.it/A.BG18

for more information and telling him how much I loved his sticks. I was blown away when I received a handwritten response from him, and I dreamed of one day being one of his product endorsers. I have been endorsing Vic Firth sticks since 1985, and I have a great relationship with the company that is going strong. I even have my own successful signature stick! I still have Vic Firth's letter, and to this day it holds a very special place in my heart. It serves as a reminder that every dream that is fulfilled must take root in the heart.

> *It is difficult to say what is impossible,*
> *for the dream of yesterday is the hope of today*
> *and the reality of tomorrow.*
> —Robert Goddard

SOLICITING INSTRUMENT COMPANIES

USE ME

The best way to seek endorsements is to solicit only those companies whose gear you love and would be proud to recommend. Many novices approach every competing company simultaneously. This is unwise, especially since many of the artist reps know each other and talk. The last thing you want is for them to find out you sent packages to all of them. Doing so would make you appear insincere and somewhat desperate—like you don't believe in anyone's equipment in particular and just want something for nothing. How can you be a great endorser if you aren't a fan of the product?

> *How can you make a great endorser if you aren't a fan of the product?*

If none of the big dogs are interested in endorsing you, take a shot at some of the up-and-coming manufacturers. Many of them have great craftsmen and excellent products, but they don't yet have the name recognition. Because they are trying to establish themselves in the marketplace, they tend to be a bit hungrier for new endorsers and would probably be more amenable to working with newcomers.

THE MANUFACTURER/MUSICIAN RELATIONSHIP

YOU'LL NEVER WALK ALONE

Take advantage of every possible opportunity to advance your career. Besides playing for a big-name artist, one of the best ways to do that is through relationships with instrument manufacturers. Just as famous athletes endorse their favorite shoes, you may have occasion to endorse your favorite instruments.

> *It is only as we develop others that*
> *we permanently succeed.*
> —Harry S. Firestone

There is a lot of confusion floating around out there about endorsements. The sole reason a company gives you equipment is to sell more of their product. So, in exchange for the use of your name and likeness in advertisements, you are given equipment and support. Exposure is the name of the game. Your job is to represent XYZ Company with a certain demographic of potential buyers.

The largest demographic of musical equipment purchasers is young people between the ages of 14 and 25. If the band you're playing in influences that particular age group on a fairly large scale, you would be a valuable commodity from the manufacturer's standpoint.

TYPES OF PLAYERS ENDORSED

EVERY KINDA PEOPLE

A player who has an agreement with an instrument manufacturer is referred to as their "artist" in the same manner that a record company would refer to a band signed to their label. This is usually the only instance when a sideman is called the artist.

Endorsements are usually offered to musicians who fall into one of five categories:

THE FIRST-TIME PLAYER WITH A BIG-NAME ARTIST:

This kind of endorsement is given to a musician who has never previously played with a big-name artist, but lands a huge gig on the first go-around. From the company's perspective, endorsing this person can be a bit of a gamble; there is no guarantee he or she will keep the gig or be able to parlay that one-time opportunity into a viable career. Due to the sheer exposure that can be gained, most manufacturers will take a chance on endorsing this kind of player hoping to realize a return on their investment.

THE RESPECTED SIDEMAN: These are musicians who have been on high-profile gigs for years and are often the pride and joy of the company's artist roster. This kind of player will always be a wise investment for the manufacturer—a proven commodity with a high degree of influence. When consumers see a world-class musician endorse a particular brand, it impacts their buying decisions. Witnessing that seal of approval from a musician the public knows and holds in high regard lends tremendous credibility to the manufacturer, translating into higher sales.

THE INFLUENTIAL EDUCATOR: Manufacturers are always looking for different markets to garner sales of their products. Highly respected educators, such as university professors, can be valuable assets to an instrument manufacturer because of the number of students under their tutelage from year to year. Many of these elite educators are also authors of educational books and DVDs, which are additional outlets for influencing potential instrument consumers.

THE UP-AND-COMING PLAYER: A manufacturer may enter into an agreement with a musician who shows a lot of promise by consistently landing better and better gigs. These are usually players who are highly talented, but who just haven't yet landed a huge gig. Just like a talent scout in sports, the job of the artist relations manager at an instrument manufacturer is to sign players who have the goods and who they believe are going to have a huge future impact in the musical community.

THE PRODIGY OR VIRTUOSO PLAYER: These rare musicians can be extremely young, as in the case of child prodigies, or somewhat older. In any case, they command instant attention because of the unbelievable ability they display on their instruments. These types of players are highly revered by manufacturers because their potential customers are wowed by their musicianship. It's not necessary for them to play with big-name artists; through clinic appearances and perhaps instructional DVDs and books, virtuosos like these have a level of influence manufacturers feel is worthy of their investment.

> *Recipe for success: Study while others are sleeping; work while others are loafing; prepare while others are playing; and dream while others are wishing.*
>
> —William Ward

TYPES OF ENDORSEMENT DEALS

WE GO TOGETHER

Endorsement deals can be structured in a variety of ways:

THE A-LIST ENDORSEMENT: This is the gold medal of deals and given only to A-list players. They are offered to extremely respected and well-known players, as well as those who became rock stars through the tremendous success and influence of their bands, such as the legendary rock groups Aerosmith and U2.

In this type of arrangement, the endorser is given all the equipment they want, within reason of course, completely free of charge. Depending on the musician's status and level of influence, A-list endorsers might be given a yearly stipend to play

> *Now, before you start seeing dollar signs, realize that there are very few companies that financially compensate an artist in exchange for an endorsement, and the ones that can afford it are usually not in the habit of handing out astronomical sums.*

the company's gear. In other cases, they are contractually required to do a specific number of clinic appearances each year. Compensation can be per clinic, per month, or per quarter, and the manufacturer pays for all the travel expenses.

Now, before you start seeing dollar signs, realize that there are very few companies that financially compensate an artist in exchange for an endorsement, and the ones that can afford it are usually not in the habit of handing out astronomical sums. This is nothing like major sports endorsements in which athletes get paid millions of dollars for the use of their name. In this industry, you are dealing with thousands of dollars and usually well under the $100 K mark.

THE B-LIST ENDORSEMENT: This deal goes to respected players who have a certain level of success, but from the company's perspective are silver medalists with good prospects for a gold medal in the near future. The benefits are similar to those of the A-list endorsement, except in this type of arrangement the gear the artist receives is limited. For instance, you might get one free drum kit, guitar, bass, keyboard, or whatever it is you play, for the length of the contract, which is usually from one to three years.

The sponsor might also contribute toward your clinic appearance fee. For instance, if your clinic fee is $500, the sponsor might decide to contribute $150 towards that fee. We'll explore clinics and clinic fees later in this chapter in more detail.

THE COST ENDORSEMENT: This deal is offered to the musician who is playing with a band that is beginning to have some notoriety, and the manufacturer is willing to take a minimal risk. At this level, manufacturers may feature artists in their advertising campaigns and support their clinic appearances to some degree. They are often given the privilege of buying their equipment near the manufacturer's cost and selecting their instruments directly from the factory. Manufacturers may also provide endorsers with replacement parts or repair their equipment free of charge.

However, since some of the larger music chains offer their valued customers prices that are close to cost, you might question how this level of endorsement will benefit you. The biggest advantage is in the relationship that is being established for the future. It's very common for a musician to go from the lowest level of endorsement and rise to the A-list category as his or her career progresses.

Even though this is the bronze medal deal, it's still an incredible opportunity if you're smart and willing to work hard.

ENDORSER WISDOM

SOMEBODY'S WATCHING YOU

There are many different ways an endorsement deal can be structured, and much of that depends on the company, who you are, and the status of the relationship between you and the artist relations manager of the company. The relationship with the artist relations manager and other key personnel at the manufacturer are very valuable, so do your utmost to connect in a positive manner. If you have someone else negotiating your deal, ordering your gear, or making your clinic arrangements with the manufacturer, you won't have a chance to develop a personal rapport with that manufacturer.

Artist relations managers at instrument manufacturers are notorious for bouncing around from company to company. You may develop a good rapport and then find out that person has been suddenly drafted to another manufacturer. When that happens, he or she may solicit you to endorse that company's product.

The endorsement game is based on relationships, so spend time developing those key connections for future opportunities. The musical instrument industry is a very small one, so it is very important to be a good endorser. A bad reputation gets around very quickly.

The only way an endorsement deal really works is if it's mutually beneficial. Many musicians look at endorsements only from the standpoint of what they can get

> *If you have someone else negotiating your deal, ordering your gear, or making your clinic arrangements with the manufacturer, you won't have a chance to develop a personal rapport with that manufacturer.*

out of it, without considering how they might contribute to the overall success of the company. Instead, adopt President John F. Kennedy's mindset when he urged the American people to serve their country in his inaugural speech: "...ask not what your country can do for you—ask what you can do for your country."

The manufacturer's success is your success. You can't take, take, take, and suck their bones dry and expect it to be a fruitful relationship. It's like a marriage; if one person is doing all the giving, resentment will eventually set in and the relationship will end. Strive to be an asset and not a liability, and your value to the sponsor will increase.

> *When you're part of team, you stand up for*
> *your teammates. Your loyalty is to them.*
> *You protect them through good and bad,*
> *because they'd do the same for you.*
>
> —Lawrence Peter "Yogi" Berra

One of the customary ways to show appreciation to the companies you endorse is to hook them up with complimentary passes to all of your concerts. It's a nice perk for them, and one of the few things you can offer them that is of value. Equipment reps love getting invited to shows. I love hooking up my friends at DW Drums, Sabian Cymbals, Evans Drum Heads, Vic Firth Sticks, Latin Percussion, Audix Microphones, SKB Cases, and all of my other equipment sponsors. We have spent so much time together over the course of my career that these people have become like family, and I enjoy every opportunity I have to be a blessing to them.

There is an awful lot of stupidity that goes on with players and endorsements. For example, if you play with a recording artist on a major television show like the Grammy Awards, there is no guarantee you will be playing on your own personal gear. Most bass, guitar, and horn players carry their main personal instruments, but amplifiers are considered back line gear. Getting the right back line gear can definitely be problematic, especially if you play drums and keyboards.

Even if you are a big-name player or you're playing for a big star, that doesn't mean you will always have the luxury of playing your own gear. It's usually due to logistics: if you are doing a one-off concert in Barcelona, Spain, there is a very good chance you will not be on your regular gear. The reason is plain and simple—money. It would cost far more to fly the band's gear to Spain than it would to just rent some of it from a local equipment company. In most cases, the rental equipment will be paid for by the local promoter of the concert or the production office of the TV show on which you'll be playing.

For the most part, the artist's management couldn't care less what equipment you are endorsing; by saving money on freight, they increase their profits. It's in your best interest to protect your endorsement and honor your commitment to help promote your sponsoring company's product everywhere possible.

In many instances you'll have to make outside arrangements with the rental company or put in a request with the artist relations manager at your instrument manufacturer's office to have the gear you want at the gig. Sometimes it's just a phone call, but sometimes it's impossible to do because the location in which you're performing may not even have access to your brand of instruments. On major tours, this is usually coordinated by the person who is teching your gear for you, but not always.

Whatever the case may be, you still have to try your best to make it happen. As ridiculous as it sounds, I have known players who had endorsements with major instrument manufacturers and were given all the equipment they wanted, but when it came time to play on a major television show, they played the competition's brand that was provided for them by the television production crew because they failed to make the necessary arrangements in advance.

> *Signing an endorsement agreement with a company you don't believe in is like marrying someone you don't love. Why would you want to do that?*

Duh—like everyone in the business is not going to be watching all of the major televised musical events. Hello—McFly!!! These widely viewed shows are your opportunity to give the brands you endorse the exposure they deserve. After all, that is precisely why they gave you the equipment in the first place! If you don't believe in the equipment, don't bother to endorse it; in the long run it won't be good for either party. Signing an endorsement agreement with a company you don't believe in is like marrying someone you don't love. Why would you want to do that?

On a personal note, I never approached a major instrument manufacturer for an endorsement if I was not on a national gig. I guess I saw how ridiculous it would have been to ask for a deal if I had nothing substantial to offer in return. These days, however, it blows my mind how many young cats try to score major endorsements without having achieved any form of notoriety. This is sheer business ignorance.

Building a strong, healthy relationship with instrument manufactures can be an important aspect of your career. The benefits are enormous since most of what you do as a player revolves around the equipment you play. Having a solid endorsement is essential if you plan to tap into the educational side of the industry as a clinician or release instructional material. Having the power of a well-known company behind you will make your life a lot easier in terms of those kinds of doors opening.

ENDORSEMENT BENEFITS

CONSIDER YOURSELF (ONE OF THE FAMILY)

COMPLIMENTARY OR HEAVILY DISCOUNTED EQUIPMENT: Paying for your musical gear is one of the biggest investments you will make in the early stages of your career. Receiving instruments that you once paid full price for is an incredible feeling and the first true perk of an endorsement deal.

FACTORY VISITS: As an endorser, you will have the luxury of handpicking your instruments from the cream of the crop. This makes choosing the right instrument a lot easier than going into a crowded, noisy music store on a Saturday afternoon with some pushy salesperson who doesn't have a clue.

CUSTOMIZED EQUIPMENT: Some sponsors will build your instrument exactly to your own personal specifications. This is a rare privilege and helps you to play your absolute best.

EQUIPMENT AND TECHNICAL SUPPORT: Equipment failures are a major hassle and can be quite a nightmare when you're on the road in the middle of nowhere or busy in the studio. Part of a good endorsement is receiving emergency support. The convenience of having parts sent to you overnight or having your gear fixed immediately is a lifesaver.

PUBLICITY: A good sponsoring company can help to further establish and build your name. This is done by including you in a variety of marketing media, including advertisements, catalogs, websites, newsletters, brochures, posters, product DVDs, blogs, and podcasts. This is probably the most vital ingredient in establishing you as a recognizable name, and that translates into notoriety and respect and enhances your money-making potential. It's a lot easier to sell a product you invented or get a good crowd at your clinic appearances if people have heard of you.

CLINIC SUPPORT: A company that you endorse will often help pay for your clinic fees or chip in for special performance events with your other sponsors. Clinics supplement the incomes of many high-profile musicians quite a bit, and without sponsor support, clinic income for musicians would be non-existent.

RESEARCH AND DEVELOPMENT: You may be given the opportunity to be a part of a team that invents new product lines or asked to beta test all the latest products. Your input and insight can have a direct impact on the end result of the product development process.

SIGNATURE LINE OF EQUIPMENT: As you rise to prominence, you may be given the privilege of having a signature product made exclusively for you that will be made available for commercial sale. It is becoming increasingly popular these days for famous musicians to have their own signature products. I have had the good fortune of having a number of signature items, including my own model of drum sticks with Vic Firth, a line of cymbals with Sabian, and a bass drum beater with Danmar Percussion. In most cases, artists receive royalties for each item sold, which is a beautiful thing! In other cases, they are paid a flat fee for the use of their name in association with that product, which is referred to as a "buyout." In either case, this is one more way to bring in revenue and further establish the value of your name. It doesn't hurt your self-esteem too much either!

LOANER EQUIPMENT: Some manufacturers will supply prominent rental equipment companies and television production crews with a sampling of their equipment to be made available to their endorsers upon request. When touring in foreign countries and larger U.S. cities, you might have the option of using this loaner equipment rather than spending the money to rent it or ship yours around. This can save a lot of hassle—and, of course, money!

> *Coming together is a beginning. Keeping together is progress. Working together is success.*
>
> —Henry Ford

ENDORSER RESPONSIBILITIES

GOT TO BE THERE

- To use the manufacturer's equipment in all playing situations including live, video, television, and studio

- To promote their equipment in any way possible and through any medium available such as doing podcasts or performing instructional demos for their websites as well as in-store and trade show "meet-and-greet," and autograph sessions

- To represent the company in the most professional manner possible

- To keep them informed and updated on all your projects

- To give them credit and mention them wherever possible in interviews, on CD and DVDs, and in books

- To supply them with usable photos and grant them permission to use your name and likeness in conjunction with any and all promotional literature

- To help them sell more product through their association with you and your circle of influence

- To hook up the company with free tickets and passes to all of your concerts

> *Sincerity makes the least man to be of more value than the most talented hypocrite.*
>
> —Charles Spurgeon

UNDERSTANDING THE BUSINESS OF CLINICS

COME TOGETHER

Clinic performances by artists on their roster are one of the key marketing strategies instrument manufacturers use to influence consumer purchases, and they are consequently among the main expenses in their marketing budgets. If handled correctly, the clinic is a powerful tool and a mutually beneficial endeavor for the artist, the instrument manufacturer, the host of the clinic, and those in attendance.

In essence, a clinic is really just a musical demonstration. There are no specific criteria for a clinic's structure; there are as many approaches as there are players performing them. What an artist wants to convey conceptually at a clinic is completely up to him or her.

From the perspectives of the manufacturers and retail stores, the important thing is that at some point in the clinic the artists mention the equipment they are playing and the reasons why they chose those brands. This generates instrument sales for the companies that are supporting the artist's clinic appearance and boosts overall retail sales for the store that's hosting the event.

Clinics also play a small part in keeping the arts alive and help to inspire newer generations of musicians to express their creativity and reach excellence on their instruments. For all parties involved, the clinic is a wonderful way to come together and share our mutual love for music. When it comes to doing clinics, my personal goal is to combine inspiration, motivation, and education in an entertaining manner.

Why do we, as a free people, honor the arts?...The arts
are among our nation's finest creations and the reflection
of freedom's light.
—Ronald Reagan

I am there to serve the host of the event and the companies I represent and to make a positive impact on all in attendance. I am not there to be a celebrity, but rather a servant to a cause that is much bigger than myself. This philosophical approach has helped achieve incredible results for all parties involved.

CLINIC BUSINESS TERMS AND INSIGHT
WHEN I THINK OF YOU

CLINIC FEE: Artists determine their fees based on name value and the demand for their appearances. The fee can range from as low as $100 up to $2,500 for a one-time appearance.

CLINIC HOST: The entity putting on the clinic is called the host. It can be a music store or chain, college, music school, high school, junior high, private teaching studio, church, or a special event of some kind such as a conference, festival, or workshop. Literally any interested party can host a clinic if they have the budget to do so.

CLINIC FEE STRUCTURE: An artist's fee can be paid in a number of ways. It can be absorbed entirely by the one specific sponsor sending the artist out to the event, or it can be split among all of the companies the artist endorses. A certain portion of the artist's fee is usually covered by the host, as well.

Compensation can come in the form of direct payment to the artist or, in the case of a music store, by accumulating points from manufacturers from the purchase of a certain dollar amount of merchandise. It works very much like frequent flyer miles, and the artist's fee is based on the accumulated points that the merchant has chosen to redeem.

In other cases, the individual music store or retail chain may pay nothing or not use any points for the clinic because of the volume of merchandise they sell of that particular manufacturer's brand. In other words, the clinic is a free perk provided to the retailer by the manufacturer as a reward for being a good customer. The artist is still paid his or her full clinic fee directly from the manufacturer.

If the host is a school, it will usually contribute to the artist's fee and travel expenses from the school's education budget since it does not sell the manufacturer's merchandise and is, therefore, not subject to the kind of perks given to music stores.

Occasionally an artist will be invited to go on a clinic tour that will be paid for by all of his sponsors. This is known as a co-op event. In many cases, however, one particular sponsor will take the lead and be the facilitator. They will act as the bank and advance the cost of all the expenses, will make all of the travel arrangements, set up advanced promotion, and book the dates with each of the hosts. Then, when the clinic tour is over, that same lead sponsor invoices the other sponsors for their agreed-upon financial commitment to the tour and cuts a check to the artist for his or her fee.

For example, if a clinic tour cost $50,000 and it was split between five sponsors, the lead sponsor would have forked out the entire $50,000 in advance. Then, each of the remaining four companies would cut the lead sponsor a check for $10,000 apiece.

If you want to be an active clinician and hit the clinic circuit, it's to your advantage to have multiple endorsements with a variety of non-competing instrument manufacturers. This way, the cost of your clinic appearances can be divided by all your sponsors, which will help keep their individual costs down and keep you busier over the long haul.

Individual commitment to a group effort—that is what makes a team work, a company work, a society work, a civilization work.

—Vince Lombardi

UNDERSTANDING THE MYSTERY OF POPULARITY

SMOKE GETS IN YOUR EYES

The instrument manufacturing and music industries are two completely different animals. It is not uncommon to be a popular player in the educational end of the music industry through clinics, teaching, books, DVDs, festival appearances, posters, ads, and interviews, yet be completely unknown in the recording and touring sides of the industry—and vice versa.

Even though you may not have heard of a particular player, this doesn't mean he or she is not prominent and influential in the world of touring and recording—typically a much more low-key side of the industry for sidemen. The reasons why many of these talented individuals are not household names amongst the musical community are many and complex.

Self-promotion certainly has something to do with it. Some busy players could care less about being known because they are just so happy to be able to make a good living in a nonchalant manner. By nature, they may not be self-promoters or interested in fame as much as they are in just making music.

Their fundamental goal is to be known by the producers, contractors, musical directors, and recording artists who hire them to play. Only a handful of sidemen are well known in both the musical instrument / educational and touring / recording camps. Either way, all players are equally important for the contribution they make to either side of the industry, whether people know their names or not.

The man is a success who has lived well,
laughed often and loved much; who has gained the
respect of intelligent men and the love of children;
who has filled his niche and accomplished his task;
who leaves the world better than he found it, whether
by an improved poppy, a perfect poem or a rescued soul;
who never lacked appreciation of earth's beauty
or failed to express it; who looked for the best
in others and gave the best he had.
—Robert Louis Stevenson

19

THE ART OF DIVERSIFICATION
EXPANDING YOUR CAREER
OPPORTUNITIES

Life is a ten-speed bike. Most of us have
gears we never use.

—Charles Schulz

Throughout my life as a creative artist, I have worn many different hats. The first money I made from music was as a DJ running my own mobile disco business. In addition to income generated by being a working musician, I have earned money as a private instructor, clinician, college professor, motivational speaker, author, magazine editor, consultant, and from royalties on products I developed. My goal has always been to make use of all my inherent gifts, so I am constantly looking for new ways to expand my horizons and challenge myself.

I consider each of these separate areas of creativity to be extensions of who I am. I want to be different tomorrow than I am today by developing more of my natural talents and continuously evolving as a creative being. I am not willing to be defined by any one particular creative skill or by any one particular era of my life, nor am I interested in living in the past or off of former glories. I appreciate my past for what it was, but I enjoy the work I am doing in the present and always look to the future.

Fortunately, from among all of these forms of expression, I have been able to maintain a good living for more than 30 years. In all honesty, though, it has never been easy, and I have had to work hard to resist the temptation to give up during tough times of transition or to be anything other than what I was uniquely created to be. I wholeheartedly agree with Ralph Waldo Emerson's proclamation, "To be yourself in a world that is constantly trying to make you something else is the greatest accomplishment."

http://4wrd.it/A.BG19

BRANCHING OUT

AFTER THE THRILL IS GONE

Once you achieve initial success as a freelance musician, there are many directions in which you can choose to go, depending upon your particular talents and interests. Many successful sidemen go on to become top-notch producers and even great songwriters. If they have business sense, they might become CEOs or A&R (Artists & Repertoire) directors for record companies, instrument manufacturers, or record company owners.

> *The successful person always has a number of projects planned, to which he looks forward. Anyone of them could change the course of his life overnight.*
>
> —Mark Caine

Some musicians are extremely gifted and have the ability to write, sing, produce, and play and may pursue all of these avenues simultaneously. Whatever the case may be, developing into a solid player first will serve as a launching pad to other aspects of the industry.

Since the music business is ever-changing, it's wise to think ahead. Always have one foot in the present and one foot in the future. If you have both feet in the future, you're in outer space, but if they are both planted in the past, you will become a dinosaur and you'll be no good to anyone because you'll be extinct!

REINVENTING YOURSELF

YOU AIN'T SEEN NOTHING YET

In order to carve out a living in this industry, you may find it necessary to diversify your skills within the broad spectrum of the music field. Doing so effectively requires a great deal of foresight, flexibility, and deliberate effort. But even through diversification, there are very few musicians who are able to make a comfortable living in the business and even fewer who earn all of their income merely by playing their instruments.

Those who have versatility with the services they provide have more options when things are slow in one area. The number-one complaint

I hear from musicians around the world is how extremely difficult it is to make a consistent living just playing an instrument. We are all united and in agreement with that truth. Diversification is one way to make the financial roller-coaster ride a little more tolerable.

If you had $10,000 to invest in your retirement and hired a top financial advisor, he or she would construct an investment portfolio that consisted of a variety of diverse equities. That way, when the market is down in one area, your assets will be growing in another and you won't suffer a total loss by having all of your eggs in one basket. The idea is to invest in equities that don't move in tandem so you can equalize the ride.

> *A good plan vigorously executed right now is far better than a perfect plan executed next week.*
> —General George S. Patton

Think of your career as a musician in the same light and you will weather the cyclical nature of the music industry much better. When the market for live playing is down, you can do studio work. When that is slow, you can teach. When teaching dries up, you can be a consultant or serve on an advisory board. When that looks bleak, you can be a music supervisor for television or motion pictures. When that's run its course, you can move into production, songwriting, or some other facet of the music industry to keep working. As a creative artist, it's important to continually expand the borders of your tents and seek out more outlets to express your gifts.

> *My interest is in the future because I am going to spend the rest of my life there.*
> —Charles Kettering

For the majority of freelance musicians, diversity is truly the key to any long-term success. Of course, there are always exceptions, but they are very few. The following list presents several opportunities that sidemen can pursue to increase revenue. This is by no means an exhaustive list, but rather some of the most typical options freelance musicians engage in after a certain point in their careers. The important thing is to always seek out new revenue sources that flow out of your natural talents and abilities. As Confucius once said, "Choose a job you love and you will never have to work a day in your life."

POPULAR SOURCES OF REVENUE FOR A SIDEMAN

PENNIES FROM HEAVEN

- Sales of your own music
- Teaching in private and formal settings, such as colleges, music schools, junior high schools, high schools, and music shops
- Conducting clinics, master classes, and workshops
- Authoring instructional books and DVDs
- Transcribing music charts as a professional copyist
- Endorsing products
- Consulting for industry-related companies, such as research and development and artist relations for instrument manufacturers, or record companies
- Selling in a music retail setting or as a rep for instrument manufacturers
- Producing recording artists or demos for music hobbyists and enthusiasts
- Arranging music
- Writing songs
- Managing a rehearsal studio
- Renting out your home studio for people who want to record
- Engineering live and in the studio
- Teching for local and national live and recorded events

ACCEPTING NEW CHALLENGES

A CHANGE IS GONNA COME

In the process of writing my first book, *The Commandments of R&B Drumming: A Comprehensive Guide to Soul, Funk & Hip Hop*, I came upon some new challenges that frightened me to death. I didn't have the foresight in school to think that I would ever have any use for typing, so I never bothered to learn. Why should I waste time learning something I would never use? I couldn't have been more ignorant if I'd tried.

The problem was that I was so intimidated by the idea of learning something new, that for a while I refused to make the necessary effort to learn. Pitifully, I relied on my wife to do the typing for me. Believe me, in her view that got old fast. My helplessness became a major source of stress for both of us.

As I got deeper into the project, there was just no way around it; I had to learn to do two things: type, and operate a computer. After a certain point in life, many of us become afraid to learn new skills, and in my case, I thought learning to use a computer was impossible.

Iron rusts from disuse; stagnant water loses its purity and in cold weather becomes frozen; even so does inaction sap the vigor of the mind.

—Leonardo da Vinci

I felt like a senior citizen who couldn't figure out how to send an e-mail, use an ATM, or program my DVR to record my favorite program, and I didn't like to think of myself in that company—in fact, I was appalled by the thought. After whining for a while, I decided to do something about my plight. I knew if I didn't get on the ball I was going to get left behind in a world that was rapidly moving past me. Since I was not mentally handicapped or dead, I was fully capable of learning to use a keyboard. If everyone else could do it, so could I. Committed to my new quest, I bought a laptop computer and a Mavis Beacon Typing Tutor program. I did a lesson each day, but I learned the most by fooling around on the computer. It was never easy for me to learn by being shown. I had to do it myself.

The key to my keyboard breakthrough was working past the frustration of learning something new. I wanted to be as good at typing as I was at playing the drums right away, forgetting that it had taken me years to hone my drumming skills. My expectations were unrealistic, and I had a good old-fashioned case of impatience. The trick was to chill out and give myself a chance to learn.

> *It's never too late to be what you might have been.*
> —George Eliot

The goal was to be a better typist each day, and as long as I made progress, that was all that mattered. Before long, I was wailing away on the computer and my typing skills blossomed.

After that, I felt as if I could learn anything new, like a portion of my brain had come alive. The way I communicated and did business was totally revolutionized; I typed letters, sent faxes, wrote e-mails, and made progress on my writing projects by leaps and bounds. It was the gateway to a new chapter in my life, a stepping-stone toward my destiny.

I can't quite express to you how great it felt to scale those mountains. For some of you, learning how to type may seem a bit trivial, but for me it was monumental. It wasn't about typing and computer skills. It was about something much heavier than that. It was about overcoming the fear of learning something new. Writing a book takes a tremendous amount of time and effort; there's no way I could have completed one in my lifetime had I not learned to type.

> *Man's mind, once stretched by a new idea, never regains its original dimensions.*
> —Oliver Wendell Holmes

Life is like a big beautiful tapestry. As we display courage to face new challenges, the tapestry is continually woven until it becomes something magnificent. The more we accomplish, the larger and more intricate the tapestry.

But without supplementing your talents with some of the essential mechanics that are necessary to flourish, your main gift will never fully blossom. Even though I had the heart of a writer and the ability to communicate, without learning how to type and operate a computer, you wouldn't be reading this book. Everyone has a mountain to climb in order to reach his or her maximum potential.

Reaching your full potential involves growing, evolving, and climbing the ladder to higher ground. I'm glad I didn't let the fact that I did poorly in high-school English class stop me from pursuing my dream of becoming a writer. Perhaps my ignorance *saved* my career as a writer. If I had realized before I started writing this book how little I knew about the technical side of writing, I may have chucked the whole idea altogether. But by the time I learned how little I knew about it all, I was almost done with this book!

Some of the world's greatest feats were accomplished by people not smart enough to know they were impossible.
—Doug Larson

THE KEYS TO LONGEVITY
THE WAY YOU DO THE THINGS YOU DO

One of the greatest pleasures I've enjoyed as a result of doing what I do for a living is that I have had the opportunity to meet a lot of wise and successful people. I've learned a great deal from pop legend Frankie Valli of Frankie Valli and the Four Seasons. The Four Seasons was inducted into the Rock & Roll Hall of Fame in 1990 and given a special tribute in *Billboard* magazine for their longevity in the industry. Frankie scored twenty-nine Top 40 hits with The Four Seasons and nine Top 40 hits as a solo artist. With The Four Seasons, his No. 1 hits were "Sherry," "Big Girls Don't Cry," "Walk Like a Man," "Rag Doll," and "December 1963 (Oh What a Night)." As a solo artist, Frankie had No. 1 hits with "My Eyes Adored You" and "Grease," and a No. 2 hit with the classic cut "Can't Take My Eyes Off of You."

The group's success spans nearly 50 years in the record industry, an unprecedented achievement in an industry as fickle as ours. Now, there's a secret to lasting that long in a business that usually spits people out just as fast as they come in, let alone being on top for so many years.

I worked with Frankie Valli for several years, and during that time we became good friends. I had the privilege of seeing firsthand some of the reasons for his enduring success. Besides his obvious talent as a singer and entertainer, I discovered that the man was relentless—a real fighter who truly believed in himself. Now, you might be thinking that we would all believe in ourselves if we had as many hits as Frankie did. But he believed in himself just as strongly when others stopped believing in him, and that is really the ultimate test.

Success is not measured by what you accomplish
but by the opposition you have encountered, and the
courage with which you have maintained the struggle
against overwhelming odds.

—Orison Swett Marden

During the time I played with Frankie, we often shared our dreams for the future with each other. I told him of my dream to write books that would inspire people. He told me about his dream to develop a Broadway musical based on his personal life story and his meteoric rise to fame with The Four Seasons.

Of course, there is a multitude of famous singers with hit records who would love to have a Broadway musical chronicling their lives and have equally compelling stories to tell. So why doesn't every famous artist have a successful musical production running? Frankie Valli had a clear vision and was willing to jump through all the hoops required to make his vision a reality.

Frankie Valli's Broadway dream, *Jersey Boys*, officially debuted in New York City in 2005 and became a huge sensation. The production won four Tony Awards in 2006 for Best Musical, Best Actor, Best Featured Actor, and Best Lighting Design, and a Grammy Award for Best Musical Show Album. In fact, it is still one of the biggest box office draws in New York City with tickets sold out months in advance. It has been so successful, that there is even talk of producing a movie based on the musical.

Despite the tremendous success he had already experienced for over 40 years in the music business, Frankie chose to dream even bigger and continue to strive for higher heights. The key to his continued success was his tenacious spirit and his willingness to accept the newer challenges that would come to oppose his dream.

> *I dread success. To have succeeded is to have finished one's business on earth, like the male spider, who is killed by the female the moment he has succeeded in his courtship. I like a state of continual becoming, with a goal in front and not behind.*
>
> —George Bernard Shaw

If I can use one word to describe Frankie it would be "committed." He was committed to everything he pursued, and he understood that there is always a cost associated with those commitments. I have tried my best to take the principles I learned from Frankie about career longevity and apply them to my life as a sideman. I made a commitment to project that fortitude and resilience onto everything I do and give myself to all of my work wholeheartedly.

> *Diligence is the mother of good luck, and God gives all things to industry.*
>
> —Benjamin Franklin

Vow to make a total commitment in all the areas highlighted below regardless of the cost, and you will undoubtedly be much closer to seeing the realization of your dreams and the manifestation of your goals.

THE COMMITMENTS

BEST THING THAT EVER HAPPENED TO ME

- Make a commitment to design a master plan for your life
- Make a commitment to practice and study your craft
- Make a commitment to reach your potential
- Make a commitment to follow through with everything you start
- Make a commitment to overcome failure, disappointments, and set-backs
- Make a commitment to achieve your goals at whatever the cost
- Make a commitment to become a better person
- Make a commitment to make excellent choices in your life
- Make a commitment to serve others with your gifts and talents
- Make a commitment to impact the lives of others and make a difference

I do the very best I know how—the very best I can; and I mean to keep on doing so until the very end.
—Abraham Lincoln

KEEPING UP WITH THE CHANGING TIMES

ROLLING WITH THE FLOW

Music is a very fickle industry filled with twists and turns that no one can accurately predict. Twenty years ago, no one could have guessed we would be seeing so much amazing technology. Technological advancements have changed the way we learn, write, play, and produce music, and this ongoing phenomenon will undoubtedly continue to do so. The fact is, popular music is constantly changing, and what's considered hip today may become passé tomorrow. Since I did not graduate from the Nostradamus School of Prophecy, I won't even attempt to make predictions about the future of the music industry or what style of music will emerge to captivate the next generations and dominate the airwaves. Still, I believe true talent and skill, when guided by vision, wisdom, and perseverance, will prevail and stand the test of time in an ever-changing industry.

> *When you can't change the direction of the wind—*
> *adjust your sails.*
>
> —Max De Pree

Sadly, there have been plenty of incredibly talented musicians left behind. Many of them simply did not stay current with the times. Perhaps they did not learn enough about business, politics, socializing, marketing, and networking. Some got strung out on drugs, others drank and smoked themselves into oblivion, and many snorted up all their profits. Quite a few lost interest or direction and got tired of the whole rat race. In some cases, the instruments they played waned in popularity and were suddenly no longer in demand.

Whatever the reason, the future belongs to those musicians who can anticipate change before it becomes obvious and are relentless in their pursuit of uncharted territory. New opportunities also come to those who commit to keeping their hearts and minds open to change. If you are so dead set on staying in the past, you will dig your own grave.

> *When one door closes, another opens; but we often look*
> *so long and so regretfully upon the closed door that we*
> *do not see the one which has opened for us.*
>
> —Alexander Graham Bell

The only way to stay on top of the music game is to stay abreast of the latest information and be hip to what's going on. This doesn't necessarily mean changing who you are with every changing tide, but you must move in the general direction things are flowing. It takes a lot of effort to follow the trends, and few people have the energy necessary to keep up with all of them.

> *Reading is to the mind what exercise is to the body.*
>
> —Sir Richard Steele

I've seen many musicians get left behind, not from a lack of talent or skill, but from laziness and complacency. They got too content with where they were, and, as a result, they lost their ambition. Eventually their progress slowed down to the point where they just didn't feel like getting back in the race. Whatever your goals may have been initially, you must be prepared to adapt your plan to the ever-changing conditions of the business. Diversify, diversify, diversify!

Let's say your original goal was to become a professional string player. After practicing for years, you discover that there are very few work opportunities for string players. This insight may cause you to move into another direction that has more potential profit.

Here's an example of what I mean. Drum machines came into prominence in the early '80s and completely revolutionized the business. This new technology also drastically changed life for thousands of drummers. Instead of hiring live drummers, many of the hit records used machines to produce the beat. As a result, a tremendous amount of the studio work for both records and demos dried up. Drum machines took over and many drummers were forced to make some serious decisions about their futures: Do I want to get into the whole computer drum programming thing, remain a live player, or get out of the business?

The point is that you have to be prepared to adapt your plans to changing environmental conditions. If you can adjust, adapt, and overcome, then you're still in the ball game. But if not, then you're out.

Opportunities multiply as they are seized.
They die when neglected. Life is a long line
of opportunities.
—John Wicker

Take a look at the medical profession. Due to incredible technological breakthroughs and increased knowledge and understanding, research and development companies are constantly releasing advanced equipment, techniques, and improved procedures for every aspect of medicine. Patients are becoming increasingly aware of all the latest developments and are no longer willing to go to a doctor who's stuck in the Stone Age. Everyone wants to go to a doctor who knows the latest state-of-the-art procedures, owns the newest equipment, and is aware of the latest information that will benefit the patient. Physicians who fail to keep up with progress will eventually get fewer and fewer calls.

It's the same for musicians; we've got to keep growing and learning all the time. Those who stay on top of things are in the highest demand, because everyone wants to work with the hippest musicians.

THE TEN COMMANDMENTS OF SUCCESS

AIN'T NO MOUNTAIN HIGH ENOUGH

- Dream
- Persist
- Believe
- Refine
- Learn
- Adapt
- Strategize
- Persevere
- Pursue
- Serve

The world around us is moving rapidly toward advanced technology that is certain to astound us. No one can accurately predict what the implications are for the future of our industry. Where it will go, nobody knows, but one thing is for certain—technology is not going away.

Modern technology will open up vast possibilities for musicians that we never dreamed possible, and the way we do business will most definitely be revolutionized in the process. Innovative ways for musicians to make money and promote themselves are being discovered daily. But these newer methods are reserved for the brave, bold, and tenacious. Take the challenge, work hard, and understand that the pathway to realized dreams is filled with many twists and turns that no one can accurately predict. The key to continued success in this business is a willingness to keep marching forward in spite of change and a refusal to let go of your dreams.

> *All men dream, but not equally. Those who dream*
> *by night in the dusty recesses of their minds wake in the*
> *day to find that it was vanity: but dreamers of the day*
> *are dangerous men, for they may act on their dreams*
> *with open eyes, to make it possible.*
>
> —T.E. Lawrence

20

The Art of Self-Control
Living Free from Addictions

*There is little that can withstand a man
who can conquer himself.*

—Louis XIV

It was painful to witness someone I loved like a brother so willingly throw his life away. Tragically, he died of a heroin overdose. This immensely talented musician was seduced by the dark side and became yet another casualty of rock 'n' roll. He was a genius whose life was cut short out of sheer ignorance and by thinking himself invincible. His senseless death bothered me for the longest time. I couldn't stop thinking about the wife and children he'd left behind because he selfishly indulged in self-destructive behavior that common sense dictates will inevitably lead to death.

*It is only possible to live happily ever after
on a day-to-day basis.*

—Margaret Bonnano

Unfortunately, I could tell many more such stories of friends who died or lost it all due to some form of substance abuse. Drug and alcohol addiction have no class distinctions; people from all ethnicities and economic backgrounds have been overtaken. Maybe I'm living in some sort of fantasyland, but I thought the dream was to work hard, achieve your goals, and have something to show for the great sacrifice it took to get there. For far too many, that dream turned into a nightmare starring the grim reaper.

The concept of denying oneself any form of pleasure is foreign to the self-obsessed world of entertainment. With "sex, drugs, and rock 'n' roll" as the mantra of

http://4wrd.it/A.BG20

the industry, the concept of restraint hardly fits into the picture. It seems as though those who live that lifestyle believe they are invincible and that death is for other people, but there's no doubt that all the casualties of rock 'n' roll had the same delusion before their untimely deaths. Sadly, too many individuals perish before reaching their full potential as artists and people. Death is just too high a price to pay for any form of escape.

> *Your life is like a coin. You can spend it any way you wish, but you can spend it only once.*
> —Lillian Dickson

My motive for speaking out on this subject comes from a sincere desire to see people reach their potential, achieve their goals, and live purposeful lives that are both rewarding and fulfilling. This subject is very personal to me as it has been a grievous experience to see many close friends die and others destroy their lives and those of their families. Regretfully, this unnecessary pain and anguish could have been avoided entirely. After all, everyone has a choice of whether or not to abuse drugs and alcohol; it's not like being born with a congenital birth defect or contracting a deadly disease that is beyond your control. The ball is fully in your court.

SUBSTANCE ABUSERS
RUNNING WITH THE DEVIL

Whether prescribed or not, drugs continue to have a profound impact on the entertainment industry. Think of some of the great jazz musicians whose downfalls were related to substance abuse on some level: Tommy Dorsey, Stan Getz, Jaco Pastorious, Chet Baker, John Coltrane, Billie Holiday, and Charlie Parker, to name a few.

Let's not leave out some of the rock legends who shared the same fate: Janis Joplin, Jimi Hendrix, Ike Turner, John Simon Ritchie (a.k.a. Sid Vicious), Jim Morrison of the Doors, Bobby Hatfield of The Righteous Brothers, John Bonham of Led Zeppelin, and Kurt Cobain of Nirvana.

Unfortunately, the list could go on and on. Each of these people was tormented as a result of self-induced addictions. The number of musicians linked to overdose, arrest, admitted drug use, or are undergoing recovery is staggering!

*A man's conquest of himself dwarfs
the ascent of Everest.*

—Eli J. Schiefer

The drug-related deaths of high profile celebrities such as John Belushi, Chris Farley, River Phoenix, Anna Nicole Smith, and Heath Ledger have done little to dissuade others from joining the party. Not to mention all of the current celebrities who are in the media on a regular basis for some form of substance abuse drama. Fortunately, they are still living, but for how long? Since many are following in the footsteps of those who have fallen before them, how can they expect their fate to be different? Beckoning musicians and entertainers of all kinds to choose this path of death and destruction is an unbelievably evil force that few understand.

I have learned a great deal about success and its delusions after working and mingling with many celebrities. Many superstars seem to have what every musician wants—fame, fortune, and respect—yet many remain unhappy, unfulfilled, and unsatisfied. There is a spiritual void and an emptiness that cannot be filled with material success. If it could, there wouldn't be so many successful entertainers with huge drug, alcohol, and personal problems.

*The foolish man seeks happiness in the distance,
the wise grows it under his feet.*

—James Oppenheim

THE LOGIC OF STEERING CLEAR OF ADDICTIONS
I CAN'T GET NEXT TO YOU

Over the course of my career, I have been around some of the biggest partiers in the business, and I have seen plenty of musicians get fired from really great gigs as a result of their habitual use of drugs and alcohol. No matter how talented you are, a drug or alcohol addiction could prevent you from getting certain gigs and experiencing longevity in the music business. Many recording artists won't want to chance working with you because the risks are too great. Even if you do end up playing with a band that likes to party, they're not going to put up with you if your partying interferes with your work and their ability to make money. If you become a known liability, chances are you'll have a very short career.

I have never been drunk or high in my entire life. I don't tell you that to make myself look like a saint or to pat myself on the back. I simply had no interest in drugs or alcohol because they looked so obviously destructive. A musician's life is a hard life in the best of circumstances, and I thought that only a fool would add to the hardship by flirting with disaster.

> *We forge the chains we wear in life.*
>
> —Charles Dickens

To me, refraining from this lifestyle was just a matter of common sense, so resisting the temptation to indulge was not difficult. I understood that the laws of sowing and reaping are always in operation in life and are not subject to my approval or even my awareness or understanding. I only needed to abide by them in order to prosper.

It is truly a blessing to be able to make a living playing music, and I would never want to do anything to jeopardize that situation. I grew up with such an intense desire to make it as a drummer that I could not conceive of letting anything destructive keep me from living the dream God placed in my heart. Like a freight train of positive energy, I was too busy trying to build something that I had no time or desire to become a demolition man.

> *One principal reason why men are so often useless is*
> *that they neglect their own profession or calling*
> *and divide and shift their attention among a multitude*
> *of objects and pursuits.*
>
> —Nathaniel Emmons

My experience with substance abuse has not been as a participant, but as someone standing on the sidelines closely observing the madness of the game. As I witnessed the whirlwind of destruction take its course, I was amazed at how many others were eager to play a game they had no possibility of winning. I was deeply saddened by how easily someone could throw away a lifetime of opportunities by letting substances become more important than their music, families, careers, or lives.

Many were duped into believing that being a major mess-up was somehow cool. I see nothing cool about purposely blowing incredible opportunities that may never come back or limiting your potential as a musician and human being. You cannot afford to mess up or else all of your impassioned efforts may end up being for nothing and you'll end up miserable. You'll stay on the ground with the beagles instead of soaring in the sky with the eagles as you were meant to do.

On the positive side, I have known several famous musicians who have traveled the long road to recovery and mustered up the courage necessary to overcome their addictions. Today they consider themselves lucky to be alive, as they admit to having tempted fate for far too long. Many of them have made a 180-degree turnaround in their lives and are now into health, fitness, and positive behavior, so there is hope for anyone who may already be struggling with addictions. But remember, the choice is ultimately yours.

> *Great is the art of beginning, but greater is*
> *the art of ending.*
> —Henry Wadsworth Longfellow

ENTERING THE MIND OF THE USER

SLIPPIN' INTO DARKNESS

In our continuous battle to overcome the massive substance abuse problem in our society, we have to logically and realistically analyze why people turn to drugs and alcohol in the first place.

In the process of writing this chapter, I had very in-depth and candid conversations with several substance abusers. Although they wish to remain anonymous, they were quite eager to help others avoid making the same mistakes they have made. The following conclusions and opinions are based on those conversations.

I WANT TO BE LOVED BY YOU

ACCEPTANCE: One of the most significant reasons people of all ages get involved with drugs and alcohol is to be accepted by their peers. The fear of being rejected by the so-called "in crowd" scares many into partying. Not being invited to the "cool" parties and welcomed into the allegedly hip inner circle can trigger a "follow the leader" mentality. People tend to be like sheep and are easily led astray by those who are assumed to be cool.

To overcome this problem, you must change your way of thinking. You are an individual, not a clone. You don't want to be like everyone else, do you? Isn't it a little embarrassing when you go somewhere wearing a hip new outfit only to find five other people wearing the exact same outfit? You see what I'm saying? You don't feel very unique, do you?

As musicians, our goal should be to achieve a unique sound and style. There is nothing gained by being an exact replica of someone else, and in most cases, you wouldn't be praised for it, anyway. Hopefully, you wouldn't jump off the Empire State Building just because everyone else was doing it, so why would you indulge in deadly substance abuse just because a few others are? If you lose friends because you won't join in with them, then they definitely aren't true friends. You're much better off without them—bad company corrupts good character.

Avoid using cigarettes, alcohol, and drugs as alternatives
to being an interesting person.
—Marilyn vos Savant

In my experience, people eventually accepted me the way I was even though I didn't party with them. Let's get real; drugs don't make you a cool person or fun to be with! Being strung out or intoxicated doesn't give you a charming personality and make you attractive, talented, or skillful.

EVERYBODY PLAYS THE FOOL

CURIOSITY: Another big reason why people start to experiment with drugs is that as human beings we are curious by nature. I suspect all who become addicts start out with the idea that they will just dabble a bit. They falsely believe they are in total control of their habit. That is a total delusion. Time flies when you just dabble, and before you know it, there go 20 years of your life.

Just as with all habits, there is a danger of becoming addicted. The best way to prevent that is to avoid experimenting in the first place. Remember the little saying you heard when you were a kid, "curiosity killed the cat." You should not experiment with some things because the end result could be detrimental to your existence.

> *Time flies when you just dabble, and before you know it, there go 20 years of your life.*

The word "fear" is often associated with something bad, but fear can also be a good thing. It is fear that keeps us from running in the middle of the freeway in front of a semi truck doing 90 miles per hour. If you did, you would be flattened like a pancake and the state troopers would have to use a spatula to scrape your dead carcass off the road.

Fear is a survival instinct. When we ignore that instinct and our sense of reason, that's when the trouble begins. Many people are addictive by nature. I recognized that I had an addictive personality at an early age, and fear kept me away from drugs and alcohol. I knew I needed to channel that energy into something that would be beneficial, so I focused my attention on music, instead. I have never regretted that decision.

YOU GOT ME GOING IN CIRCLES

PROBLEMS, PROBLEMS, PROBLEMS: People often resort to drugs and alcohol as a form of escape from the hassles of daily life or to numb the effects of a major crisis. But once again, let's use our brains. It doesn't take a genius to figure out that getting drunk or stoned isn't going to do a single thing to help solve your problems or lessen the pressure. Once you come back down to earth and you're off that artificial high, you are still faced with the same dilemma and usually further in the hole.

People with high-stress jobs claim to indulge in drugs or alcohol because of the intense pressure. That's their excuse to partake, and to me that's a total cop-out. Life will always have trials and tribulations and one must decide to deal with them logically as they arise, but most people tend to magnify their problems rather than dwell on the possible solutions.

Many problems have solutions and can be overcome by optimism, hard work, perseverance, faith, and prayer. None of us can control what life dishes out, but we can certainly control our responses to those things. Learn to move forward despite what you are going through.

> *We can't solve problems by using the same kind of*
> *thinking we used when we created them.*
> —Albert Einstein

Partying is simply irresponsible. How can you solve your problems by being irresponsible? All that does is create an even bigger problem. Accept the challenges of life so that you may feel the glory of victory.

CLOUD NINE

LOW SELF-ESTEEM: Many people turn to drugs and alcohol as a quick way to heal the wounds of early childhood. That is like trying to put a band-aid on a huge open sore—it will never work. A lack of affirmation throughout one's formative years can certainly be the cause of a low self-image. Bad parenting, negative experiences, a lack of good role models, and a lack of attention can all contribute to emotional dysfunction. Unless you deal with those issues, you will always struggle with them. They won't just go away.

> *Circumstances are the rulers of the weak; but they are*
> *the instruments of the wise.*
> —Samuel Glover

Low self-esteem also leads to an unhealthy need to impress others as a means of self-validation. Behaving recklessly is a way of crying out for desparately needed attention. People with low self-esteem tend to abuse substances in an attempt to bury deeply rooted hurt and pain, but running away from problems won't solve them. Counseling is the key to getting over the ghosts of your past. It takes honesty to face problems head on and courage to undergo the process necessary to be set free from bondage.

DAZED AND CONFUSED

THE RUSH: The euphoric feeling of being high is another trap that catches people. How can you really feel good from something you know is artificially induced? It's not reality, it's an altered state. It's fake, and it doesn't last. Once you come down from an artificial high, you feel 10 times worse than before. Choose to get high on something that lasts—an accomplishment, a friendship, or anything real, for God's sake!

Take full account of the excellencies which you possess and in gratitude remember how you would hanker after them if you had them not.
—Marcus Aurelius

I get a natural high every time I play my drums, play with my children, or hang out with my wife or close friends. There are so many healthy alternatives that can make you feel great, but you'll never embrace them as long as you buy into the false reality of substance abuse.

I LOVE THE NIGHTLIFE

BOREDOM: For musicians on the road or in the studio, boredom can become a big problem. People with too much unproductive time on their hands are notorious for getting into trouble. You need to have something healthy to occupy your heart, mind, and soul when your working environment becomes mundane.

Do not allow idleness to deceive you; for while you give him today, he steals tomorrow from you.
—Crowquill

Boredom can happen no matter what you do or where you live, which is one reason why it's so important to use your free time to do something that leads to fulfillment.

OTHER IMPORTANT FACTS TO CONSIDER
I CAN'T GO FOR THAT (NO CAN DO)

YOUR HEALTH: In addition to all the other negatives, abusing drugs and/or alcohol is extremely harmful to your physical body, your mind, and your spirit. We are living in a world on the brink of environmental disaster, and it's hard enough to stay healthy as it is. If you indulge in drugs and alcohol, you might as well throw your health out the window. Sooner or later you are going to encounter medical problems due to the poison you are putting in your body. Respect yourself enough to take good care of your body; no one else will do it for you.

MONEY: If nothing else convinces you to stay away from drugs and drinking, consider this fact alone: these indulgences are expensive! We've all heard horror stories about people who have sold all their possessions and stolen from loved ones just to support an addiction. In desperation, users financially bankrupt themselves and burn bridges with people who once trusted them. Money is hard to come by these days, so don't waste it.

If you count all your assets you'll always show a profit.
—Robert Quillen

There must be a million things to spend your hard-earned money on that can benefit you in some way. What about new musical equipment, a new sound system for your home or car, private lessons, music school, or building your music library with iTunes downloads? Invest your money in developing the talents and abilities you were given and towards the fulfillment of your dreams. Don't invest in something that yields no dividends, or worse, something that produces a deficit in your life!

THE TRUTH ABOUT SUBSTANCE ABUSE
WASTED DAYS AND WASTED NIGHTS

If I said you couldn't be a successful musician if you have an alcohol or drug problem, I would be lying. There have been many great musicians who were known addicts all throughout their careers. In most cases, however, abusing substances will eventually catch up with you and negatively affect your life—personally, spiritually, and professionally. The former addicts I spoke with agreed on two things: they wish they had never gotten into substances, and they had no regrets when they finally quit.

Young people are often operating under the delusion that if they emulate the drug and alcohol addicted behaviors of their rock star idols, they too will be successful. They associate those behaviors with success, but the mistake is in emulating their addictions rather than their work ethic and tenacity.

Hold yourself responsible for a higher standard than anybody else expects of you. Never excuse yourself.
—Henry Ward Beecher

Think of how much farther those rock stars could have gone in every aspect of their lives without destroying their potential with substances. You won't suddenly grace the cover of a music magazine, drive a Ferrari, or blow everyone away with your musical talent just because you get high. I have never met anyone who can attribute his or her success to drugs or drinking! That behavior does not promote your success: only talent, vision, hard work, and persistence can do that.

I have tried to present logical reasons to keep you off the path of substance abuse. I hope you make the right choice and enjoy the beautiful gift of music and life. Abusing drugs and alcohol will not bring anything but trouble and serious regret to your life. Addiction is one of the most evil forces known to man, and it has shattered the hopes and dreams of countless people.

Our culture's fascination with the dark side deceives too many people into thinking that being a user is somehow romantic and full of glorious light. The doom and gloom of being a junkie has been made into something chic and glamorous, but it eventually gets ugly. Unfortunately, cool images in books, movies, magazines, and videos don't jibe with the reality of addiction.

*That's all drugs and alcohol do, they cut off your
emotions in the end.*

—Ringo Starr

Consider the massive destruction addiction has on so many lives, careers, families, finances, relationships, and health, not to mention the devastation to our minds through a lost sense of hope. Anything that can account for all this damage is surely not something to greet with open arms. Play with fire and you'll get burned every time. When something is more powerful than you are, it's best to stand back and leave it alone.

You have to choose whether you are going to build or destroy. It's imperative to have a mission that motivates you and a positive inner force that gives you purpose. Invest your time, energy, and money in that purpose and in the pursuit of your dreams and goals by developing the talent you were given. You are responsible for your own destiny. Build your future with desire, determination, and discipline, and let nothing negative stand between you and your dreams. Drugs and alcohol lead to disconnection, destruction, discontentment, and disaster.

*The only true happiness comes from squandering
ourselves for a purpose.*

—William Cowper

21

THE ART OF COMMITMENT
THRIVING IN YOUR PERSONAL RELATIONSHIPS

If we discovered that we only had five minutes left
to say all that we wanted to say, every telephone booth
would be occupied by people calling other people
to stammer that they loved them.

—Christopher Morley

It was a stunningly beautiful California afternoon, and one of the most special days of my life. Our close friends gathered in our backyard on that crisp autumn day to witness my wife, Renee, and me renew our wedding vows in honor of our first decade of marriage.

This ceremony was even more special than our wedding day had been because our two children were in attendance and were able to see us renew our commitment to one another. Our son, Jarod, was the ring bearer, and our daughter, Jordan, was the flower girl. All dressed in white, they looked like precious little angels. It was a huge celebration!

I have thoroughly enjoyed the wondrous joys of making music and have always maintained a deep appreciation for all of life's other incredible gifts, but when I think of the greatest gift God ever gave to mankind, it was clearly our capacity to love and be part of a family.

The deafening sound of screaming fans simply cannot compare to the angelic sound of my family welcoming me home from a long trip. Hearing my children yell, "Daddy, daddy, daddy, daddy, you're home!" with genuine excitement, and seeing the warmth of my wife's smile drowns out the resonance of every other competing noise. That echo of love is truly the sound of music to my ears; I wouldn't exchange it for anything in the world.

Thriving in one's personal relationships is the hallmark of meaningful living—the greatest of all human

http://4wrd.it/A.BG21

achievements. Accomplishing this, however, is also one of the greatest challenges you'll ever face in your life. For those of us in the entertainment industry especially, solidarity in personal relationships can seem elusive.

The magic allure of show business can be attractive to those who haven't seen the smoke and mirrors behind the scenes. It's definitely not all the glitz and glamour many have been led to believe. The deeper innocent bystanders delve into this world, the more disconcerting they may find it.

> *Thriving in one's personal relationships is the hallmark of meaningful living—the greatest of all human achievements.*

Dating a musician can seem fun and exciting in the beginning stages of a relationship, but maintaining that relationship over the long haul can be very challenging.

The unpredictable nature of a musician's lifestyle can make it difficult to earn a living, but the musician at least makes it by choice. For all the garbage we put up with in this business, we are at least able to enjoy the privilege of expressing ourselves and doing what brings us the greatest joy—playing music. But to be romantically involved with a musician can be far less exciting and tremendously challenging. The freelance lifestyle is filled with uncertainty, and some people are simply not designed for this type of ride.

NAVIGATING THROUGH ROMANTIC RELATIONSHIPS

WHY CAN'T WE LIVE TOGETHER

Unless your love interest is experiencing the same kind of spiritual high that comes from doing what they love for a vocation, there can be the tendency to become envious of what you do. While you are sun bathing on the beach in the South of France, your partner could be back at home fixing the hot water heater. While you're going back onstage for an encore in Athens, Greece, your significant other may be apologizing to the phone company for a late payment and begging them to reconnect your service.

Household emergencies have an uncanny way of happening when you're too far away to do anything about them. If you throw children into the equation, it can get crazy! Then there are the huge phone bills you incur in an effort to keep your relationship afloat while you're away. Even though you have the option of texting, instant messaging, or doing an online video chat, there are times when talking on the phone the old-fashioned way is far more convenient and absolutely necessary.

In order to endure a relationship over the long haul, the partner of a freelance musician must possess a very unique and rare kind of strength not found in most people. To increase your odds of relationship success, look for someone with an independent nature and plenty of self-confidence—he or she will quite often have to deal with things alone that most couples have the luxury of tackling together.

Over time, the stress and strain of a musician's lifestyle can cause resentment. Your love interest won't always understand you, your music, or what seems to be ridiculous ambitions. The moment the sobering reality of living with a musician kicks in, the honeymoon is over.

> *There are three keys to more abundant living: caring about others, daring for others, and sharing with others.*
> —William Ward

Music is certainly not the only profession that requires frequent travel, but if you are a professional athlete or a business executive, you are at least making serious money, and that makes the ride a little sweeter for your mate. The financial struggle experienced by many musicians and those who love us can be very taxing.

Resentment can also be a big issue, and it can manifest in many forms. It's not uncommon for the partners of struggling musicians to earn quite a bit more money, and if they start to feel like they are bankrolling a music career that isn't really taking off, resentment can take root.

Because people in the creative arts garner so much attention, partners may feel insignificant. Even though what your partner does for a living is just as important as what you do, people tend to get more excited about you being a musician. Your partner may also have to contend with fans and groupies. This kind of adulation can be a huge barrier in a relationship if your partner happens to have a strong need for that same kind of attention. It can then become a competition of sorts, which can cause tension and frustration.

> *Adversity is another way to measure the*
> *greatness of individuals.*
>
> —Lou Holtz

I have seen this business destroy many relationships, marriages, and families. Sexual promiscuity is one of the main culprits, as is excessive partying and a general lack of responsibility. Relationships take work, and not being around often enough to nurture them causes many break-ups. Financial hardships also take their toll.

PRIMARY REASONS FOR RELATIONSHIP PROBLEMS

GO YOUR OWN WAY

- Self-centeredness
- Lack of quality time together
- Unwillingness to work things out
- Financial hardship
- Lack of hope
- Lack of courage
- Jealousy
- Resentment
- Infidelity

Because relationships are an essential part of everyone's life, giving some serious thought to how much of yourself you are willing to invest in others is crucial to the success of those relationships.

To love and be loved is the greatest need of every human being. The personal choices you make in terms of how you express that love will have a huge impact on your overall happiness and your music. It's hard to focus and make beautiful music when you are miserable.

*In my experience, the best creative work is never done
when one is unhappy.*

—Albert Einstein

The following is a list of partner traits that are not conducive to a healthy relationship for someone pursuing music as a career. If any of these is displayed for any length of time in your significant other, your relationship could end up shipwrecked.

THE RELATIONSHIP RED FLAGS

LOVE ON THE ROCKS

- Someone who is not very self-reliant or comfortable being alone

- Someone who likes to plan everything in advance and greatly detests plans being changed or canceled

- Someone who demands excessive attention

- Someone who absolutely demands financial security and stability

- Someone who is not secure with themselves

- Someone who is unwilling to endure the tough times

- Someone who does not understand what it is to have extreme passion for something

---

*Constant kindness can accomplish much. As the sun
makes ice melt, kindness causes misunderstanding,
mistrust and hostility to evaporate.*

—Albert Schweitzer

BUILDING A SUCCESSFUL RELATIONSHIP

I WILL ALWAYS LOVE YOU

We live in a world that is totally narcissistic. The word "self" permeates our society in toxic amounts. It rears its ugly head in common terms like self-centered, self-absorbed, and self-indulgent, all of which describe the root source—selfishness. There is even a magazine called *Self*. With selfishness as the cultural mantra, it should come as no surprise that ravaged marriages and broken homes are commonplace. It's no wonder so few relationships last.

Still, despite all of the relationship challenges we face in our society, I do believe with the right heart, a positive attitude, and a willingness to put the needs of your partner ahead of your own, that freelance musicians can thrive in their personal relationships. I experienced one failed marriage very early on in my career and learned a lot from that experience.

> *Selfishness is the greatest curse of the human race.*
> —W. E. Gladstone

I was on the road traveling through Europe for about three months when my first marriage began to fall apart at the seams. After I got back from the tour, my wife informed me on my birthday that she was having an affair and wanted a separation. That was the most terrible way to celebrate what had always been treated as a special day. It rocked my world.

Nevertheless, I was willing to forgive her and tried my best to reconcile. It was my sincere hope that we could start all over and try to salvage the marriage, but she was unwilling and wanted to go through with the divorce. My heart was completely broken in two and it was the worst emotional time of my life.

> *Loyalty is rare. It can only be proven under test.*
> —Alfred Armand Montapert

Reflecting on that relationship, my first big mistake was to marry someone who was not able to handle being alone very well. I can see we didn't have a very healthy relationship in the first place, but we were young and didn't really know any better. After the divorce, I vowed I would look much more closely at the character of the women I was interested in pursuing.

As they say, time heals all wounds, and in time I opened my heart once more and was ready to take a chance on love again. I am so glad that I didn't let that first failure prevent me from believing that faithful people can still be found and that true love does conquer all. Fortunately, I found Renee, the love of my life, and asked her to marry me. It proved to be the smartest decision I have ever made, and our relationship has gotten better with each passing day.

> *One word frees us of all the weight and pain of life:*
> *That word is love.*
>
> —Sophocles

Even in the best of circumstances, marriage is no easy undertaking. Ultimately, you get out of it what you put into it. It has taken an incredible amount of hard work, selflessness, and perseverance to get my marriage to where it is today. Marriage is not for quitters, cowards, the lazy, or the unfaithful. Committed relationships are for those who want to mature and grow, and for those who are eager and willing to learn the true meaning of love.

Building a great marriage in the midst of the music industry doesn't happen by accident. I have learned two important things about building a solid relationship: I need to serve my wife by giving her my absolute best, and I need to be faithful to her in all ways. A marital relationship requires a true personal sacrifice from both people. The goal is for the two of you to become one so that the sum is greater than the parts.

This kind of thinking is so countercultural to our "Me, me, me—instant gratification" world. The only relationships that truly work are those in which both people put the needs of the other before their own. To many people, that sounds like the language of aliens. A good marriage has so many incredible benefits that are so often overlooked in today's Hollywood "live for the moment" mentality; a world where people jump from one partner to another just as soon as they get bored. Stubborn individuals refuse to deal with anything difficult or address their own shortcomings, because everything is about them.

So rather than changing themselves, they change partners and start the dance all over again. But just like the process of working on weaknesses in our musicianship, tremendous joys result from being willing to address and work on our personal weaknesses. It's called personal growth, but unfortunately there are many people who are content with remaining unchanged.

> *Two are better than one, because they have a good*
> *return for their work: if one falls down, his friend can*
> *help him up. But pity the man who falls and has no one*
> *to help him up!*
> —Ecclesiastes 4:9-10, NIV

Marriage in its optimum state is a place to share all of life's struggles and victories with that special someone you love. A genuinely loving marriage is a safe haven of trust where you can be vulnerable and share your innermost feelings.

You are far better equipped for dealing with all of life's challenges when there are two of you than going it alone. With each of you pulling your own weight, you and your spouse can split the overwhelming daily responsibilities that keep 21st-century life moving forward. My wife and I are a team. Our own unique strengths add to the success of the marriage and family. It's hard to imagine navigating through the obstacle courses that life presents without having someone you love and are committed to by your side.

> *It is better to be faithful than famous.*
> —Theodore Roosevelt

Being in a happy marriage has not only given me unspeakable joy in my heart and soul, it has also increased my productivity. Because I am stable and centered, I am able to get a laser-sharp focus on my personal, spiritual, and vocational goals and pursue even bigger dreams. Being in constant pursuit of the next one-night stand consumes copious amounts of time and still leaves you empty and disconnected from the deeper relationships we are meant to experience as human beings.

I look at my marriage the same way I look at playing a song. My role in both cases is that of a servant. If I serve my wife well, I will enjoy the benefits of marriage through the incomparable gifts of love, peace, joy, trust, and fulfillment.

> *If a man hasn't discovered something that he will die for, he isn't fit to live.*
>
> —Martin Luther King Jr.

THE KEYS TO A SUCCESSFUL RELATIONSHIP

I WOULD DIE 4 U

- Love
- Sacrifice
- Kindness
- Faithfulness
- Trust
- Listening
- Friendship
- Time
- Communication
- Commitment
- Self-Control
- Reliability
- Wisdom
- Hope
- Patience
- Forgiveness
- Perseverance

> *Love is patient, love is kind. It does not envy, it does not boast, it is not proud. It does not dishonor others, it is not self-seeking, it is not easily angered, it keeps no record of wrongs. Love does not delight in evil but rejoices with the truth. It always protects, always trusts, always hopes, always perseveres. Love never fails.*
>
> —1 Corinthians 13:4-8 (NIV)

RAISING CHILDREN

MY FATHER'S EYES

One of the most daunting tasks you will ever encounter is raising emotionally stable, well-adjusted children. I absolutely love everything that I do for a living, but nothing gratifies me more and gives more depth to my life than being a father! Having grown up without one, I am whole-heartedly committed to being the best father I can be. When I was a young boy, I vowed that I would never let my children feel the pain of abandonment that I endured.

Since being on the road so much makes parenthood a challenge, I made some sacrificial choices early on in my role as a father to lessen the sting of my travel and give my children as much of my time as was humanly possible.

When my children were very young, I averaged between 50 and 100 dates per year, including one-off concerts, clinics, and speaking engagements. To minimize the impact on my home life, I traveled strategically. For example, if I had a one-off engagement on Saturday afternoon in New York, I took the latest flight possible from Los Angeles on Friday night. Most of the time, I arrived at my destination in the wee hours of the morning on Saturday, and by the time I picked up my bags and settled at my hotel, it was time to head to the gig for sound check.

> *Having kids has been a fantastic thing for me. It's meant that I'm a little more balanced. In my twenties I worked massively, hardly took a vacation at all. Now, I, with the help of my wife, I'm always making sure I've got a good balance of how I spend my time.*
> —Bill Gates

After flying all night on the plane I was totally exhausted, so it was hard to go right to work and play my best. It was taxing on my body to be sure, but by leaving on the red-eye, I had all day Friday with my children. Most of my colleagues left on Thursday so they would have one day to get acclimated and settled in New York before having to play the gig. That certainly would have been less wear and tear on my body, but I was willing to make the sacrifice to give my children another full day with their daddy.

Everyone else booked flights back home much later in the day so that they could sleep in after the gig, but I was always on the earliest flight possible back to Los Angeles. By the time the gig was over and I got something to eat and went back to the hotel to pack, it was already 2:00 a.m. Then I would set up a wake-up call for 3:30 a.m. to catch a 6:30 a.m. flight. It was pretty brutal, but by arriving on Sunday morning I had the full day with my wife and kids. Most of the other dads lost three days with their families by choosing to fly at the times they did, but I only lost a third of that. If I had 70 one-off dates in a particular year, my wife and kids only missed me for 70 days instead of 210 days!

> *Perhaps the very best question that you can memorize and repeat, over and over, is "what is the most valuable use of my time right now?"*
>
> —Brian Tracy

Even though it was extremely tough to endure that kind of travel schedule, the sacrifice was well worth it. I knew how important it was for me to be home as much as humanly possible during the all-important formative years of my children's lives. As a result, my family has grown strong and extremely close in an industry that is filled with casualties in the arena of family life.

I am living proof that it is possible to be a busy working musician who travels around the world and still has a happy family life at home.

> *A happy family is but an earlier heaven.*
>
> —George Bernard Shaw

In order to accomplish this kind of personal success, you must work very hard to ensure that love permeates your home in real ways. It takes a bona fide effort, but to me family is everything, and no one had to talk me into spending more time with mine. Over the years, many people have asked me what my favorite gig is. My answer has always been the same—my favorite gig is being a father!

LEARNING HOW TO MULTITASK

WE CAN WORK IT OUT

One of the biggest dilemmas for a musician is maintaining some semblance of order in his or her life. Because the life of the average musician is inconsistent, achieving balance is an extremely challenging proposition—it certainly has been perplexing in my own life. How do you find time for all the professional demands and still accommodate your personal needs?

If you do find a way to attend to all your present responsibilities and strive toward your future goals, it won't be by accident. I tend to have tunnel vision, and because of that I was not a good juggler in my early days. It was much easier for me to dig wholeheartedly into one thing than it was to work on a few different things at the same time.

Modern life, however, requires multitasking. If you want to get the most out of life, you must learn to drop whatever you are immersed in at a moment's notice and take care of each crisis that demands your immediate attention. Over the years, I've worked very hard to become a master juggler; now I can keep several balls in the air at the same time.

For example, I would have loved to have been able to concentrate on the writing of this book with no major interruptions, distractions, or responsibilities competing for my attention. Instead, I had to learn how to keep this project moving forward while working, traveling, spending time with my family, handling domestic obligations, and of course eating, exercising, and sleeping. I had to juggle like a clown if I wanted to stay employed in the circus of life and accomplish all that I envisioned.

> *If you can't ride two horses at once,*
> *you shouldn't be in the circus.*
> —American Proverb

To accomplish a great deal in your life, you must learn to be like a shepherd. The job of a shepherd is to guide his or her flock so the animals are moving toward greener pastures. At times, shepherds have to go after lost sheep, but they always go back to the flock. It's the same with life; you may get sidelined by events or circumstances, but you should always maintain focus on the main event.

Maintaining balance is no easy feat, and despite the number of balls I have in the air at every moment of the waking day, I have learned when to drop everything and just chill out. Since I have learned how to effectively utilize my time, I no longer feel guilty about taking time out for fun. After all, what's the point of all this hard work if one can't occasionally take time out to enjoy some of the other great gifts of life? Work will always be there waiting in the wings.

> *You must master your time rather than becoming*
> *a slave to the constant flow of events and demands*
> *of your time. And you must organize your life to*
> *achieve balance, harmony and inner peace.*
> —Brian Tracy

Although too much work will put you into an early grave, squandering too much time will dwarf your potential and limit your achievements and your ability to impact others. Choosing to live totally carefree will lead to low self-esteem, boredom, and complacency and will zap your purpose for living. Each of us must strive to maintain a healthy balance between work and play; that is the ultimate recipe for happiness.

THE IMPORTANCE OF TRUE FRIENDS

LEAN ON ME

The creative life of a musician is filled with love and laughter, but it is also plagued with great pain and sorrow. In order to withstand the hardships that come with the territory, you need true friends who will be there during the tough times and when you have victories to celebrate. Accomplishments mean very little without friends with whom to share them.

There is a vast difference between casual acquaintances, business partners, and genuine friends. True friendship is based on unconditional love. In order to ensure success from a business standpoint, it's necessary to establish relationships with as many industry people as possible, but you also need to have a few real friends with whom you can share your struggles and bare your soul; people who will not judge you, but encourage and affirm you.

True friends will shoot it to you straight and level with you honestly when you veer off track. We all have blind spots that only our closest friends can see. It's hard enough to make it in this world with good friends, but it is virtually impossible to make it without any.

> *Trust men and they will be true to you; treat them greatly and they will show themselves great.*
> —Ralph Waldo Emerson

Congressman George Adams once noted, "Everyone who has ever done a kind deed for us, or spoken one word of encouragement to us, has entered into the makeup of our character and our thoughts, as well as our success." I have been very fortunate to be able to accomplish many of the goals I set for myself throughout my life, but a few special people helped to make it all possible. I am grateful for my mother, wife, brothers, and sisters, and the friends who enabled me to overcome temporary failures. Each of them helped me in the fulfillment of my dreams, and each gave greater meaning to my successes.

No one ever really makes it alone; we are meant to thrive as part of a community rather than fly solo. Our greatest needs are met when others help us realize our full potential and we are doing our part to help others realize theirs.

THE DANGER OF ENVY, JEALOUSY, AND COVETOUSNESS

SMILING FACES

One of the greatest tests of your true character will be whether you can be happy for the success of your friends during times when you are struggling. Because of envy, I have lost close friends during periods of my life when my wife and I were prospering. What hurt most was that these periods of prosperity were supposed to be times when those you trusted with your heart genuinely celebrate your accomplishments. We all want to honestly believe that our close friends would be rooting for our victories, but instead, those of less-than-noble character are shamefully and secretly hoping for our downfall, and they are always the first ones to spread the news when we fail.

> *When an envious man feels another praised,*
> *he feels himself injured.*
>
> —English Proverb

Insecure and jealous people are consumed with hidden desires to be elevated just above their friends. Their wish is for everyone in their close-knit circle to be a little less successful than they are. They are the kind of people who thoroughly enjoy the times when they can one-up everyone, because they like being the big cheese or queen bee. Rather than honoring the victories of their friends, they put on pity parties for themselves behind closed doors and are often consumed with jealous anger.

In the end, the competitive nature of those friends made it too difficult for them to remain friends with my wife and me. This was very disheartening on so many levels, but I chose to forgive them and move on despite my sadness for the loss of those friends. Those who covet will always be poor in spirit and rob themselves of the joy that comes from earnestly celebrating the achievements of others.

Jealousy, envy, and covetousness bring about bitterness and torment to the one who has given into these bitter vices. If you don't want to be tormented with them, never give these emotions a doorway to your heart. This industry—and life in general—will give you ample opportunity to become jealous of others, including those whom you call friends.

Human nature is such that people tend to make unnecessary and useless comparisons, and that is dangerous ground. There is always someone more talented, attractive, successful, and wealthy, and someone will always be pulling ahead of you. Warning: if you take the bait, you will destroy your very soul.

Few of us can stand prosperity. Another man's I mean.
—Mark Twain

Remember that it is highly unlikely that you and your friends will advance at the same exact times in your lives. Each of us has a different destiny and a unique path toward it, and everyone's appointed time to catch a break and shine is different. Making comparisons converts positive energy into a deadly poison that will destroy you. Cultivating a competitive spirit will inevitably give rise to all kinds of destructive emotions that will wreak havoc upon your relationships, your health, and your potential, and it will prevent you from experiencing genuine love.

Of all the passions, jealousy is that which extracts
the hardest service and pays the bitterest wages.
Its service is to watch the success of our enemy;
its wages, to be sure of it.
—Charles Caleb Colton

If we can't be truly happy for the success of our friends and colleagues, even if they pursue similar dreams or share the same profession, then we must question what kind of friend or person we really are and honestly examine the state of our hearts.

In the final analysis, the earnest friendships we build will become far more valuable than the notoriety we achieve. At the end of our lives, we will come to understand that people are what matter most. Invest yourself fully into a few others who you feel compelled to support, but find a few important individuals who want to invest in you, as well. If you are lucky enough to find a couple of true friends who would be honestly happy to see you succeed, then consider yourself blessed. Do your best to love and support them well, and by all means, celebrate their achievements as they arise—the ultimate proof of your genuine love.

You'll always have everything you want in life if you'll
help enough other people get what they want.

—Zig Ziglar

WEATHERING TOUGH TIMES TOGETHER

WITH A LITTLE HELP FROM MY FRIENDS

My friend Butch Thomas used to call me from New York City with painfully sad stories about how he couldn't find gratifying work. Butch was a monster sax player who could also sing, as well as play percussion and keyboards. He had already played with quite a few artists, including the legendary jazz-fusion bassist Jaco Pastorius. Butch and I played together for five years; first with Lenny Kravitz, then with French pop star Vanessa Paradis.

After our tour with Vanessa Paradis ended, Butch went back to New York City and I went home to Los Angeles. Not long afterward, I was fortunate enough to begin a tour with Grammy Award-winning recording artist Jody Watley. I saw on my itinerary that we were scheduled to play in New York City, so I called Butch to invite him to the show.

Few things in the world are more powerful than a
positive push. A smile. A word of optimism and hope.
A "you can do it" when things are tough.

—Richard De Vos

When we got together, I could tell Butch was happy to see that I was already working again, but at the same time he was a little bummed out that he wasn't doing the kind of work he wanted. For nearly two years following the Vanessa Paradis tour, Butch had to play club and corporate gigs in New York, New Jersey, and Connecticut just to pay the bills. None of them was particularly fulfilling from his standpoint. We talked a lot during that time and I always encouraged him to hang in there; it was just a matter of time before he would be right back on top. Friends can help each other persevere when self-doubt sets in and times are tough.

Being out of the limelight is a depressing thing for a musician who has had a taste of the good life. First, you feel like you're someone, then you're back to feeling like a nobody all over again. That can be a real ego crusher.

Unfortunately, most of the value that we place on ourselves as freelance musicians is based on how much we are in demand. In reality, employment status should never be the gauge you use to determine your self-worth. Butch refused to quit during his time of tribulation and he carried on with as much optimism as he could muster. That mindset really paid off.

> *How many a man has thrown up his hands at a*
> *time when a little more effort, a little more patience*
> *would have achieved success?*
> —Elbert Hubbard

When I least expected it, I got a surprise phone call from Butch that was filled with emotion. He called to tell me that after his two-year dry spell he had just landed the gig of a lifetime with Sting! Sting, the former lead singer of the enormously successful rock group The Police, was a huge solo artist at the time. As you can imagine, Butch was thrilled, and I was truly happy for my friend who had hung in there for so long.

I saw Butch on television later that very week! He was performing on *Saturday Night Live* with Sting, and it was really cool to see him on the tube knowing how he had struggled over the previous couple of years.

> *Shared joy is double joy; shared sorrow is half sorrow.*
> —Swedish Proverb

There are very few high-profile gigs for sax players, so this opportunity was a big deal for Butch. He wasn't merely one player in a large horn section like most gigs would be for a sax player; since Sting was only using a six-piece band, Butch was a featured player and very prominent in the show. Plus, Butch was making serious money for a freelance musician and was being treated like a king! As if that weren't enough, Sting put his band up at first-class hotels and they flew on his private plane everywhere they went.

I remember how excited I was when Butch called to invite me to see Sting in concert at the Greek Theater in Los Angeles. When I saw him backstage after the show, Butch introduced me to Sting and gave me some more good news. He and his wife, Sandy, had just had a baby and purchased a house in London!

The big gig couldn't have come at a better time for Butch. When I saw him that night, he thanked me for being such an encouraging friend when he had been down and out. The only way to successfully navigate through the storms of life is to surround yourself with true friends who will help you weather them.

> *Obstacles cannot crush me. Every obstacle yields*
> *to stern resolve. He who is fixed to a star does not*
> *change his mind.*
> —Leonardo da Vinci

22

THE ART OF GIVING
LIVING A LIFE OF PURPOSE

*One thing I know; the only ones among you who
will really be happy are those who have sought and
found how to serve.*

—Albert Schweitzer

When I think of individuals who selflessly gave of themselves, I am reminded of four great men I was fortunate enough to know: Louie Bellson, Ed Thigpen, Jim Chapin, and Joe Morello. Each was a legendary drummer and teacher, and each touched my life in a meaningful way.

What I remember most about these men was their loving nature and the incredible talent they generously shared with everyone who came across their paths. Besides being humble and gracious, they intuitively understood that their calling in life was to be a blessing to others through the gifts God had given them. They walked in that calling to the highest degree, and knew the secret to life was in the giving and caring rather than the prize.

As I dwell upon the significance of each of these men's lives, I am reminded of the words of author Robert Louis Stevenson, "Every heart that has beat strongly and cheerfully has left a hopeful impulse behind in the world, and bettered the tradition of mankind." Upon the passing of these men whom I loved and admired, I was reminded of my own mortality. What will my legacy be when I pass into eternity?

Not all people who are endowed with undeniable talent choose to live life the way those four men did. Like many other gifts in life, music can be used for good or evil. Of course, it is not the music that is inherently one or the other. A song is like a piece of metal that is forged into its purpose by the hands of the craftsman who creates it.

That metal can be tempered into a beautiful instrument or a weapon of mass destruction, and the way an individual chooses to use that alloy determines how it will serve its master.

Music is a powerful medium; it is doubtful that we will ever fully understand the magnitude of its powers on this side of eternity. Those who create it have a great responsibility. Use your gift wisely and make sure everything you do is motivated by the purest of love, for in the end, that's the only thing that will endure.

> *The only thing that walks back from the tomb with*
> *the mourners and refuses to be buried is the character*
> *of a man. This is true. What a man is survives him.*
> *It can never be buried.*
>
> —J. R. Miller

THE POWER OF MUSIC

I'VE GOT YOU UNDER MY SKIN

Try imagining classic movies like *The Sound of Music* or *Jaws* without an accompanying soundtrack. Envision battle scenes in *Lord of the Rings* or *Star Wars* without the sound of an orchestra. You can't, because without the undeniable effects of music, the medium of film would cease to awaken the spirit within you that intuitively responds to the majestic nature of music.

All great film directors would tell you that music is half of their movies; without it, they could not evoke the desired emotions from their audiences that they seek. Without the jangle of music, there would be no jingles in commercials to subliminally connect us to the product being advertised. Music is truly one of the greatest gifts that has ever been bestowed upon mankind, and we can't imagine living without it.

> *Music gives a soul to the universe, wings to the mind,*
> *flight to the imagination, and life to everything.*
>
> —Plato

From laughter to tears, music awakens senses that could not otherwise come to the surface. When I hear a magnificent melody or a masterful instrumental solo, I am often moved to the point of tears. They are not tears of sadness, but rather tears of joy that the music is able to summon from within my heart. Music is a supernatural force that no one fully comprehends. Much like love, passion, laughter, and forgiveness, music is visible only to the soul. It touches our innermost beings unlike anything on the planet.

We are the wire, God is the current. Our only power is
to let the current pass through us.

—Carlo Carretto

Music is spiritual by nature, supernatural by design, and connective by intention. It transforms, transcends, and transfigures into a beautiful tapestry upon which inspiration of every kind is born. Even though I play an instrument, I have always felt like I am the instrument, and that a divine flow of energy is playing through me as I yield myself to it. It is only when I surrender to this powerful force that music is able to profoundly affect my heart, as well as those who are listening.

Music is a sacred, a divine, a God-like thing, and was
given to man by Christ to lift our hearts up to God, and
make us feel something of the glory and beauty of God,
and of all which God has made.

—Charles Kingsley

IMPACTING THE LIVES OF OTHERS

ALL YOU NEED IS LOVE

In his play *As You Like It,* William Shakespeare coined this timeless phrase: "All the world's a stage, and all the men and women merely players." My interpretation of that famous quote is that the whole world is but one continuous gig, and what we contribute to each and every gig is what ultimately leads us to our destinies. Our efforts determine the level of impact our gigs—or rather our lives—will have on others. I view everything in my life as an opportunity to be a conduit for the expression of love, and that manifests itself in a multitude of tangible and creative ways.

In the end, I know that my time on earth will be short in comparison to eternity. The purpose of my big gig is to leave behind positive impressions as a living legacy that will go on through the lives of others whom I was able to influence, inspire, and uplift in some way.

> *The true meaning of life is to plant trees under whose shade you do not expect to sit.*
>
> —Nelson Henderson

Those of us who possess the gift of music did not give it to ourselves; we are merely recipients of a divine power that was pre-wired into our DNA. We are given the freedom to choose how we will use that gift. In and of itself, music has no power to be good or bad; it needs a conduit, and that conduit is you. Examine the spirit that is behind all you do. The condition of your heart and the personal desires you cultivate within yourself will determine your choice.

Peter Marshall once said, "The measure of life is not in its duration, but in its donation. Everyone can be great because everyone can serve." To serve others with humility and graciousness is the divine path chosen by few. But those who do will receive the greatest reward; an inexplicable sense of satisfaction that comes from knowing they are fulfilling their purpose.

> *A life is not important except in the impact it has on other lives.*
>
> —Jackie Robinson

At the end of your life, true success will be measured by what you have given, versus what you have acquired. Will your journey have been one of self or service? Self-absorption, or self-denial?

When you leave this planet, all you will leave behind are the seeds you planted in others through the gifts you possess. You will either leave behind a well-tended and fruitful vineyard with life flowing through it, or a dried-up vineyard that is incapable of producing more grapes.

*A day lived without doing something good for others
is a day not worth living.*

—Mother Teresa

There are always more blessings in giving than in receiving, and by choosing to serve others you will find the true meaning of life. If you serve only yourself, you will find only emptiness and dissatisfaction, and you will end up living a very shallow existence.

Way down deep inside, I believe that we all have a desire to feel what I call the four A's: attention, acceptance, admiration, and applause. We have a strong need to be affirmed, but that doesn't mean we have to live exclusively for ourselves. History gives us so many examples of how those who lived for self eventually self-destructed, and Hollywood's mantra of sex, drugs, and rock 'n' roll continues to validate that truth on a daily basis.

*No person was ever honored for what he received.
Honor has been the reward for what he gave.*

—Calvin Coolidge

THE BIG GIG IS YOUR LIFE

OVER THE RAINBOW

Throughout this text, my goal has been to share personal experiences that have allowed me to accomplish my childhood dreams of making it as a drummer in the music industry. Because life is so short, I'm committed to spending the majority of mine doing what I feel I was created to do, and that gives me a tremendous sense of inner fulfillment. Despite all the hardships I have endured along the way, I wouldn't exchange what I've experienced for the world.

If you possess the necessary talent, and the principles revealed in this book are properly applied, you will have a great chance of success as a musician or in any other vocation you choose to pursue. There are always many paths to success, of course, but I believe these core concepts can become a part of your arsenal in the battle of life if you embrace them.

One central truth I have been trying to convey throughout this book is that your efforts must be strategic and intentional if you hope to score the big gig or sustain any kind of success as a player and as a person. The way you get the bigger gigs in life is by giving every seemingly insignificant gig your very best effort.

The big gig is not just one dream gig, nor should it be viewed as merely external success. It is really the inward journey of your life, and what transpires from yours will be determined by your attitude and your stewardship over the talents and opportunities that have been given to you.

The future is purchased by the present.

—Samuel Johnson

How you conduct yourself on the stage of life will determine your effectiveness and the kind of impact your life and talents will have on the world at large. You will make the most of your opportunities by being faithful to every assignment that life presents; you will only reap what you have sown in the garden of music and in life.

DISCERNING THE TIMES AND SEASONS

SEPTEMBER OF MY YEARS

In today's all-too anxious world, there are many young people in the spring of their lives who desperately want to be in the autumn of life and reap a huge harvest. However, the universal laws that the Almighty Creator put into place do not allow for you to reap a harvest of something later in life that you never planted in an earlier season.

Likewise, many older people who are in the fall of their lives are desperately trying to navigate backwards into the spring or summer when they were young and lived with less responsibility and accountability. They long to live in Peter Pan's Never Never Land and refuse to grow up because they are smitten with self-centeredness. Their self-serving natures and immaturity cause them to miss golden opportunities to sow into others. They fail to discern that the next season of their lives after fall is winter, and after winter comes death. The fall is the time to deposit what we have learned into others and prepare to leave a worthwhile legacy.

What you leave behind is not what is engraved in stone monuments, but what is woven into the lives of others.
—Pericles

The key is to recognize the seasons in your life and be willing to do what is called for to make the most of each season. There is no guarantee that growing older will give way to more wisdom. Strive to do the right thing in each and every season of your life, and wisdom will follow.

REACHING YOUR FULL POTENTIAL

DIAMONDS ARE FOREVER

Diamonds are the most coveted gemstones in the world. Wealthy people from every prosperous nation will pay incredible sums to possess these things of true beauty.

Almost everyone knows what a diamond looks like when it is displayed on top of a gorgeous piece of black velvet and set inside an expensive glass case at a high-end jewelry store. But most are not aware of how ugly and unglamorous the diamond is initially as merely a chunk of coal found miles beneath the earth's surface. Until it goes through each of those stages that bring forth its true beauty, no one sees its potential.

Each of us is a diamond, and each of us possesses a diamond's worth of potential. Sadly, very few individuals allow themselves to go through the rigorous process that it takes to become more than a diamond in the rough. It takes 100 tons of mud to produce one carat of diamond.

If you are willing to sift through the mud of your own life, you will display tremendous beauty and be all you were created to be. This is achieved by carefully doing all that is required of you. There is so much more potential in all of us than most people seem willing to mine out of themselves.

*One of the rarest things that a man ever does
is the best he can.*

—Josh Billings

Diamonds are rated by what the industry refers to as the four C's: carat, color, clarity, and cut. A "carat" refers to the size of the diamond. The color of a diamond is determined by examining it face-up and then face-down, and contrary to the average consumer's knowledge, diamonds come in many colors. Clarity is the degree to which a diamond is free of blemishes and inclusions. Cut is the human touch to the diamond's beauty.

Whether you remain a lump of coal or become a flawless, brightly shining diamond is determined by the choices you make throughout your life. There are four C's that will enable you to reach the highest state of clarity: courage, cooperation, confidence, and commitment. Regardless of what stage of life you are in, you can always make a decision to be all that you're capable of being. It is never too late.

GIVING YOUR VERY BEST

CLIMB EVERY MOUNTAIN

How you start the race is not nearly as important as how you finish it. Your life is a limited-time offer, so remember to give it all you've got. Each of your days should end in utter exhaustion because you have given it your best. Live each day to the fullest and approach each day as if it were your last. One day, when you least expect it, it will be that final day of all your days. Giving your best is the ultimate act of gratitude for the wonderful gift of life you've been given.

By the end of my life, my goal is to have given away all that was freely given to me with a humble spirit, and to have brought joy, inspiration, and hope to all who have crossed my path and partaken of my gifts.

*And in the end, it's not the years in your life that count.
It's the life in your years.*

—Abraham Lincoln

It is my deepest wish that you live out the dreams that God has placed in your heart, and that you never forget that the journey itself is far more important than the actual destination.

It is my sincere hope that this book has inspired you to give every day, experience, and opportunity your personal best, and that you are encouraged to face each challenge life brings you with the will to overcome it. None of us is exempt from adversity; you can be sure that your life's journey will be filled with trials and tribulations.

The good news is, however, that if you allow these difficulties to develop and strengthen you, they will deepen the art that flows from you. Your ability to touch people in the depths of their hearts will come, in part, from the pain you have endured. As much as we don't like it, only resistance can build strength, and only hardship and anguish can produce depth of character.

> *Character cannot be developed in ease and quiet. Only through experience of trial and suffering can the soul be strengthened, ambition inspired, and success achieved.*
>
> —Helen Keller

We only grow in times of intense battle, and the flames produced from the pressures of life will forge the depth of expression that emanates from your soul. Stay strong, stay focused, stay the course, and always let light shine from you so others can also find their way.

> *God created the universe in order to hear music, and everything has a song of praise for God.*
>
> —Louis Ginsberg

Most important of all, never, ever stop singing your song. You have a song to sing, your own secret melody that God gave only to you. Like a present waiting to be unwrapped, the joy of life is in the discovery of that special song He has hidden for you. Your purpose is to discover your song day by day and to sing it at the top of your lungs for all to hear. Your melody will ripple into eternity, and the world will be a far better place for having heard it!

With faith, hope, and love,

> *The height of your accomplishments will equal*
> *the depth of your convictions. Seek happiness for*
> *its own sake, and you will not find it; seek purpose,*
> *and happiness will follow as a shadow comes with*
> *the sunshine.*
>
> —William Scolavino

THE BIG GIG QUIZ
50 QUESTIONS TO DETERMINE YOUR CHANCES OF SCORING THE BIG GIG

Take the following quiz to find out just how good your chances are of making it as a musician. To the best of your ability, answer truthfully "yes" or "no" to each of the questions below and total your "yes" answers at the end of the quiz. You get two points for each question with a "yes" answer. Your score reflects your chances of making it. For example, if you answered "yes" to 25 of the questions, you have a 50 percent chance of success. If you answered "yes" to 40 of the questions, you have an 80 percent chance of success.

For best results, enlist someone who knows you really well—and has the necessary musical knowledge—to answer the test questions as they pertain to you. With two quiz results, you can compare the scores and evaluate where you both honestly feel you need the most work.

Due to unforeseen and unpredictable circumstances that surround the music industry and life in general, no quiz can determine whether someone will succeed as a musician. However, this quiz can tell you quite a bit by raising serious issues that should cause you to examine your efforts, habits, and level of commitment in a most thorough manner.

I have broken down the questions into five categories: vision, commitment, skills, character, and business. The point of this quiz is to get you to realize how many necessary components it takes to complete your puzzle of success. The most important aspect of piecing together your puzzle is to understand what pieces are missing. You do this by conducting serious self-examination to realistically see where you are with regard to each of these crucial categories and then making a strategic effort to improve upon all weaknesses or deficiencies.

http://4wrd.it/A.BGQuiz

Don't be discouraged if your score is low. The important point to remember is that most of your answers can be changed simply by your desire to change and your willingness to do what's necessary. If you really want to succeed, you must do all that is within your power to have a fighting chance. Work hard, stay positive, keep after it, and never give up. Best of luck on your musical endeavors!

50 QUESTIONS
TO DETERMINE YOUR CHANCES
OF SCORING THE BIG GIG

*"Our goals can only be reached through the
vehicle of a plan, in which we must fervently believe,
and upon which we must vigorously act.
There is no other route to success."*

—Pablo Picasso

VISION

1. Do you consider yourself musically gifted?

2. Do you have an overall vision for your career?

3. Have you set short-range goals for your career?

4. Have you set long-range goals for your career?

5. Have you defined the objective of your
   musical career?

6. Do you have someone to keep you accountable
   for your goals?

7. Do you believe it's possible for your dreams
   to come true against all odds?

COMMITMENT

8. Do you study your instrument regularly via method
   books, the Internet, or instructional DVDs?

9. Are you taking private lessons with a master to develop
   your talent and improve on your instrument?

10. Do you regularly read music industry magazines or publications that pertain to your instrument?

11. Do you regularly read books about the music business or musicians?

12. Do you regularly read motivational books that inspire you to pursue your dreams?

13. Do you have a mentor within the music industry?

14. Do you practice your instrument for long periods of time on a daily basis?

15. Are you constantly immersed in listening to and analyzing music?

16. Do you know all standard songs for the genre of music you wish to succeed at playing?

17. Are you studying all the greats who defined the genre of music you wish you master?

18. Is the majority of your extra money invested in the pursuit of your musical dreams, such as studying your instrument, purchasing musical equipment, music CDs and downloads, and books?

SKILLS

19. Are you extremely proficient on your instrument?

20. Can you adapt quickly when musical changes are made in an arrangement?

21. Are you an excellent sight-reader?

22. Are you an extremely versatile musician?

23. Do you come prepared for each gig or opportunity?

24. Do you know how to contribute to the musical success of others, and do you enjoy doing so?

25. Do you believe your musical skills are highly marketable?

CHARACTER

26. Do you have a strong work ethic?

27. Would you say you are a flexible person?

28. Do you consider yourself an optimistic person?

29. Are you a reliable person on whom others can always depend?

30. Are you punctual?

31. Are you a humble person?

32. Do you have a good attitude?

33. Do you take criticism well?

34. Can you work effectively with differing or abrasive personalities?

35. Do you take instruction well?

36. Do you deal well with competition?

37. Do you handle rejection well?

38. Do you do well with unpredictable schedules?

39. Do you mind having someone else dictate how you spend your time?

40. Are you living free from drug and alcohol overuse or addiction?

41. Do you consider yourself a determined, focused, and ambitious person?

BUSINESS

42. Do you have excellent-sounding equipment?

43. Do you have reliable transportation?

44. Are you willing to live in or near one of the major music market cities of Los Angeles, New York, Nashville, Atlanta, Chicago, or Miami to increase your chances of landing the big gig?

45. Are you are a good money manager?

46. Do you know how to market and promote yourself at each subsequent stage of your career?

47. Are you routinely building a network of contacts within the music industry?

48. Do you know how to capitalize on current situations to advance your career?

49. Are you willing to learn how to be your own manager to ensure your success as a musician?

50. Are you willing to do everything necessary to make it in the music business?

Groove Masterpieces
of Biblical Proportions

CHECK OUT THESE BEST-SELLING, AWARD-WINNING DRUM PUBLICATIONS

By

As the foremost authority on R&B drumming, Zoro provides a historical and in-depth study, from soul to funk to hip-hop. Topics include practice tips, developing the funky bass drum and hi-hat, creating and playing with loops, and what are considered the Ten Commandments of Soul, Funk, R&B, and Hip-Hop.

The Commandments of R&B Drumming
Book & CD (00-0110B)
DVD (00-903185)
Modern Drummer Reader's Poll Winner for No. 1 Educational Drum Book

The Commandments of R&B Drumming Play-Along
Book & MP3 CD (00-32444)

The Commandments of Early Rhythm & Blues Drumming
By Zoro and Daniel Glass
Book & CD (00-30555)

Buy them today at alfred.com/zoro

 Alfred Music Publishing
LEARN · TEACH · PLAY

THE BIG GIG PICTURE BOOK
A FANTAZMICAL ADVENTURE

Mom filling my little heart with big dreams!

Official start of the incredible journey.

Playing with Philip Bailey of Earth, Wind & Fire.

Performing for nearly 1 million people in Washington D.C.

Grooving with
Bobby Brown
at Madison
Square Garden.

Posing with Frankie Valli
just before our show.

With renowned
music producer
Quincy Jones at
a fundraiser.

Chillin' with basketball legend
Magic Johnson in Los Angeles.

Backstage with Julia Louis-Dreyfus
from *Seinfeld*.

Rocking out in concert with Lenny Kravitz.

Meeting Regis during
Live! with Regis & Kelly.

On set of the
Arsenio Hall Show.

Katie Couric posing with my Vic Firth
Zoro signature drumsticks.

Hanging with Jay Leno
before his show.

SCAN THIS
QR CODE
WITH YOUR
SMART
PHONE TO
SEE MORE
PHOTOS!

http://4wrd.it/A.BGPhotos

Sharing my passion
on the *Joyce Meyer Show.*

Biggest and best gig ever—
husband and father!

ABOUT THE AUTHOR
ZORO: MINISTER OF GROOVE

He is the consummate definition of the rare man who marches to the beat of a different drum.

Zoro has sat on the drummer's throne commanding some of the most famous stages in the world of rock and R&B music. Z has toured and recorded with Lenny Kravitz; Bobby Brown; Frankie Valli and The Four Seasons; The New Edition; Jody Watley; Philip Bailey of Earth, Wind & Fire; Angie Stone; Vanessa Paradis; Sean Lennon; Lisa Marie Presley; Tommy Walker; Lincoln Brewster; Phil Keaggy; Barlow Girl; and many others.

Throughout his career, Zoro consistently has been voted the No. 1 R&B drummer and clinician by premier music industry publications such as *Modern Drummer*, *Drum!*, and *Rhythm* magazines.

Often called the "Minister of Groove," Z authored the No. 1 award-winning and best-selling book and DVD package *The Commandments of R&B Drumming* (Alfred Music Publishing). *The Commandments of Early Rhythm & Blues Drumming*—his latest effort in collaboration with Daniel Glass—is another masterpiece of biblical proportions and the winner of a Drummie! award for Best Drumming Book in *Drum!* magazine.

All heart and soul, Zoro is a sought-after musician, clinician, instructor, and motivational speaker simply because he's real, relevant, relatable, and connects with all generations. Z is passion personified and motivated to serve people as well as inspire his audiences with all he has and does.

http://4wrd.it/A.BGAuthor

Zoro is a spokesperson for Compassion International and Big Brothers Big Sisters of America. He recently established Zoro International Ministries, a nonprofit organization for the vital work of equipping young adults ages 18–29 to reach their potential and fulfill their purpose on earth. (For more information, visit zoroministries.org.)

Zoro is a kinetic bundle of human energy and enthusiasm. His heartbeat is in the groove itself, earning him the distinction of being a groove for the generations.

To learn more about *The Big Gig* and connect with Zoro, visit the following sites:

THEBIGGIGBOOK.COM

ZOROTHEDRUMMER.COM

FACEBOOK.COM/ZOROTHEDRUMMERMUSIC

TWITTER.COM/ZOROTHEDRUMMER

FACEBOOK.COM/ZOROMINISTRIES

Zoro is available for speaking engagements, music-related performances and clinics, career consultation, and media interviews. To book Zoro, please contact his promotions representative, Lisa Cieslewicz, through Lisa@CieslewiczCorpCom.com.

Big Brothers Big Sisters

ABOUT THE BOOK

The Big Gig is an intriguing and comprehensive insider's guide for independent musicians who want to break into the highly competitive music industry. And it's much more! *The Big Gig* is a metaphor for the big picture of life. Channeling music industry savvy from the stage to the page, Zoro provides a template for success—for everyone, regardless of career—by covering the vocational, personal, and spiritual aspects of achievement.

Readers will be given backstage access with Zoro's refreshing straight talk and colorful anecdotes. Go deeper with Z as he gives personal interviews at the beginning of each chapter via Quick Response Code technology, which allows smartphones and dedicated QR readers to scan two-dimensional barcodes to activate video recordings. Think you have what it takes to make it? Check out The Big Gig Quiz, which can be found at the conclusion of the book, on the back cover, and at alfred.com/TheBigGig.

Grammy-winning recording artist Lenny Kravitz writes in his foreword to *The Big Gig*, "Zoro's heart, discipline, and passion are what propelled him to greatness."

Now, Z wants to share those traits so success is within reach of everyone.

Inspiring readers to aspire higher, the Minister of Groove reveals the true power behind the art of success. With more than 400 motivational quotes, *The Big Gig* is certain to awaken the dreamer in all of us and help lead the way to purposeful living and personal fulfillment. It's nothing short of life changing.

THEBIGGIGBOOK.COM

http://4wrd.it/A.BGBook